VEGANISM SEX AND POLITICS
tales of danger and pleasure

VEGANISM SEX AND POLITICS

tales of danger and pleasure

HAMMER/ON

C. LOU HAMILTON

VEGANISM, SEX AND POLITICS: TALES OF DANGER
AND PLEASURE

British Library Cataloguing in Publication Data
A catalogue record for this book is available from the British Library

ISBN-13: 978-1-910849-12-5
ISBN-10: 1910849125

Veganism, Sex and Politics: Tales of Danger and Pleasure/ C. Lou Hamilton
1. Veganism 2. Animal Rights 3. Consumerism 4. Environmentalism
5. Queer 6. Feminism

First published in 2019 by HammerOn Press
Bristol, England
https://www.hammeronpress.net

Cover design and typeset by Eva Megias
http://evamegias.com

CONTENTS

In this beautifully written book, C. Lou Hamilton explores the politics of veganism through the lens of her own experience as a queer vegan. She uses science, philosophy, storytelling and more to examine the use of animals for food, clothing, medicine, sexuality and identity. Her approach is refreshingly open. There are no unambiguous heroes or villains in her story. She approaches all subjects, including herself, with the same critical yet generous perspective, which allows her to move beyond simplistic frames and arrive at a more complex, ambivalent set of truths. This book does what we need many more books to do: show what it looks like for a particular individual in a particular context to aspire to resist oppression in all its forms, while still living a life full of joy, individuality and community.

Jeff Sebo, New York University

Veganism, Sex and Politics is a wonderful and inspiring contribution to the ethics and politics of veganism as a practice. Hamilton has produced a gorgeously written, careful and sensitive text. This book deftly weaves sophisticated contemporary debates together, giving readers a wonderful opportunity to gain insight into the complexities of pro animal politics and veganism. Importantly, this unique volume offers visions for veganism as a non-normative ethical and political practice that goes well beyond individual ethics and move us towards large scale social and political transformation.

Dinesh Joseph Wadiwel, The University of Sydney

INTRODUCTION

Sometime around midsummer 2014, a few months after I started practising veganism, I strolled home from a party in the wee hours, heels in one hand, bag thrown over the opposite shoulder. A hint of sunlight squeezed through the trees. In my head I was still dancing. As I reached the corner near my flat, a fox crossed the empty street and stopped on the pavement some fifty metres before me. She turned my way, looked me in the eyes, and slipped under a bush.

I'd had countless encounters with foxes before this one. London's vulpine population is thriving, and the animals are second only to squirrels and pigeons for wildlife in my neighbourhood. But this meeting felt different. As I looked at the fox and fancied that she returned my gaze — intentionally, knowingly — I sensed a sudden connection that I intuitively attributed to the fact that I had stopped eating animals.

I am well versed in the concept of anthropomorphism, and in the magic born of dawn dreaming. I have long since abandoned the fantasy that a vegan diet means a human body free from the traces of dead animals, or non-complicity in the exploitation of animals. What I have not lost is that sense of curiosity about other creatures and my kinship with them. While I examine, in the pages that follow, some of the ways that veganism gets tangled up in politics — sexual politics in particular — and what those knots tell us about contemporary identities and other conflicts, I carry with me the memory of this and other trans-species encounters. I open this book with my crossing with the fox because, as I ask a series of sometimes difficult questions about what it means to practise veganism in the early twenty-first century, I want to keep alive this sense of wonder, my ongoing amazement at veganism's always more-than-political powers.

Why veganism now?

Veganism is hot.

During the second decade of the twenty-first century, veganism in the West has gone from a political practice associated first and foremost with animal rights activism to an increasingly popular approach to eating and living. According to one survey from early 2018, in the United Kingdom 7% of the population now identifies as vegan, a substantial rise since 2016.[1] A year later *The Economist* announced that 2019 would be "the year of the vegan."[2] While surveys and New Year's predictions need to be taken with a grain of salt, it is clear that more and more people are implementing or considering a plant-based diet.

Veganism's rising popularity can be attributed to a range of factors. In the first place, it is evidence of the success of animal rights and welfare activists in documenting, publicising and challenging the exploitation of animals raised for food, especially on modern industrial farms, since the second half of the twentieth century. In Western countries such as Britain and the United States, agriculture underwent a transition to greater intensification after World War Two. Technological developments, pesticides, new breeding techniques and the use of vitamins and antibiotics facilitated the rapid expansion of intensive animal agriculture.[3] By the 1960s and 1970s, animal advocates were increasingly concerned about the conditions on what were soon dubbed "factory farms." Ruth Harrison's 1964 book *Animal Machines* and, a decade later, Peter Singer's *Animal Liberation: A New Ethics for Our Treatment of Animals*, were instrumental in raising awareness of welfare issues related to industrial farming in Britain and the U.S.[4] During the same period, scientific research increasingly demonstrated that the animals raised for food or used in scientific experimentation are intelligent and sentient beings who experience and express emotions and feel physical pain.[5]

By the early twenty-first century there is also increasing evidence that animal agriculture is dangerous for people's health and for the very future of the planet. The survey cited above names the growing concern about climate change as the most significant factor in veganism's newfound popularity.[6] Parallel to this we have seen a growth in movements for clean eating and living that often promote plant-based diets. In the digital age, information about the negative impacts of animal agriculture and the consumption of animal products, along with alternatives, circulate readily and rapidly to large audiences, increasing access to information about veganism.[7] According to the presenter of a BBC radio programme on vegan diets broadcast in February 2019, "When I ask people why they would like to give it [veganism] a try they usually say that something they saw on the television or on social media has changed the way they'll think about meat and dairy forever."[8] Some people celebrate the growing enthusiasm for veganism as proof of increased compassion for animals and greater awareness about the dangers of climate change, especially among younger people. But not everyone is happy about veganism going mainstream. Some fear that it is losing its political edge, becoming just another middle-class lifestyle choice, complete with celebrity backers. Evidence that a preoccupation with healthy eating and the environment is behind veganism's popularity prompts some to fear a loss of focus on animal rights.[9]

There is certainly room for criticism of vegan consumerism. But in this book I argue that it is a mistake to assume that veganism is nothing more than a lifestyle choice. I am also wary of accusing some vegans of having self-centred rather than properly political motives, or of being driven by the wrong kinds of politics.[10] It is not possible, or desirable, to think of the lives of other animals, human health, economic inequalities and environmentalism as separate issues. If discussions about climate change teach us anything, it is just how deadly the ideology of limitless economic growth, and the day-to-day activities of many of us living in the West, have become — for ourselves, the rest of the world's human population, other creatures, and the planet as a whole. The deadliness of many aspects of Western culture and consumerism is hardly news. But it is given new dimensions by the current planetary crisis. The turn towards veganism is one expression of a growing consciousness about the enormous costs of global capitalism and anthropocentrism — the worldview that promotes human beings and our interests as the centre of the universe.

As it becomes more popular, veganism has become a hot topic. We can find a plethora of vegan cookbooks, blogs and online cooking classes, veganism is in the news on a regular basis, and there is even an emerging academic subfield of vegan studies.[11] Activists, journalists and scholars debate the pros and cons of veganism for human health, animal welfare, food security (the ability to feed the world's growing human population), food justice (equal and fair access to healthy food for people) and the earth's future. So veganism

4

is also hot as in "hot potato." It attracts attention because it reflects changing attitudes towards animals, food and the environment; but it also creates anxiety in relation to other social, economic and political issues, including class, race, gender, sexuality, disability, gentrification, globalisation and environmental protection. Why does veganism raise hackles? In this book I explore some ways we might think critically about veganism so that we can appreciate its values and better understand the controversies it causes, without equating it to those. Amidst the sometimes stifling debates, I want to give veganism some space to breathe.

I define veganism as an ethical commitment to live, as far as possible, without commodifying or otherwise instrumentalising other animals for our own human ends. Adapting Deane Curtin's theory of "contextual moral vegetarianism," I advocate the practice of contextual ethical veganism. Although I believe it is impossible to draw a sharp distinction between the care of other animals and care of one's self and other people, I follow common usage among vegans by using "ethical veganism" to signal a commitment motivated by compassion for other creatures and not primarily a concern about human health. While "ethical" and "moral" are used largely interchangeably in everyday speech, I choose "ethical" in order to avoid the easy slide of "moral" into "moralism," a term sometimes (incorrectly in my view) associated with veganism. Following Curtin, I include the word "contextual" in my definition in order to signal a recognition that veganism defined in strict dietary terms may not be appropriate to all situations, given significant differences among people, our histories and our circumstances.[12] Those who are able to practise strict veganism need not — indeed, should not — adopt a universalist position by arguing that *everyone*, regardless of material and cultural context, must practise veganism in a particular way. Finally, following common usage in writing on animal rights and welfare, I refer collectively to nonhuman species as animals, while remaining aware that people too are animals. I try to avoid lumping all other-than-human animals together by being specific, wherever possible, about which species I am referring to.

In practical terms, in contemporary Western societies, practising contextual ethical veganism means avoiding as far as possible the consumption of products made from animals instrumentalised for human ends, and seeking to minimise other practices involving the exploitation of other species. Whereas in popular parlance veganism is normally associated with diet, this book goes beyond food to consider some of the other ways people consume or instrumentalise animals, including for clothing, medicine, pleasure and work. While the book offers a defence of veganism, it draws attention to what I consider unsatisfactory or even dangerous arguments in its favour. It also examines the merits of some arguments against veganism and takes into account some of the challenges of practising veganism today.

The book's objective is twofold: to invite readers from different backgrounds to take veganism seriously as an ethical practice with important political implications, and to encourage readers to think in ways they may not have before about the relationship between veganism, sexual politics and other political issues, including anti-racism, environmentalism, anti-capitalism and anti-colonialism. My words are neither the first nor the last; I draw on existing discussions, try to take them in different directions, and hope to keep the conversations moving.

Veganism, sex and politics

Sex is also a hot topic, but in a more obvious way than veganism. Why sex, politics *and* veganism? If you picked up this book hoping for tips on how to find your ideal vegan lover, or help to boost your sex life through a plant-based diet, you're likely to be disappointed.[13] I'll leave the hottest vegan competition to others.[14] Instead, I set out to examine some of the ways veganism crosses paths with sex and other political topics. Sex, sexuality and sexual politics provide examples of how ideas about veganism and people's relationships with other animals get caught up in complex questions about intra-human relations.

I use "sexual politics" in a broad sense, incorporating sexuality, sexual orientation and sexual relations, as well as power dynamics among different groups of gendered human beings (women, men, transgender and non-binary people). To many readers, sexuality and veganism may not seem immediately related. Yet both share the widespread and persistent perception, on the left as well as the right, that they are luxury issues, not serious political questions. This book begs to differ. Perhaps the most obvious connection between sexuality and veganism is that both are linked to bodies, our own and those of others. These days it is something of a cliché to say that "food is the new sex"; food and sexuality have become intimately tied through the themes of desire and identity.[15] But when we expand the scope of veganism beyond food we relate to bodies in different ways: through the medicines we take, the clothes we wear, the intimate relationships we form with human and other creatures, and the ways we travel and move in the world. Thinking about veganism in relation to sexual politics has helped me better to understand the extent to which eating, dressing, playing and taking care of our bodies and those of other people depend and impact upon the bodies and lives of other animals.

The book also examines how different power relations among people — including, but not exclusively, gender relations — intersect with definitions of animality and humanity. In the early twenty-first century most people who study the history of human-animal relations agree that there are ideological and historical connections between the ways in which animals, women and other oppressed human groups — people of colour, Indigenous people, Jews, queers, workers, disabled people — have been represented and treated as less-than-human by people with power. There is also a recognition that the construction and treatment of certain people and collectives of people "as animals" is structurally connected to the (mal)treatment of other animals. Where there is less agreement is how exactly these connections work, and where and when it is appropriate to make comparisons between different forms of intra-human and human-animal relations.

I look at some of the controversies surrounding these comparisons in chapter 1. There I explain how my approach to the sexual politics of veganism differs from the theory of "the sexual politics of meat," a term coined by the American ecofeminist Carol J. Adams in 1990. Adams's understanding of the relationship between vegetarianism/veganism and feminism continues to hold considerable sway in Western writings on veganism.[16] While "the sexual politics of meat" model of feminist veganism is useful for understanding how cultures of misogyny and meat-eating are entwined in the contemporary United States and other parts of the West, I find its understanding of gender relations and its reliance on anti-pornography feminism reductive and restrictive. The approaches I adopt in this book are critically queer and feminist. I have been influenced by older arguments about animal rights and more recent writings on veganism, especially by queer activists and feminists of colour.[17] Recognising that violence — against women, gay men, transgender, non-binary people, among others — is an important element of power relations, the queer feminism I embrace does not take sexual and other forms of violence to be the main basis for feminist action. My subtitle — "Tales of Danger and Pleasure" — is a nod to a landmark feminist volume on sexual politics, *Pleasure and Danger: Exploring Female Sexuality*, which challenged anti-pornography feminism's interpretation of sex as dangerous for women.[18] By adopting and adapting this title, I signal that although veganism is a site of potential danger — especially when it is misunderstood as being in competition with the interests of oppressed groups of people — it is also a source of pleasure.

My queer feminist veganism embraces transpecies kinship and relations, and is open to the powers of veganism to help us challenge and revise our sense of what it means to be human. But I do not claim that veganism is by definition feminist or queer. In his "Queer Vegan Manifesto" Rasmus Simonsen argues that veganism is queer because, in an overwhelmingly omnivore culture, it is deviant and non-normative.[19] I am inspired by the utopian thrust of Simonsen's text, but I am aware that most vegans do not identify as queer and vice versa. My approach to queer feminist veganism seeks to examine the points of encounter and mutual influences among different kinds of relationships rather than emphasise similarities. I broadly follow an intersectional approach that, in Jeff Sebo's words, "there are respects in which different issues, identities, and oppressions interact so as to make the whole different from the sum of its parts."[20] When veganism comes into contact with other social and political issues it often becomes a flashpoint for debate. These flashpoints provide valuable opportunities for reflection on the multiple and sometimes conflicting meanings of veganism. The book combines an attention to vegan flashpoints — moments of crisis in the present — with an analysis of sticking points, ideas about veganism that recur, time and again, especially when it is seen in relation to other social and political movements, including feminism, queer politics, anti-racism and anti-colonialism. By exploring flashpoints and sticking points alongside a series of personal and other stories about veganism and sexuality, I aim to draw attention to ways of practising veganism that do not pit it against other personal and political priorities.

Veganism in a nutshell

This book is by and large about veganism as it has arisen in the West since the mid-twentieth century, and most of the material it discusses is drawn from Britain and North America. The bias towards English-language Western sources reflects the situation I live and write in. It is also important to grasp the historical context in which contemporary veganism has developed in order to understand the shapes it takes and why it continues to cause controversy. The book is not an examination of plant-based diets and animal ethics *per se*. Numerous traditions outside Europe have long histories of vegetarian/vegan diets and understandings of human–animal relations that differ substantially from those of Europe. At certain points in these pages I bring in examples from different cultures via stories of vegan activists from those traditions.

The term "vegan" — formed by the first three and the last two letters of the word "vegetarian" — was coined in the United Kingdom in 1944 by founders of the Vegan Society.

These people wished to distinguish themselves from those who avoided the flesh of animals but might eat dairy and/or eggs.[21] Both veganism and vegetarianism had longer histories. In Britain, the avoidance of meat and other animal products had been promoted, since at least the nineteenth century, by some supporters of campaigns against cruelty to animals as well as feminist, socialist, and alternative health and spiritual movements.[22] By the 1960s and 1970s veganism was increasingly practised among activists of the postwar animal rights movement.[23] In 1975 arguments in favour of veganism got a significant boost with the publication of Singer's *Animal Liberation*.[24] A philosopher in the utilitarian tradition, Singer compared the struggle against "speciesism" to civil rights and feminism.[25] He argued that there was no rational reason why moral arguments in favour of equality among human beings should not be extended to other animals, so long as those animals could be proven to be sentient and capable of suffering pain. Much of *Animal Liberation* is dedicated to a detailed account and critique of the exploitation of animals in scientific experimentation and industrial agriculture, and the final chapter of the book is a defense of vegetarianism. Although in subsequent editions of *Animal Liberation* and other writing Singer shifted his position on where the line between sentient and non-sentient creatures should be drawn, his main argument was clear: the rearing and slaughtering of sentient animals for food and their use in scientific testing causes unnecessary suffering and is therefore unethical.[26]

Singer's emphasis on evidence of suffering as the basis for including many animals in the moral community— drawn from the late eighteenth-century utilitarian philosopher Jeremy Bentham— has been controversial. Most notoriously, it has led Singer to argue that some disabled human beings have less value than some sentient animals.[27] A number of feminist animal advocates have criticised Singer for providing a rationalist basis for vegetarianism that ignores the emotional dimension of human-animal relations.[28] These are serious problems with Singer's framework. Yet it is difficult to overestimate the impact of *Animal Liberation* on the development of veganism and the animal rights movement over the past four decades. Published at a time when animal rights activism was on the rise in Britain and the United States, the book is probably the most widely-read argument in favour of vegetarianism/veganism in the contemporary West. For all its association with animal rights, however, Singer is not a rights philosopher and never advocated rights for animals as such. That argument was made by another philosopher, Tom Regan, in his 1983 book *The Case for Animal Rights*. Regan argued that the rights of animals are violated when they are raised for food and experimented upon and, in consequence, advocated "obligatory vegetarianism."[29] Singer's and Regan's books are cited time and again as the main contemporary philosophical defences of animals. They come up regularly in writings about veganism, their arguments sometimes used to represent the views of all vegans. The association of veganism with the work of Singer and Regan has helped to tie veganism to a very particular, and Eurocentric, tradition of rights, rationalism and moralism. This in turn helps to explain why veganism sometimes becomes a flashpoint in debates about animal ethics. Singer and Regan come out of a European humanist tradition that pays insufficient attention to differences among people. Their work has sometimes been used to make univeralist arguments about how all people should live with other animals, arguments that ignore the distinct cultural and economic contexts in which human-animal relations develop in practice.[30]

While their philosophical defences of animals have been important for the development of vegan ethics, the theories of Singer and Regan have by no means been the only factors. There is a history of vegetarianism and veganism in feminist activism and writing that does not rely on utilitarian or rights philosophy. Just as in the nineteenth and early twentieth centuries vegetarianism was associated with a number of alternative political and social movements, in the late twentieth and early twenty first centuries veganism has been practised in some anarchist, feminist and queer movements. The African-American civil rights activist Dick Gregory is sometimes cited as an influence for Black vegans, as is the Rastafarian tradition of Ital.[31] Followers of Hinduism, Buddhism and Jainism have used predominantly plant-based diets for centuries, as did some of the Indigenous peoples of the Americas before the Spanish Conquest of 1492. Those communities that relied on hunting and fishing did not share a European, Christian worldview that placed human beings above other animals.[32] Veganism as widely understood today arose in response to a specifically Western history of human exploitation of other animals. While it is now followed by many people outside this context, veganism should not be used by Western thinkers and activists as a universal moral baseline, to be adopted in a particular way by all people, including those populations colonised by European nations and whose traditions may have involved less exploitative human-animal relations. It is this colonialist conceit that has sometimes made veganism a flashpoint in debates about animal advocacy, racism and imperialism.[33]

This book acknowledges the importance of the pathbreaking work of Singer and Regan, as well as early animal activists. But it dedicates more space to new generations of vegans who are changing what it means to practise veganism in the contemporary world. The pages here are especially inspired by feminist and queer theories that emphasise veganism as an embodied practice or an expansive expression of care for other-than-human kin.[34] It is informed by writers who understand veganism as a contextual and ever-changing practice, an aspiration rather than a moral absolute, an ongoing process of questioning one's place in the world rather than a secure sense of self. I follow those who understand veganism not as a rationalist calculation of right and wrong, but an expression of the recognition of our dependencies on other animals. The vegan artists, activists and thinkers I cite draw on a range of cultural and intellectual traditions, including, but not exclusive to, animal rights discourse. They recognise that practising veganism does not mean avoiding all forms of death or violence against other animals.[35] And they understand veganism as a practice integral to, rather than in competition with, struggles for justice for human beings.

While I welcome wholeheartedly the rise in numbers of people practising veganism, I am wary of turning "vegan" and "veganism" into modern myths, frozen in history and ceasing to be open to change.[36] The word "vegan" proliferates on the windows and menus of eating establishments in my East London neighbourhood, and in many of the cities I have visited in Europe, Canada and Mexico. While this trend makes veganism more accessible to some, it also helps to associate veganism with consumerism and healthy, expensive eating. Likewise, the internet is an important resource for vegans and I have used it substantially in this book to access contemporary debates. But I am concerned that the word "veganism" sometimes circulates in social media as a static concept defined exclusively as a plant-based diet. At the same time, I am conscious of the productive use of "vegan" in activist circles in a range of contexts. My own first regular contact with veganism came in turn-of-the millennium queer anarchist circles in London, where vegan food was shared among activists engaged in migrant solidarity, sex worker rights and anti-capitalist campaigns. More recently, on a trip to Mexico in early 2018, I discovered that many animal rights activists use the terms "vegan" and "anti-speciesist" strategically to signal their opposition to animal exploitation in the context of neocolonialism, rather than as a form of consumerism or identity politics. Practising contextual ethical veganism means recognising and being open to these differences, as well as to changing definitions of vegan and veganism.

Beyond moralism and identity

One of the most frequently repeated clichés about vegans is that we are are self-righteous and believe ourselves holier-than-thou. In a world in which moralism plagues so much of political discourse, in which righteousness so easily slides into self-righteousness, it is notable that vegans take the rap for this more than most. As someone who practises veganism I have much more frequently been accused of being moralistic (or of being in cahoots with moralisers) than I have been for supporting any struggle against the oppression of people, even though feminist, queer and anti-capitalist movements are by no means free from obnoxious ranters. In fact, as I show in chapter 6 of this book, vegans can be accused of being moralistic even without opening our mouths. Our very presence is enough to provoke accusations of moralism. This suggests that the gripe is not with vegans ourselves, but with our message. As the philosopher Cora Diamond wrote over four decades ago: "I do not think it an accident that the arguments of vegetarians have a nagging moralistic tone. They are an attempt to show something to be morally wrong, on the assumption that we all agree that it is morally wrong to raise people for meat, and so on."[37] It is perhaps also not an accident that as arguments in favour of veganism become more forceful — in the light of evidence of animals' abilities to feel and express pain, the abuses of animal agriculture and climate change — enthusiastic meat- eaters find it easier to dismiss the messengers than to engage seriously with the message.

When I say that veganism is not a form of moralism I am resisting not only the bad arguments of some omnivores, but also the bad arguments of some vegans. I am thinking in particular of claims that veganism is a "moral baseline" or "moral imperative" for anyone who cares about the rights of animals. This view is put forth by the vegan legal scholar Gary Francione and the philosopher Gary Steiner, for example, and can be understood as a universalist argument that goes against the principles of the contextual ethical veganism espoused in this book.[38] Similarly, I reject claims that veganism is a form of self-sacrifice.[39] While veganism does mean giving up certain things, it does not mean giving up a part of ourselves, our most cherished values or interests. Nor should veganism be understood as a form of moral or physical purity. It can only ever be an aspiration, never a perfection. Vegan bodies are not free from the traces of other animals, for many reasons.[40] There is no being in the world without killing and death. As Sunaura Taylor puts it: "vegans are not opposed to death. We are opposed to the commodification and unnecessary killing of animals for human pleasure and benefit."[41] Practising veganism means recognising that as human beings we have much to do to minimise violence in the world, even if we can never eliminate it entirely.

By measuring the credentials of individual vegans, arguments in favour of moral baselines or self-sacrifice actually deflect attention away from animals and back onto people. I do not say "I am vegan" in order to emphasise my own impeccable ethics. I usually say "I am vegan" for practical reasons. If I want to coexist with other human beings in an omnivorous society I constantly have to tell them what I do and do not eat and the activities involving animals (dead or alive) I do or do not participate in. I do not conceive of veganism as a statement of who I am — in short, as an identity — though it is sometimes understood in this way. For example, Laura Wright, author of the book *The Vegan Studies Project*, begins from the premise that "vegan" is a "culturally loaded term" which signals both an identity and a practice. Wright acknowledges that as an identity "vegan" is unstable. There is a "tension," she writes, "between the dietary practice of veganism and the manifestation, construction, and representation of vegan identity" because "vegan identity is both created by vegans and interpreted and, therefore, reconstituted, by and within contemporary (non-vegan) media."[42] In this sense, we could compare vegan identity to categories such as gender, sexuality, race and class — identities that are constructed through the ongoing, complex interaction between self-identity and wider social forces and discourses.

Without wishing either to dismiss the experience of vegans for whom veganism is experienced as an identity, or to create a hierarchy of different identity categories, I think it is fair to say that vegan differs in important ways from, for example, gender, "race, sexual orientation, national origin, or religion."[43] For one thing, although the latter categories are all historically contingent, they nevertheless carry a substantial historical weight and collective meaning in a way that vegan does not. Few people are born into vegan families, are assigned vegan at birth or experience discrimination or privilege for being vegan. Some may object that it is just a matter of time before veganism becomes something inherited, complete with a recognised community history and collective memory; and others might claim that vegans can be the targets of discrimination. Yet I suggest that vegan is less an identity than an ethical, and for some political, commitment to end the exploitation of other animals. In that sense, "vegan" has more in common with "feminism" than "woman," is more akin to "anti-racist" than "Black." But even here there is an important difference: while one can certainly identify as a feminist without identifying as a woman (to give one example), to "be" vegan is by definition *not* to belong to the community of beings whose oppression one seeks to end. I would go further: when "vegan" is understood as a category of human identity it actually takes attention *away* from animals and centres it on people. For that reason identifying "as vegan" carries the risk of anthropocentrism.

The philosopher Chloë Taylor writes of ethical vegetarianism that "it is always constitutive of the vegetarian's identity. We do not say that we eat vegetarian but that we *are* vegetarian."[44] Extending this observation to veganism, we could say that it too is "always constitutive of the (vegan)'s identity." But in order to avoid reductive or static uses of "vegan" and "veganism," it would perhaps be useful to think of veganism as something we practise or *do* rather than vegan as something we *are*. This would allow us, in the words of Dinesh Joseph Wadiwel, "to explore veganism as a set of imperfect practices which are situationally located as forms of resistance to the war on animals, rather than as a mode of identity."[45] Our ethical and political commitments, what we eat and wear, the company we keep — these are all expressions of complex collective and individual identities. They say something about who we are or want to be; in the contemporary world they can form part of what Taylor, following Michel Foucault, calls self-fashioning.[46] In this sense, the practice of veganism is entangled in our identities without in itself *being* an identity. Similarly, we can recognise that practising veganism involves an ongoing process of personal transformation, and impacts on the ways in which we live our lives, even while veganism is much more than a lifestyle. One of the things I want to try to convey in these pages, against a negative representation of veganism either as trendy lifestyle choice or moralistic holier-than-thouism, is the joy of striving to live as people, caring for ourselves and others, without depending upon the endless exploitation of other animals.

Vegan stories

> Stories are a great way to educate, share information, pass on pearls of wisdom in ways that can adapt to each individual that hears them, and our ability to reflect on our own stories, integrate the learnings and then reframe them and share them with our insights are powerful acts of magic.[47]

I am not the first to tell my vegan story. Over the past several years more and more people are writing or talking about veganism, including its relationship to gender, sexuality, race, class and disability. Their tales appear in blogs, online magazines and social media; newspapers and television; documentary and fiction film; PhD theses, academic books and journals; and at conferences where academics and activists converge.[48] There is also a popular tradition to be found in zines and pamphlets, and in the recorded oral histories of animal rights activists, as well as autobiographical writing by vegans. This book draws on a number of these sources, interweaving them with my own autobiographical experience and reflection.

The stories I tell look at veganism from different angles: how and why people come to practise veganism; how we face different difficulties, including practical challenges and those of combining veganism with other priorities in our lives; how veganism relates to our different identities, including sexuality and gender; people's encounters with other animals — dead, alive and imaginary — and how these shape our ideas about veganism; and some of the pleasures of practising veganism. The topics I cover include: comparisons between violence against animals and violence against women and other human groups (chapter 1); feminist arguments for and against veganism (chapters 1, 2 and 4); the relationship between veganism and environmentalism, including climate change activism (chapter 3); how some people have confronted the ethical dilemmas of practising veganism in the face of serious illnesses, and other issues related to caring for ourselves, other people and other animals (chapters 4 and 5); real and fake fur and leather, especially their use and meanings in some queer subcultures (chapter 5); anti-colonial and anti-racist arguments for and against veganism (chapters 5 and 6); the mainstreaming of veganism and the rise of vegan consumerism (chapter 6); and fictional representations of vegans and vegan futures (interludes 1 and 2). This list is not exhaustive. New research, writing and artistic work on veganism — and, in the academic context, critical animal studies — are appearing on a daily basis, and I apologise in advance for missing any important new evidence or arguments. Many themes are not covered in detail in the book: religious arguments for and against veganism; the dilemmas of vegans sharing our lives with carnivorous companion animals; veganism and debates about women's eating and body image. Where I have not trod this time other writers have, and more will surely follow.[49]

At points in the subsequent pages the reader may say, "What on earth does this have to do with a plant-based diet?" The sections on sex work, naturopathic cancer treatments and queer leather communities (in chapters 1, 4 and 5 respectively) might make a few readers squirm. So let me say from the start that mine is a personal, and hence idiosyncratic, take on the sexual politics of veganism. I have followed my experiences, desires and passions as well as the stories and theories of others who have sparked my interest. By retracing my particular path I aim to present aspects of veganism that I believe are underexplored, especially in relation to queer politics and feminism. As veganism becomes more popular and widespread I think it is vitally important to honour its longer associations with radical political movements and alternative communities. And against the common perception that veganism is only for the young and the fit, I want to provide some insight into the peculiarities of coming to veganism in middle age, and about the forces and factors that enable us to change our ways at different stages in our lives. In my own reflections and those of others I have tried to find tales that go against the grain either of stereotypes or mainstream writing. By taking some unexpected turns, I encourage readers to think of veganism from different perspectives, and above all to be open to its powers, possibilities and pleasures, as well as its necessities.

Chapter 1

DREADED COMPARISONS AND OTHER STORIES

The Vegan Papers

August 2014
London

It's almost six months since I stopped eating animal products. This short voyage into new habits has been accompanied by fits of writing, sorting thoughts and observations. I am going to call this haphazard diary "The Vegan Papers." I'm writing because I want to make sense of why, at this relatively late stage in my life, I became vegan virtually overnight. What was behind and around this personal and political turning point? What were the connections between this change and my other ideals and commitments? These questions are striking: posing them reminds me that in the omnivore culture in which I grew up and continue to live, eating, wearing and otherwise using animal products for our human-centred ends is the norm. Giving up the habit of exploiting animals is abnormal. A little deviant even.

I also need to make sense of others' opposition to this giving up. I write in part because I want to understand why veganism sometimes encounters resistance, even provokes other people to anger. The most difficult anger to face has been the accusation that vegans don't care about people. That by not eating meat, milk and eggs, or not buying leather or wool, we are complicit in violence against other human beings. The first time I heard someone accuse me directly of being a privileged vegan who didn't care that millions of people in the world don't have enough food to eat it felt like a kick in the gut. Red rage rose to my cheeks, anger shielding against anger. But after the defensive reaction came the questions: How could choosing to minimise my complicity in violence against other-than-human animals be equated with complicity in violence against other humans? Why does veganism sometimes become a flashpoint for anxiety and anger about differences and power relations among people? And how can vegans and animal advocates tell stories about our relationships to other animals that honour the lives of those creatures without making simplistic comparisons to the ways in which human beings do harm to one another?

Shortly after starting "The Vegan Papers" — excerpts from which appear throughout this book — I started to look for answers to these questions by investigating veganism's connection to feminism. I took that focus because feminism was the broad movement and community in which much of my political formation had taken place. My aim was not to come up with a singular theory or explanation of how and why sexual politics and veganism are related. And because it is impossible to separate sexual politics and human-animal relations from other forms of power relations among people, I also had to examine the ways that some vegans reference histories of racism and genocide in their attempts to raise awareness of the exploitation of animals. The purpose of this chapter is to examine some of those examples and to explain why big-picture analyses that make sweeping claims about similarities among different forms of oppression, while sometimes useful, also run the risk of reductiveness.

Following the wisdom of the animal rights activist and

performance artist Mirha-Soleil Ross, I argue that we should be wary of forcing connections and obsessively trying to bring everything together at the expense of being faithful to the specificity of each issue.[1] While keen to see links where they exist, my storytelling technique in this chapter and the rest of the book is designed less to tie things up than to follow threads to see where they meet, all the while paying attention to webs of power and struggle. I understand veganism as inseparable from feminism and other struggles for justice among people because I believe these movements share a commitment to an ethics of non-violence and a recognition that we are all responsible for, as well as dependent upon, other animals, including people.[2] Understanding the ways hierarchies, power structures and systems of exploitation operate against different bodies and groups is an important step towards challenging them. Although those systems are interlocking, extending an ethics of non-violence to all creatures does not depend upon demonstrating that people and other animals are exploited or violated in similar ways. On the contrary: it requires that we pay as much attention to difference as similarity. It also requires that we avoid pitting different forms of violence against one another by, for example, implying that one is more urgent than another. Finally, it requires that we be aware of what comparisons might obscure as much as they clarify.

Vegan feminist stories

My first regular contact with vegans and veganism was in London's hodgepodge queer anarchist communities around the turn of the millennium. Preparing and sharing plant-based food was part of a wider social and political project that also incorporated a critique of neoliberal capitalism, migrant solidarity, campaigns for affordable safe housing, and alternative sexual relationships. Although not active in animal rights campaigns or practising veganism at that time, I recognised that there was an ethos in these communities that emphasised solidarity with people and other animals alongside what I would call a politics of pleasure. We were committed to struggles against different forms of violence without reducing our personal experiences or those of others to the status of victimhood.

When I started to investigate the relationship between feminism, sexuality and veganism I was surprised to find that much writing on the topic emphasised similarities in the ways animals — especially those raised for food — and female human beings were victimised. The main reference for this theory was *The Sexual Politics of Meat: A Feminist-Vegetarian Critical Theory* by Carol J. Adams, published in the United States in 1990. In this book Adams "examines the connections between male dominance and meat eating" and argues that "animals' oppression and women's oppression are linked together."[3] Although she was not the first to demonstrate a connection between meat-eating and masculinity, Adams made an original contribution by extending theories of objectification and male violence against women to human violence against other animals, claiming that these processes are related and reinforce one another.[4] Adams's book was important in uncovering the misogynist underpinnings of meat advertising in the U.S. and in showing how, in Anglo-American societies, dominant forms of masculinity are partly constructed in violent opposition to an undervalued femininity and to other animals. Although the contemporary U.S. is not representative of all omnivore societies, Adams's thesis remains relevant to Western popular culture, in which meat-eating and aggression towards animals and women are often represented as part of a tough-guy masculinity.[5]

Adams explained the connection between violence against women and other animals with something called the "absent referent." When live animals are butchered, wrapped up in plastic, sold and eaten by people, they are metaphorically as well as literally repackaged. The act of erasure involved in this process is particularly evident in the English language: cows become "beef," sheep become "lamb," pigs become "pork," and so on. As a result, the living, breathing animals become absent to the people eating them. The theory of the absent referent stresses not only human beings' capacity for violence, but also our ability to deny that violence and, along with it, the history of the other beings against whom we commit it. We don't have to feel responsible towards the animals we are eating, because we have already erased them from our memories. Of course, not all meat-eaters try to forget that they are consuming what was once a living being; some actually promote this fact. In the most voraciously carnivorous corners of contemporary North America, for example, meat-eating is sometimes celebrated through the *present* referent. Kelly Struthers Montford demonstrates this in her analysis of beef advertising in the Canadian province of Alberta, which often features images of living animals.[6]

The theory of the absent referent explains some, but not all, the ways people relate to live and dead animals. It also rests on a simplistic understanding of human gender relations. *The Sexual Politics of Meat* divides people into two groups — men and women — and presents these in a fairly rigid power hierarchy. The book has little to say about the experiences of men who reject hegemonic forms of masculinity (for example, gay men or vegetarians), about transgender people, about how and why some women may take pleasure in eating animal products, or about cultural traditions in which masculinity is not associated with meat-eating. Adams's work also overemphasises female biological reproductive capacity as a point of identification between women and female animals of other species. I do not think women have a particular identification with the suffering of cows and hens, or a special investment in avoiding milk and eggs because these are forms of "feminized protein."[7] Such claims reinforce the idea that womanhood is defined by motherhood and that females across species are united in victimhood. In Adams's version of the world, men are consumers of flesh — literal and representational — while women and animals are objectified and consumed.

The absent referent is a valuable concept for helping us to understand the doublethink sometimes involved in consuming animal products. But the theory has too often been used as an overarching explanation for the interconnections between the oppressions of women and animals.[8] In much writing on veganism and feminism published in English, the absent referent has taken on the status of common sense, as defined by the early twentieth-century Marxist Antonio Gramsci and further developed by the cultural critic Stuart Hall. Gramsci defined common sense as thinking that has the status of "traditional truth or wisdom of the ages" and is therefore taken for granted.[9] Common-sense thinking is apparent anywhere an argument takes on the air of a universal explanation. When this happens the history of a particular idea — the context in which it was first formulated, why and under what circumstances — is forgotten or ignored. When certain explanations are repeated time and again they take on the power of timeless truths, resistant to evidence of changing circumstances. For this reason it is important to ask about where arguments come from, how they have been passed down, and what may have gotten lost in transit.

The Sexual Politics of Meat is a book of its time and of a very particular kind of feminism. The language and theory Adams uses to explain the relationships between violence against women and other animals draws substantially on feminist critiques of pornography as they were developed in the U.S. in the decade before the book was published. In the 1980s a number of American feminists — most famous among them Andrea Dworkin and Catharine MacKinnon — argued that pornography was a main cause of women's oppression. In their understanding, pornography was much more than a series of representations of certain sexual practices; it was in itself a form of violence that affected all women. Not only did anti-pornography feminists like Dworkin and MacKinnon call for the legal censorship of pornography; they implied that *all* forms of sexuality, especially penetrative sex, were violent, and that all women were potential victims of violence.[10] Sex, in their account, was basically dangerous for women.

Anti–pornography feminism was challenged by many other feminist activists, in the U.S. and elsewhere.[11] But the work of Dworkin, MacKinnon and their allies was influential in some feminist circles in the West in the late twentieth century. This influence is very much discernible in *The Sexual Politics of Meat* and the later work of Carol Adams.[12] It is important to recognise this because the world as seen through the eyes of anti-pornography feminism is a limited one. It excludes the perspectives of entire groups of people, most notably those who work in pornography and other parts of the sex industry. And by emphasising women's experience of victimhood the theory of the absent referent presents women as having little agency. This is a problem for those of us who believe that women are active sexual beings, and it is a problem for vegans. This is because Adams's writing does not explain the significant *differences* between the representation of women in pornography and advertising, on one hand, and the confinement and slaughter of farm animals for meat, on the other. It is just not possible to understand the complexities of either sexism or animal exploitation with reference to how some women and some animals are represented in a small range of cultural texts. When vegan activists cite *The Sexual Politics of Meat* they should keep this in mind: although the book has some valuable reflection on points of connection between sexism and the exploitation of animals, the theoretical framework and examples it draws on are limited. Ultimately, Adams's reliance on anti-pornography feminism obscures and simplifies the experiences of women and animals. We could say that they both become absent referents in her work.

An early critic of the comparison between pornography and the fate of farm animals was sex worker, performance artist and animal rights activist Mirha-Soleil Ross:

> I was always offended that women who are prostitutes or who work in pornography could be compared to animals in factory farms and slaughterhouses. Frankly we are talking about two different things. Yes there's this image that appeared in a magazine a decade or two ago of a woman's body going through a meat grinder but that was an image, big deal! There are real animals going through that grinder! What animals are enduring on factory farms, during transportation to the slaughterhouse, and during the slaughtering process is absolutely incomparable to our experiences as women consenting to being paid — and quite well thank you — for providing sexual services. Women who work in the sex industry do not think of themselves as pieces of meat and frankly if one did, she'd need a serious reality check. She would need to be dragged to a shed where hundreds of thousands of hens are piled up and rotting in battery cages. She would need to smell and hear and feel the blood and the fear and the agony that goes on 24 hours a day, 7 days a week, 12 months a year for billions

of animals in thousands of slaughterhouses across this continent. So I always found that the comparison was offensive and really minimizing what the animals are actually going through.[13]

Ross highlights the dangers of making comparisons that focus on similarities at the expense of exploring differences among diverse forms of violence. In the next section I turn to some of the other comparisons that have been made in arguments in favour of veganism — those that cite historical examples of mass racism and genocide — and the problems they raise.

"Dreaded comparisons"[14]

Comparisons have a long and controversial history in the movements for animal welfare and rights. For over two hundred years, animal advocates in the West have relied on comparisons between the maltreatment of animals and oppression of certain groups of human beings. In nineteenth-century Britain and the U.S. some slavery abolitionists made links between the abuse of animals and human slavery, and animal advocates in turn took lessons from the campaign to end slavery.[15] Later in the nineteenth century some female anti-vivisectionists noted similarities in the methods used in live experimentation on dogs and other animals, and those employed in the gynaecological examinations of poor women. If women as a whole were considered less rational and therefore more like animals than men, literature published at the time sometimes portrayed working-class women as wild animals who needed to be brought under the control of male doctors.[16] A hundred years later, in his landmark philosophical and political treatise *Animal Liberation*, Peter Singer proposed that animal liberation was a natural extension of the Black civil rights and women's liberation movements, advocating the use of the term "speciesism" as an equivalent to racism and sexism.[17] Singer was proposing, in effect, that the exploitation of animals was comparable to the oppression of women and African Americans. While these are very different kinds of comparisons, they demonstrate that violence against people has, historically, sometimes been justified on the grounds that those people are no more than "animals," and that different movements against the mistreatment of animals have drawn analogies with violence against people.

In the early twenty-first century it is not uncommon to find animal advocates comparing animal abuse to histories of racial violence and genocide. Most notoriously perhaps, the campaigns of the largest animal rights non-governmental organisation in the U.S., People for the Ethical Treatment of Animals (PETA, founded in 1980), have drawn analogies between the fate of farm animals and the historical enslavement of African Americans. Other activists have compared animal slaughter to the murder of Jews and other prisoners in Nazi concentration camps. These comparisons have often received harsh criticism from people who argue that they trivialise the historical experiences of human victims of racism and genocide and reinforce racist stereotypes associating Blacks, Jews and other racialised groups with animals.[18] These comparisons and criticisms have been given so much air time that it might seem redundant to revisit them here. However, in the course of researching this book I became aware that slavery and Holocaust analogies have taken on new life in the age of social media, circulating far and fast.[19] I am also aware that some vegan activists believe that such comparisons, when made carefully, can be useful guides for understanding how different forms of power and violence relate to and reinforce one another. For these reasons, I think it is worth considering briefly how these different kinds of comparisons work and why they continue to cause controversy.

The Black vegan writer Christopher-Sebastian McJetters provides an example of what I would call a useful comparison. He argues that the "mindset" that allowed for the justification and continuation of chattel slavery for several centuries in the United States and elsewhere is comparable in some ways to that which enables the widespread justification today of the raising, slaughter and consumption of animals. Note that McJetters is not comparing human slaves to animals; he is comparing the ways certain kinds of oppressive attitudes and systems are formed and become the norm.[20] In a similar vein, the vegan writer and activist A. Breeze Harper approaches comparisons between human slavery and animal agriculture with caution and open-mindedness. In her book *Sistah Vegan*, an anthology of writings by Black female vegans in the U.S., Harper discusses the controversy surrounding a 2005 PETA campaign entitled "The Animal Liberation Project." PETA has removed the link to their online version of the exhibit, so I quote Harper's description of it:

> images of human suffering juxtaposed with nonhuman animal suffering: a painting of Native Americans on the Trail of Tears positioned next to a photo of herds of nonhuman animals being led to their demise; the atrocity of a Black man's lynched and tortured body next to a picture of an animal that had been burned; a black-and-white Jewish Holocaust photo next to animals in confined, crammed structures on a meat-production farm.[21]

From my observation of individual photos still available online I can add to this that the historical photographs of violence against people are in black and white while the contemporary images of animal abuse are in colour, and the juxtaposed images are emblazoned with words including "Enslaved," "Hanging" and "Beaten." These images were exhibited in public places throughout the United States, including on university campuses, where they were often met with protest.[22]

The PETA campaign is different from the analysis of McJetters. Even if it implies a comparison between systems of oppression, the juxtaposition of violent images can readily be interpreted as a comparison of certain groups of people with animals. In the words of Claire Jean Kim, "Jews, blacks, and others have historically been constructed as liminal figures standing at the boundary between humanness and animalness precisely in order to justify their enslavement or extermination."[23] The PETA exhibit draws on this history, not to raise awareness of the persistent use of the tropes of bestiality in contemporary racist language, but as a publicity stunt to get people to think about the suffering of animals. PETA's use of sensationalist imagery fails to take into account that these will have different meanings for different groups of people, most notably those whose ancestors are represented in them. While recognising that such representations were aimed at raising viewers' consciousness, Harper argues that they are oppressive to people of colour because the "images and textual references trigger trauma and deep emotional pain."[24]

Harper contrasts the "lack of sociohistorical context" in PETA's video and photo campaign with what she calls the "sensitive, scholarly explorations" of Marjorie Spiegel and Charles Patterson, who have written books analysing the historical interconnections between the violent instrumentalisation of animals in farming and scientific experimentation and, respectively, slavery and the Holocaust.[25] In *The Dreaded Comparison: Human and Animal Slavery,*

Spiegel takes the reader through a brief account of the different ways chattel slavery was interlinked in the past with the forced keeping of animals, especially those destined for human consumption. She shows that white writers often compared Africans, as well as Indigenous Americans, to other animals ("brutes"), how similar instruments of control (for example, muzzles and chains) were used to restrain slaves and animals, and draws parallels between the forced breeding practices used on human slaves and farm animals. Based on such evidence, Spiegel makes a compelling case for comparing the *institution* of chattel slavery to industrial farming, and for taking the experiences of those oppressed by these systems as the impetus for change. "It is vital to link oppressions in our minds," she writes, "to look for the common, shared aspects, and work against them as one. To deny our similarities to animals is to deny and undermine our own power."[26] In *Eternal Treblinka: Our Treatment of Animals and the Holocaust* Patterson makes a similar case that ideologies and practices of white Christian supremacy are historically interconnected to human control and abuse of other animals. Christian vilification of Jews as beasts and vermin went back centuries; National Socialist propaganda drew on and expanded these anti-Semitic metaphors. Patterson also examines the interwoven histories of forced breeding and sterilisation, eugenics and industrial slaughter that were developed and used on different species of animals and on millions of people during the Nazi genocide.[27] *Eternal Treblinka*, like Spiegel's *Dreaded Comparison*, draws out these interlocking systems, without insisting they are the same. Nor does either book claim that the histories of slavery or the Holocaust can be explained entirely with reference to similarities with the violent instrumentalisation of animals, or that a myriad of other factors did not contribute to these histories of genocide.

In contrast, all too often comparisons between animal abuse and genocide are made in sensationalist ways that reduce complex historical processes to dramatic images, slogans or simplistic analogies that emphasise similarity over difference. Some such bad comparisons can be found in contemporary defences of veganism. For example, in 2009 the vegan philosopher Gary Steiner published an article in the *New York Times* in which he made a reference to Isaac Bashevis Singer's short story "The Letter Writer" (the story also inspired the title of Patterson's book). Steiner wrote that Singer "called the slaughter of animals the 'eternal Treblinka.'"[28] Singer did indeed explore the theme of human maltreatment of animals in a number of his short stories, frequently drawing comparisons with the Holocaust.[29] However, to use the term "eternal Treblinka" as a shorthand for animal exploitation belittles the complexity of meaning in Singer's fictional work. The "Letter Writer" is not a political tract; it is a moving tale about a Holocaust survivor and his multiple relationships with the human and other-than-human world, including a mouse who inhabits his house.[30] Following some objections by readers to his use of the phrase "eternal Treblinka," in a chapter entitled "Cosmopolitanism and Veganism" Steiner excused himself, saying he "had absolutely no intention of belittling the hideous fate of the Jews."[31] This strikes me as a defensive reply that demonstrates a lack of willingness to listen and engage, in Harper's words, with other people's accounts of the "painful history of racially motivated violence."[32]

But Steiner persists — going beyond the use of the comparison between animal slaughter and the Holocaust to make it into a competition:

> when we occupy the anthropocentric standpoint, we do something that is *arguably much worse*: we fail to

appreciate the fact that this sacrifice of innocents is so woven into our everyday practices and values that we tend to shudder at the characterisation of this regime as being in any way comparable to large-scale human tragedies.[33]

Steiner seems to suggest that one history of mass violence — the Holocaust — enjoys greater recognition than the other — mass animal slaughter. The implication is that the anti-Semitism and other forms of racism that enabled the Nazi genocide are now fully recognised and therefore not as urgent as the issue of mass animal slaughter. A similar problem was on display in the PETA campaign "The Animal Liberation Project." As one critic observed, the juxtaposition of *black and white* photos of historical violence against African-Americans, Jews and Indigenous people with *colour* photos of violence against animals created a visual image "implying that 'hey oppression of minorities is in the past. It's over!'"[34] In both cases, there is a failure to acknowledge and confront the realities of persisting forms of racial discrimination and violence.

In Steiner's usage, the Treblinka extermination camp is shed of its historical specificity and the realities of the people who perished there. It becomes instead a catchphrase to promote veganism as part of a philosophical argument. There are other examples of vegan and animal rights activists making similarly reductive references to Nazi camps. During the protests against the live export of veal calves from England to the European continent in early 1995, some activists carried placards reading, simply, "AUSCHWITZ."[35] Other campaigns have employed photographs of a pile of animal corpses next to a photograph of a pile of skeletal human bodies.[36] As with the examples from PETA and Steiner cited above, these campaigns imply that anti-Semitism — like racism generally — has been overcome and allocated to history. These signs and representations try to promote animal rights by exploiting painful pasts of violence against human beings, without regard for how these campaigns will impact people living with the legacies of that violence. The political scientist Claire Jean Kim has argued that the PETA "Animal Liberation Project" is morally defensible, because it draws attention to an urgent moral issue — the mass exploitation of animals — but that it is politically indefensible "because it may complicate the project of building cross-group alliances in the context of fighting 'interlocking structures' of domination."[37] But I don't think these two elements are so easily separable. It is precisely because these comparisons fail to address "interlocking structures" of domination that they are morally unjustifiable. In order to be morally defensible they would have to give full recognition to the different forms of violence referenced in the comparisons, including recognition of the ongoing forces of racism. This is where the analogies used by PETA and Steiner differ from the more carefully contextualised comparisons of Spiegel and Patterson, which are attentive to how "interlocking systems" of violence affect different species, including human beings.[38]

Kim is right that, ultimately, the uncritical circulation of images and words that imply or directly make comparisons between factory farming, animal experimentation and Nazi death camps is politically counterproductive. One reason for this is that competitive comparisons can never do justice to *either* element being compared. We cannot extend solidarity to other animals by pitting their needs against those of different groups of people. Competitive comparisons obscure the details that we need to understand in order to appreciate what is at stake in confronting violence against different groups. It feels almost absurd to have to point out that the forced breeding, raising and slaughter of farm animals for human consumption on a mass scale is not a form of genocide.[39] This does not mean that it should not be opposed. PETA spokespeople claim that they make comparisons with the Holocaust and slavery in order to drive home the point that people, too, are animals, and that we have a moral obligation to *all* animals, not just to our own species.[40] This is an important argument. But their campaigns can also be read to imply that other animals are only worthy of our consideration if we can imagine them as suffering *as people have*. Moreover, photographs or words that present animals as little more than distressed victims may actually reinforce rather than challenge anthropocentric attitudes by implying that human beings are the heroes who should save poor helpless creatures. When presented with endless images of animal suffering we get no sense of animals as complex beings with agency. Nor are we enlightened about the institutional powers behind animal agriculture, why the slaughter of animals for meat continues to rise precipitously throughout the world today, and how we might end this.[41] If the reason for using comparisons between different forms of oppression is to encourage people to rethink our relationship to animals in the present and to stop abusing them, the analogies we need are those that open people to new information rather than close us down. And even this is not sufficient: it is not enough that comparisons raise awareness about violence against other animals. They need to do the work of challenging oppressions against people too. Only then can we rid ourselves of the competitive logic which, as Spiegel so convincingly argues, can only support master narratives and the forces of oppression against all beings.

From dreaded comparisons to strategic images

It is never good enough to stop at a critique of bad language or representations. One task of activists is to consider in what contexts particular comparisons might work well, and what kinds of language and images we might use most effectively to promote positive change. Used with careful consideration, provocative representations might promote reflection that prompts people to treat animals in more humane ways. The historian Hilda Kean emphasises the importance of visual imagery in changing attitudes and actions towards animals in the past. Focusing on the rise of campaigns against cruelty to animals in Britain in the nineteenth century, she argues that there was a close relationship between the act of *seeing* the mistreatment of animals and campaigning to end it. Similarly, in her discussion of the English live export protests of the 1990s, Kean insists that demonstrators were affected both by witnessing the suffering of caged veal calves as they were transported to ports and airports, and by the hidden cruelty they imagined the animals would undergo at the end of the voyage.[42]

According to the artist and critic Steve Baker, animal advocates should not be in the business of recycling old images, but instead should try to create new ones that will promote more ethical inter-species relations. In a world saturated with images of animals, Baker wonders "whether and how things might be changed — to the advantage of the animal — through the constructive use of representations." In his book *Picturing the Beast,* Baker makes a useful comparison between two posters used by the British Royal Society for the Protection and Care of Animals (RSPCA) for the launch of its advertising campaign for dog registration in 1989. The first poster — which, significantly, Baker does not reproduce — features a picture of "a huge pile of dead dogs." The photograph "(i)conographically," and presumably on purpose, recalled images of heaps of human bodies from concentration camps, similar to the one described above, and, according to Baker, "understandably caused controversy and offence." A second poster — which does appear in Baker's book — shows a photo of a black bin bag (a "doggy bag") filled with something and tied at the end. Although this second image was "superficially, more restrained" than the first, Baker argues that by "the very act of leaving it to the viewers' imaginations to picture the final body which the bag concealed, thus denying them the catharsis of responding to its literal depiction, the image arguably remains more potent and more horrific than the pile of dogs."[43] Baker implies that a political image may have more currency when used in a way that trusts the human viewer to make the imaginative link herself rather than having it thrust upon her.

When animal advocates turn expressions like "eternal Treblinka" into slogans, carry signs emblazoned with the word "Auschwitz," or circulate photographs of dead chicken bodies in heaps, they literalise and force analogies, reifying them and presenting them as perpetual truths. In so doing, they simplify the historical specificity of the Holocaust and of the exploitation of animals alike. While representations of violence committed against animals have a certain shock value that may motivate people to change, such images also carry dangers. When they try to impose a particular message on an image or word, animal advocates do something similar to anti-pornography feminists: they tell us that there is only one way of interpreting the images around us. If we sincerely want to change what Baker calls the "contemptuous attitudes and painful practices to which animals are still too often subjected," we may be better off with powerful but subtle representations of animals that allow room for people's careful contemplation and consideration.[44] All vegans would do well to keep this in mind when we choose the images and language we use.

Alternative animal metaphors

Baker's approach to images that might help to disrupt anthropocentric attitudes acknowledges that people's understanding of animals always relies to a certain extent on our imaginations. We understand animals as symbols as well as living beings. This is apparent in the use of animal metaphors in language. While some metaphors reduce both human and other animals to one-dimensional stereotypes, others may help people to identify with animals in more positive ways, and even to challenge the boundary between human and other species. An example of the former is those metaphors used to deride certain groups of people by associating them with despised creatures. When political activists call the security forces "pigs" they mean to insult the police, but they denigrate the real animals as well. The expression "fat cats" similarly degrades the wealthy people who are meant as its target, but insults and belittles felines and fat humans in the process. The English language is full of such metaphors. Even when they have a poetic ring, they do little to help us to understand animals as living beings worthy of our care.

The performance artist Mirha-Soleil Ross has used her art "to ask some hard questions regarding our use of animals as 'metaphors' for human suffering."[45] In her description of preparing for and writing her one-woman performance piece, *Yapping Out Loud: Contagious Thoughts of an Unrepentant*

Whore, Ross provides a useful contrast between animal metaphors that draw attention to human causes without adequately taking into account the experiences of animals, on one hand, and those that offer the potential for transforming human-animal relations, on the other hand:

> One of the first and most prominent prostitutes' rights organizations in the United States was called COYOTE (Call Off Your Old Tired Ethics) founded in 1973.There are several stories about why the name COYOTE was chosen but the most popular one is that there was a parallel to be drawn between how coyotes are used as "scapegoats" by ranchers and others — and nowadays even in cities like Toronto and Vancouver — for everything that's going wrong and also how prostitutes are blamed for everything that's going wrong in our neighborhoods. So a year ago I just felt this coyote presence crawling into my life and I decided that I had to explore that metaphor more profoundly. I think there is a link between how coyotes are treated and how prostitutes are treated and perceived. But I have an issue when people appropriate another group's oppression to make a statement about their own if they're not going to also speak about that other group's oppression.[46]

Yapping Out Loud explores examples of violence against sex workers through seven monologues, two of them featuring linguistic and visual images of wild canines:

> Coyotes are very powerful animals, beautiful animals. And they can also be intimidating animals. You cannot help but feel something when you're in the presence of a coyote either on video or in real life. Just like prostitutes

also. When people are in our presence, we can come across as powerful people. So I wanted to have this very beautiful and strong and grounded coyote presence.[47]

Ross's coyote metaphor does not insist on parity or even similarity between the persecution of coyotes and sex workers. Her description of feeling "this coyote presence crawling into my life" is an example of what the late Gloria Anzaldúa, in her short essay "Metaphors in the Tradition of the Shaman," called the "working of [...] the imagination act(ing) upon the body."[48] For Anzaldúa, images and words communicate with the body's organs, reshaping them in the process. The way our imaginations work, the kinds of metaphors we choose or have imposed upon us, can make us sick. This is especially true of racist and other oppressive metaphors (for example, comparing people of colour to animals). But metaphors can also heal and open the way for transformation. One task of the poet is to cure societies by purging dead, harmful metaphors and replacing them with new, healing ones:

> Like the shaman, we [poets] transmit information from our consciousness to the physical body of another. [...] If we've done our job well we may give others access to a language and images with which they can articulate/ express pain, confusion, joy and other experiences thus far experienced only on an unarticulated emotional level.[49]

I detect in Ross's story of the coyote entering her life echoes of Anzuldúa's transformative poetry. And I learn from the words of queer artists such as Ross and Anzaldúa that animals can work their way into our imaginations and bodies, helping us to see the world in ways that may empower us to change it. As

Ross insists, other creatures are always *more* than metaphors for human existence and dreams. Similarly to Baker's call for animal representations that offer alternatives to the violent, anthropocentric images of animals that saturate Western society, Ross's coyote metaphor reminds us that the use of animal symbolism need not be reductive and oppressive for human beings or animals. At different points in this book I consider how we might use animal imagery, as well our everyday encounters with animals, to learn more about the lives and experiences of other creatures, in the process thinking about how we might construct new, less oppressive relationships to them.

The history of the use of animal metaphors and comparisons between people and animals shows that these can sometimes be transformative. But they can also be dangerous, for people and animals alike. Making comparisons between different forms of oppression and violence can be a useful way of prompting people to examine more carefully the gaps in our thinking and compassion, to draw attention to our inconsistencies and our hypocrisies. But in order to do that effectively, comparisons need to be done in ways that recognise differences as much as similarities. This includes, crucially, the fact that comparisons of different kinds of past atrocities will have very different meanings for different people. If the aim of veganism is to encourage people to end the exploitation of all animals, including humans, we need to be careful and conscious about the kinds of comparisons we use, and how. And we need to be honest about whether certain metaphors and comparisons are likely to promote change, or whether they carry the risk of injuring others while keeping the hierarchical status quo firmly in place.

Chapter 2

EATING AND BEING EATEN

September 2017
Alicante, Spain

Ideas that have been swimming around my mind for some time — less a school than an anarchic assembly of finned creatures — are starting to sway to the rhythm of my peculiar temporary office space. The location is a rather rustic sailboat, moored in a Mediterranean marina, bobbing up and down, rocking me and filling my ears with the assorted sounds of flapping sails, lapping water and, most insistent and persistent, the scrape of the hull against the wooden dock. Between rushes of rapid jotting on my laptop I become aware of the movement and soundtrack outside, amplified at times by flashes of heat from inside and outside my body.

This morning a different kind of bodily sensation disrupted and then coloured my thinking: during my dawn dip in the sea I was stung by a jellyfish. It was quick as lightening — brief confusion followed by the shock of realisation, then panic as I kicked the innocent offender away and swam quickly back to shore. The calf and knee of my left leg swelled rapidly under the hot red stripes left by the tentacles I had managed to tear away. After a do-it-yourself treatment — dosing the injured leg in vinegar, followed by a hot shower — the sting subdued to a dull ache as I continued to write.

The body of this particular animal — whom I had glanced but briefly, a faint swirl of cloud dispersing underwater — stayed with me.

Later, walking to lunch under the scorching sun, I reflected on my irritation with this small beast of the sea. After all, it was I who had trespassed in her home. Though I had escaped with minor pain and discomfort, I didn't know what had become of her. Do jellyfish have a sex? Do they live after they sting? A quick tour through Google taught me that most jellyfish are male or female and sting to defend themselves and catch their prey, so do not normally die after striking out. I seem to have come off lightly — no tentacles stuck in my flesh. Yet as the swelling died down I felt blessed to carry a light trace on my skin of this encounter with a real-life medusa.

Being prey and being predators

My brush with the jellyfish in the warm waters of the Mediterranean brought to mind a tale of a much more dramatic — and infinitely more dangerous — underwater encounter with a predator. In a brief narrative written in the mid 1990s, the late ecofeminist philosopher Val Plumwood recounts the story of her near-death experience with a saltwater crocodile during a solo canoe trip in Australia's Kakadu National Park.[1] Plumwood's description of how she escaped — just — three consecutive crocodile death rolls is also an account of how, while she fought for her life, her sense of self was shattered. This is no heroic tale of human survival in the face of the unpredictable brutality of "nature," no reaffirmation of what it means to be human in the face of adversity. Instead, Plumwood's crocodile tale is a humble reflection on herself as prey. It is also the occasion for asking about how we as people categorise different species, deciding what counts as food and what does not — questions with important ethical and political implications for vegans, vegetarians and omnivores alike.

An experienced canoeist and bush traveller, Plumwood had ventured out alone into the lagoon on a wet day in search of an Aboriginal rock art site. As the rains got heavier she and her canoe were pulled out of the backwaters into the main river channel that the camp ranger had warned her to stay away from: "'The current's too swift, and if you get into trouble, there are the crocodiles. Lots of them along the river!'" As she looked cautiously towards the banks — "Edges are one of the crocodile's favourite food-capturing places" — Plumwood realised the seriousness of her situation: "As a solitary specimen of a major prey species of the saltwater crocodile, I was standing in one of the most dangerous places on earth." Guiding the canoe steadily and carefully to avoid the shore, Plumwood saw with alarm that what she had thought was a stick ahead of her was actually a crocodile lurking at the surface of the water. In retrospect, Plumwood imbues her story with an element of fate: "Although I was paddling to miss the crocodile, our paths were strangely convergent." Before she could change tack, the crocodile began to strike at her small vessel. "For the first time," Plumwood writes, "it came to me fully that I was prey." Just as she was steering the canoe to shore to get out onto dry land "the crocodile rushed up alongside the canoe, and its beautiful, flecked golden eyes looked straight into mine." In the next instant the animal had Plumwood in a tight grip, dragging her underwater.

Plumwood attempts, with hindsight, to make meaning of her thoughts during the three death rolls that followed:

> In its final, frantic attempts to protect itself from the knowledge that threatens the narrative framework, the mind can instantaneously fabricate terminal

doubt of extravagant proportions: This is not really happening. This is a nightmare from which I will soon awake. This desperate delusion split apart as I hit the water. In that flash, I glimpsed the world for the first time "from the outside," as a world no longer my own, an unrecognizable bleak landscape composed of raw necessity, indifferent to my life or death.

Against the odds Plumwood remained conscious through these short bursts of terror ("The crocodile's breathing and heart metabolism are not suited to prolonged struggle," she explains, "so the roll is an intense burst of power designed to overcome the victim's resistance quickly") and managed to come back for air after each roll. Following the third, she scrambled her mangled body up the shore, away from the river and crocodile. But she was far from her trailer and had sustained serious wounds. In the goriest segment of the story, but also one of the most telling, Plumwood stops to inspect the extent of her physical injuries: "The left thigh hung open, with bits of fat, tendon, and muscle showing, and a sick, numb feeling suffused my entire body." In this moment of relief mixed with fear and pain, Plumwood sees part of her own body as raw meat.

Yet the experience of being torn physically and existentially proved to Plumwood that she was *something more than* meat:

> As my own narrative and the larger story were ripped apart, I glimpsed a shockingly indifferent world in which I had no more significance than any other edible being. The thought, "This can't be happening to me, I'm a human being. I am more than just food!" was one component of my terminal incredulity. It was a shocking reduction, from a complex human being to a mere piece of meat. Reflection has persuaded me that

not just humans but any creature can make the same claim to be more than just food.

Plumwood does not call her story "Being meat," though that would have been a catchier title. The point of her account is precisely that "being prey" — potentially food for another being — is not the same as "being meat" — being *nothing more than* food. The realisation that one can be meat and also be a complex being led Plumwood to conclude that other beings — including the ones that people typically eat — can be our food and *more than* our food. The act of violence is not in predation itself, but in treating other creatures as mere meat.

In order to put her traumatic experience into words, Plumwood had to overcome the pressures and powers of dominant narratives about animal attacks on people. Although "[f]ew of those who have experienced the crocodile's death roll have lived to describe it," Plumwood was determined not to play the heroine. When the camp ranger finally found her and she began the long journey to hospital, Plumwood overheard the rescuers' boastful plans to return to the river and hunt down the crocodile. She resisted this plan forcefully: "I was the intruder," she writes, "and no good purpose could be served by random revenge." Having survived the attack, Plumwood faced a threat of a different kind — "the cultural drive to represent it in terms of the masculinist monster myth: the master narrative."

> The imposition of the master narrative occurred in several ways: in the exaggeration of the crocodile's size, in portraying the encounter as a heroic wrestling match, and especially in its sexualization. The events seemed to provide irresistible material for the pornographic imagination, which encouraged male identification with the crocodile and interpretation of the attack as sadistic rape.

There are echoes in this quotation of Carol J. Adams's thesis in *The Sexual Politics of Meat*.[2] But Plumwood rejects what she sees as the reproduction, in Adams's work, of the dualistic thinking that characterises the master narrative. In the American ecofeminist tradition of Adams and others, Plumwood claims, all hunting is condemned as predatory, violent, masculinist and morally corrupt, set in opposition to a supposedly more ethically and environmentally sustainable female gathering culture. Hunting and gathering thus correspond to a preexisting assumed male/female dualism. This model ignores forms of hunting that may not be based on the instrumentalisation of animals, and idealises and universalises women's gathering activities, overlooking evidence of female hunters, for example in some Indigenous societies.[3] Drawing on examples from Australian Aboriginal culture, Plumwood is careful neither to associate hunting exclusively with men nor to demonise it or predation.[4] Her point is that in the mainstream Australian media the crocodile attack could be readily assimilated into a patriarchal plot that anthropomorphised the crocodile as a sexual hunter and reduced her, Plumwood, to a victim devoid of agency.

While challenging the masculinist adventure tale foisted upon her by the Australian press, Plumwood reminds the reader — and herself — of her arrogance at venturing into crocodile waters without seeking the advice of "the indigenous Gagadgu owners of Kakadu." Plumwood's rendering of her own tale, like much of her philosophical writing, is indebted to the teachings of Aboriginal Australians. From them she learned the value of stories as collective, transgenerational meaning-making, as well as a holistic way of thinking about death that "sees animals, plants, and humans sharing a common life force."[5] She contrasts this worldview with Western anthropocentrism and individualism, and "Being Prey" presents a forceful challenge to those traditions. As the philosopher Matthew Calarco writes, the importance of Plumwood's tale lies in her "effort to think not simply her *death as such*, but her willingness to accept her indistinction from the world around her, the loss of her human propriety."[6] For Calarco, "Being Prey" is a radically anti-anthropocentric account of what it means to be human, one that makes room for being animal and being food for others.

Val Plumwood's contextual vegetarianism

Plumwood's reflection on the shattering experience of being prey provided one basis for her particular kind of ecofeminism. At the heart of this lies a critique of dualistic thinking, the Western philosophical tradition that divides the world into a series of hierarchal binary oppositions: reason/nature, man/ woman, human/animal, human/nature, European/Other and so on.[7] Plumwood identifies what she calls "ontological" vegetarianism or veganism — which categorises some beings as food and others as not food — as an extension of, rather than a challenge to, such dualisms.[8] Her critique of ontological veganism focuses on two areas of thought: utilitarian and rights philosophies, on one hand, and American cultural ecofemimism, on the other. Plumwood argues that utilitarian and rights theories are extensionalist, that is, they extend moral consideration — and with it the status of not food — to those animals most similar to human beings. While human omnivores draw the line between what is food and what is not at the boundary between humans and all other beings, including other animals, Plumwood accuses thinkers like Peter Singer and Tom Regan of moving the distinction further along the chain, replacing the human/animal dualism with a another binary opposition: sentient/non-sentient, or those deserving rights and moral consideration/those not. Some animals are thus afforded moral status while the majority of the other-than-human world is excluded from the moral community. The unstated assumption in utlitarianism and rights theory is that human beings can never be food. In contrast to what she understands as this anthropocentric position, Plumwood proposes what she calls "ecological animalism," defined as "re-envisaging ourselves as ecologically embodied beings akin to rather than superior to other animals."[9]

Plumwood also detects ontological veganism in the work of Carol Adams and some other American ecofeminists. Plumwood is one of the few thinkers to highlight the problem with Adams's comparison between violence against women and animals.[10] Plumwood challenges the parallel that Adams draws between the reduction of farm animals to meat and the reduction of women to sex objects. In both cases, Adams mistakenly conflates use with instrumentalisation. Just as it is possible to imagine non-exploitative sexual relations, Plumwood insists, it is possible to imagine animals being used by human beings in a way that is not purely exploitative. Against a veganism based upon the premise that *all* use of animals for food or human benefit is exploitative and instrumentalist, Plumwood argues that it may be possible for people to use animals without reducing them to mere instruments for our own ends.[11]

When we human beings take ourselves out of the food chain, refusing to be food for other creatures (including as rotting corpses), we take from other living beings — including plants — without giving back.[12] Plumwood does not object to human beings eating plants, though her critique of ontological veganism anticipates recent critiques of moral vegetarianism based on scientific evidence of plant sentience.[13] Nor did she espouse the eating of meat. Her experience of being potential prey for the crocodile confirmed her vegetarianism. However, Plumwood argues that it is wrong to privilege animals above other forms of life and to prioritise animal advocacy over other forms of political commitment. She stresses the inseparability of the struggle against anthropocentrism and campaigns to end the exploitation of people, calling upon animal rights activists to form political alliances with workers' movements, radical health movements, environmental organisations, small farmers and movements against neoliberalism. According to Plumwood, proponents of ontological veganism put too much emphasis on the actions of the individual activist, forestalling the kinds of alliances necessary for the construction of an effective ecological ethics. Her contextualised ethics of eating, in contrast, targets "the most extreme examples of distortion and instrumentalisation of animal lives — the intensive farming practices that treat animals as no more than living meat or egg production units."[14]

Plumwood contrasts the unethical reduction of factory farmed animals to "no more than living meat" with her own moment of revelation, following the near-death experience with the crocodile:

> We are edible, but we are also much more than edible. Respectful, ecological eating must recognize both of these things. I was a vegetarian at the time of my encounter with the crocodile, and remain one today. This is not because I think predation itself is demonic and impure, but because I object to the reduction of animal lives in factory farming systems that treat them as living meat.[15]

If people can become meat to other predators while retaining the complexity of our humanity (being more than food), as a predatory species we humans must recognise that all living entities that can be eaten — people, other animals, plants — are both potential food and always more than that.

Plumwood provides a sophisticated critique of both the utilitarian and rights traditions, and of American cultural ecofeminism. She also offers an attractive alternative in the form of contextual veganism or ecological animalism. Her argument against a universalist moral veganism echoes in some ways the work of Deane Curtin.[16] Her advocacy of an embodied ecological animalism and her emphasis on the need for coalition building among animal rights and other activists has echoes in some of the new writing on veganism in the twenty-first century. Unlike some critics of veganism, who provide a cursory reading of the canonical works of utilitarianism, rights theory and ecofeminism, Plumwood engages in depth with the work of Singer, Regan and Adams. But by calling for animal activists and vegans to form broader coalitions with environmental, workers and food justice movements she implies that these coalitions were not in place at the time she was writing, around the turn of the millennium. If she had investigated the anti-capitalist activist groups around the globe in those years she would likely have come across more than a few vegans putting that coalition work into practice.

Because she claims that there is a difference between making other animals prey and treating them as nothing more than meat, Plumwood argues that vegans should "prioritise action on factory farming over less abusive forms of farming."[17] For all their differences, in this she and Singer are on the same page.[18] Plumwood is convinced that it is in "flesh factories" that animals experience total instrumentalisation.[19] Her contextual vegetarianism opposes any attempt to impose Western veganism on cultures with less exploitative human-animal relations. This is an important anti-imperialist and anti-anthropocentric argument. But by associating non-instrumentalising animal relations with Indigenous cultures Plumwood fails adequately to address the question of whether it would be possible to implement less abusive farming systems in the context of the contemporary West. I look in more detail at this questions in the next chapter. There are other simplifications in Plumwood's distinction between ontological and contextual vegetarianism/veganism. For example, while her claim that the animal rights movements in the West suffers from an "over individualized and culturally hegemonic vanguard focus on veganism" has some merit, she presents at times a familiar caricature of *all* vegans as people obsessed with personal purity, self denial and "unhealthy elements of self righteousness and holier-than-thouism."[20] In what is otherwise a nuanced argument, Plumwood falls for a series of clichés about veganism that are more commonly found in mainstream media.[21] She gives little space for practices of veganism grounded in collective movements for change.

According to Cora Diamond, one of the main ways in which people learn how to be human is through eating other animals — '*WE* eat *THEM*'.[22] Veganism challenges this dominant definition of humanity by disrupting the action of us eating them. Val Plumwood provides us with a potentially more egalitarian formulation — *WE* eat *THEM* and *THEY* eat *US*. Like Diamond, Plumwood challenges what she understands as overly simplistic or rationalised defences of vegetarianism based upon self-confident understandings of the categories "animal" and "human." Neither philosopher argues against the animal rights position in order to delegitimise vegetarianism. On the contrary, like Diamond, Plumwood homes in on what she perceives as the weaknesses in some philosophical defences of vegetarianism as part of a project for developing an ethical practice of eating.

In the end, Plumwood may protest a bit too much. She recognises that contextual vegetarianism is available — culturally and practically — to many living in the West and strongly implies that it is the best ethical option for most.[23] Although I find her philosophical critique of ontological veganism laudable, it is her reflection on being prey that provides the most original contribution to the project of constructing an ethical contextual veganism.

Eating sex

Elspeth Probyn is another feminist writer interested in the relationship between eating and being eaten, albeit from a perspective markedly different from that of Val Plumwood. Over the past few decades Probyn has developed a corpus of writing on bodies, sex and food that is, from the perspective of this vegan reader, both enticing and infuriating. Notwithstanding her avowedly non-vegan starting point, and her celebration, even eroticisation, of an omnivore diet, Probyn's ponderings are provocative in ways that prove, perhaps in spite of her own best intentions, useful for thinking about the sexual politics of veganism.

In *Carnal Appetites: FoodSexIdentities* (2000), Probyn offers some novel takes on the old axiom "we are what we eat." By following the not-always-predictable paths that stretch out from the points where food and sex meet, Probyn suggests that we can open ourselves up to new ways of thinking about identities. Food, Probyn points out in refreshingly vivid imagery, travels through us. Envisioning the ingestion, digestion and excretion of food draws the mind to the other functions of the organs involved in eating. The cavity that gobbles up nourishment, for instance, is the same one that spits out words. The "mouth machine" thus "brings together the physical fact of what goes in, and the symbolic production of what comes out: meanings, statements, ideas."[24] But some of the arguments dished up in *Carnal Appetites* stick in the throat. In particular, Probyn's take on vegetarianism is so reductive as to make any good vegan turn up her nose in disgust. As Chloë Taylor writes: "Probyn quickly dismisses ethical vegetarianism as a rule-bound dogmatism that strictly dictates what everyone should and should not eat."[25]

Probyn is at pains to acknowledge that not *all* vegetarians are moralising zealots who naively divide the world into good vegetarians and bad carnivores. But her hasty dismissal of two iconic vegetarian texts — Carol J. Adams's *The Sexual Politics of Meat* and Peter Singer's *Animal Liberation* — reflects a deep suspicion of ethical plant-based diets. According to Probyn, vegetarians like Adams and Singer inhabit a "stark moral universe in which the individual measures him or herself against a set of strict guidelines. Succinctly, what this produces is a moral subject, not necessarily an ethical person."[26] I have my disagreements with both Adams and Singer, but this neat synopsis does not do their respective work justice. For all its shortcomings, *The Sexual Politics of Meat* grapples with some of the challenges of being a vegetarian in human-centred political movements, including feminism. As for Singer, whether we regard *Animal Liberation* as presenting a "stark moral universe" depends largely on how we read it. Originally published in 1975, the book grew out of a preoccupation with the place of animals in the history of Western philosophy, and more specifically the mass maltreatment of animals in science and agriculture in much of North America and Europe in the twentieth century. To apply the arguments of *Animal Liberation* uncritically outside that context is to propose that the system at the heart of the problem is the one most adept to solve it. But read within its context, Singer's book provides an important critique of industrial farming and animal experimentation, and proposes a number of practical suggestions for what people can do to challenge these. Far from laying down an inflexible set of rules, *Animal Liberation* takes the reader through the different steps of adopting a vegetarian diet, even including some sample recipes. Singer considered vegans "the living demonstrations of the practicality and nutritional soundness of a diet that is totally free from exploitation of other animals." But he added that "in our present speciesist world, it is not easy to keep so strictly to what is morally right."[27]

Probyn's treatment of the work of Singer and Adams, and her references to alternative accounts of how to live as vegetarian or vegan, are short and sour compared to her exploration of what she considers more complex and ethically and aesthetically attractive approaches to food. She draws a sharp contrast between the supposedly queer celebration of food culture epitomised by the 1990s British TV chefs the Two Fat Ladies — with their "excess and extravagance" and avid anti-vegetarianism — on one hand, and what she interprets as the condescending, do-gooder earnestness of vegetarian food justice activists on the other.[28] *Carnal Appetites* thus replaces the "stark moral universe" of vegetarianism with an equally stark world in which hearty carnivorous consumption constructs complex human subjects while restrained plant eating creates simple selves.

The repeated association of plant-based diets with simplicity, restraint and moralising is similar in some ways to Plumwood's reductive representation of "ontological" vegetarianism, and echoes claims in more popular portrayals of veganism.[29] These representations raise an important question: why is the proposal to encourage a plant-based diet sometimes dismissed as facile, unrealistic or even ethnocentric, while other ways of eating and doing politics ostensibly are not? The remainder of this chapter swims around these questions, as I follow Probyn's line in new directions. In her most recent work she immerses herself and her reader in the world of ocean life and the ways it runs through human lives. Although often overlooked in analyses of rearing and eating animals, fish and other marine creatures offer important insights into the challenges of ethical, sustainable eating in the early twenty-first century.

Fishy tales

December 2014
London

Last night, another disastrous date. Even after I said I would have dinner beforehand (avoiding the awkward "What can I eat?" moment as manifestly unsexy), my internet date insisted on going to a sushi joint. She sat across from me like some selfish god, stabbing at the pink and black corpses flayed and displayed before her, banging on, between chomps, about one life drama after another. I felt like I was being force fed someone else's minor traumas. I sipped my beer and tried to close my ears. Anger rose like bile in my throat, hotter than the ball of green fire globbed on the plate that marked a border between us.

These words were written as a kind of purging, a visceral reaction to an encounter that left me feeling physically and emotionally out of sorts. I don't want to paint a picture of a sensitive vegan who cannot stomach dead fish in her presence; I have learned to plug my nose and hold my tongue (as many, many vegan and vegetarian friends did with me for years). My diary entry was a way of disgorging a memory of an encounter with an obnoxious human whose bad dinner table behaviour I cannot separate from my visual memory of the pieces of salmon and tuna being pierced in rhythm to the monologue, munched and swallowed between rants. Let's set aside the rather obvious question of why someone would be so rude and unattractive on a first date (on any date for that matter). On the level of romance, I put this ugly experience down to an episode in what I subsequently dubbed my "year of dating disastrously," a period in which I had a go at online hook-ups and assorted rendezvous, most of which ended sourful and sexless, and involved fraught moments over food — specifically fish food. The bad sushi date with a cute but verbally objectionable butch dyke forced me to swallow a chunk of my own pride and acknowledge a kernel of truth in Carol Adam's argument that flesh-eating sometimes goes hand-in-hand with macho posturing. The fact that this was a bravado performance of carnivorous female masculinity adds a queer dimension to Adams's argument, in spite of its best radical feminist intentions.

Dinners and dates are full of potential for delights and fights. If the supper table is one of the places where human beings affirm, over and over and over again, that we are the eaters of others but never the eaten, it is also a location where we learn to love and hate each other, and relate to other human beings more generally. From the perspective of this particular human, these unpleasant unromantic encounters were on one level reminders of the unhappy sensations vegans can experience when we choose to witness people eating the dead bodies of other creatures. But I want to resist the temptation to focus on my initial individual reaction to the corpses spread out in front of me. Instead, following Probyn, I wish to understand these failed attempts to flirt over dead fish as unexpected occasions where eating and sexuality come into contact, meeting across and through bodies in ways that can lead in unanticipated directions.[30] Not satisfied with the explanation that vegans and omnivores don't get it on because we inevitably fall out over incompatible diets, the lack of chemistry, empathy and conversational flow on my disastrous dates prompted me to reposition my body towards

sea creatures and the particular politics of (not) eating them.[31]
Inspired by the work of Icelandic anthropologist Gísli Pálsson,
Probyn puts an interesting spin on seasickness, proposing
that it can be good for thinking with. "[T]he moment of
fundamental queasiness in the world," writes Probyn, gives
us an "embodied lens" that allows us to spot connections
between things that are often perceived as separate: "emotion
and cognition, body and mind, human and fish."[32] My
queasiness at the sushi joint was not the nausea induced
by a rocking boat. But my reaction to the consumption of
small pink and grey fleshy bits through the same "mouth
machine" that sounded off alerted me on a visceral level to
interconnected forms of aggression. I have never thought of
sushi, or internet dating, in quite the same way again.

Wading into the waters of human-fish encounters involves
reading Probyn contra Probyn. In her most recent book,
Eating the Ocean, she argues that there is a terrestrial bias
in contemporary writing on food, environment and human–
animal relations.[33] Probyn is right to claim that inadequate
attention has been paid to the sea, a significant oversight
given that the oceans cover the majority of the earth's
surface and are home to — literally — countless numbers of
species.[34] Given the sheer richness of life underwater, going
below the surface offers many different lines of thought, as
does the inevitability of human-fish encounters, including
consumption. Ultimately, as Probyn argues, it is not possible
entirely to opt out of fish, even if we don't eat them directly.
Different parts of fish bodies make their ways into almost
everything we eat, including some breads and fertilisers
used to grow vegetables. But Probyn goes further, arguing
that "[t]he idea that you can resolve such intricate and
complicated human-fish relations by voting with your fork
is deluded narcissism." Veganism is singled out for special
mention: "the choice to proclaim oneself vegan often seems

to act as an opting out of the structural complexities of food provisioning, production, and consumption."[35] Here Probyn conflates consumer politics — which elsewhere she dubs "feel-good food politics" — with a political and ethical commitment to ending animal exploitation.[36] Anyone who believes that personal and political change are possible will likely be jarred by the implication that the desire to construct a more ethical and egalitarian world makes one naive or prone to narcissism. These clichés may nibble at the feelings of individual vegans, but the real damage they do is on the collective level, dividing the world into good, ethical, real and realistic activists, on one hand, and bad, deluded and self-centred ones, on the other. Ironically the derision aimed at "feel-good" activism also makes its way into the writings of some vegans who wish to distinguish between proper, morally upright vegans and those of us who aren't quite up to scratch.[37] The derision of some people as engaging in nothing more than "feel-good" activities is an example of moralism masquerading as political argument.

The caricature of vegan politics as fuzzy feel-goodedness suffuses Probyn's speculation about the imbalance between concern for the fate of land animals and solidarity with those who live in the sea. "Is this simply because," she wonders, "it's easier to care about a cow than a lobster?"[38] When I read these words I was reminded of the provocative piece "Consider the Lobster" by the late David Foster Wallace. The article began as a seemingly straightforward assignment to cover the Maine Lobster Festival for *Gourmet* magazine, but soon morphed into a rather more interesting treatise on the ethics of killing and eating large crustaceans. Wallace addresses those people who have swallowed, along with the buttered–up limbs, the myth that being thrown live into boiling water does not induce pain, entreating them to consider how the lobster might feel about all this. He does not mean "feel" in some vague anthropomorphic way, but in relation to anecdotal and scientific evidence that lobsters suffer on their own terms. A large dose of lobster's kudos as posh foodstuff comes from its association with freshness. This is derived from the brief time that elapses between the prospective eater's observation of the creature swimming around (well, trying to crawl with bound claws) in its "natural habitat" (that is, a saltwater tank in your local upscale supermarket or seafood restaurant) and appearing on the plate. The fresh factor is further enhanced by the fact that killing and cooking are achieved simultaneously through boiling.[39]

Wallace's description of the lobster's responses to being tipped into boiling water while still alive — claws clinging to the edge or banging on the sides of the pot — certainly tends to validate the theory that lobsters feel pain. We could even say that whether or not lobsters experience pain like human beings do, their attempt to escape is evidence of their determination to live and avoid suffering. Or, in Wallace's terms, by trying to clamber out of the pot, lobsters demonstrate their preference *not* to be boiled.[40] Other witnesses to lobster boiling have reported that the animals "scream" when dropped into the water. Brian Luke recalls that the first time he cooked a lobster he "kept imagining being boiled alive." When the moment of reckoning arrived for the lobster, Luke "gingerly picked him up, lifted the lid off the large pot, dropped him in and then ran from the room, with my hands over my ears." Luke subsequently interprets his actions as a failure to allow himself to be guided ethically by his emotions. Had he acted based on his feelings of agony he could have taken definitive action by freeing the lobster instead of hiding from the screams. In other words, a consideration for the lobster would have opened the possibility for a different kind of relationship between a person and a lobster.[41] As for Wallace, in the end he confesses that, having concluded that lobsters feel pain and distress when they are caught, kept in crowded tanks and boiled alive, he remains doubtful about what it means to eat ethically. For that particular writer, then, the recognition of animal sentience and ability to feel pain leads not to moralism or a search for simplistic solutions, but to confusion.[42]

The question of lobster pain is by no means marginal to veganism. Crustaceans are at the edge of philosophical debates about which animals should or should not count as food. As Probyn reminds us, "Peter Singer's *Animal Liberation* hesitated about where to draw the line" between sentient and non-sentient animals.[43] In the original 1975 publication, Singer wrote that the nervous systems of shrimp, prawns and lobsters

> are complex enough but so differently organized from our own that it is difficult to be confident one way or the other about whether they feel pain. ... Crustaceans do act as if they feel pain, in the appropriate circumstances. There may be room for doubt, but it does seem that crustaceans deserve the benefit of the doubt.[44]

Mollusks (including oysters, clams, mussels and scallops) are a different story: "Most ... are such rudimentary beings that it is difficult to imagine them feeling pain, or having other mental states ... [S]omewhere between a shrimp and a lobster seems as good a place to draw the line as any, and better than most."[45] Probyn remains skeptical of Singer's reasoning (as do I, but for reasons closer to those Plumwood), speculating that animal ethics revolves less around scientific evidence of sentience than the fact that some animals have the "good looks and good luck to be more anthropomorphically cute than others. It's hard, though not impossible, to cuddle a fish."[46] Probyn seems to me unduly preoccupied by the cuddliness of furry animals over shelled and scaled creatures as the basis for the — by implication highly arbitrary and anthropocentric — distinction between the vegetarian or vegan and the pescatarian. Singer's rationalist approach, on the other hand, makes him entirely dismissive of anything approaching an emotional attachment to animals as the basis for animal advocacy. In the introduction to the first edition of *Animal Liberation* the utilitarian philosopher deliberately distanced himself from lady animal lovers who pat their pets while chomping down on ham sandwiches.[47]

Singer's defence of animals is certainly not based on whether or not they are cute and cuddly, or evoke human sentiment. As Plumwood argues, it is extentionalist: Singer takes the human capacity to feel pain as the point of departure and extends the category not-food only to those other animals who, according to existing scientific evidence, can also experience pain. Plumwood argues that this is an anthropocentric position because human beings remain the main point of reference against which is made the claim to extend moral status to some animals and not to others. Sunaura Taylor agues that the emphasis on sentience is also ableist, because the criteria used to exclude some animals from moral concern are also used to question the moral status of some people.[48] In fact, Singer's preoccupation with sentience has led him to argue against the full moral status of some disabled people.[49] The high-profile nature of Singer's arguments have sometimes made it difficult for disability activists to engage with animal rights. By looking at the human mistreatment of other animals through the lens of disability activism, Taylor demonstrates not only how wrong Singer is, but how much we can learn about both disability and animal rights by considering them in relation to one another. One example she gives is debates about whether oysters can feel. Citing the biologist Mark Bekoff, Taylor argues that human knowledge of animal consciousness and sentience has tended to underestimate rather than overestimate the capacities of other animals. We do not need to rely on scientific evidence of whether or not oysters feel pain in a way comparable to people. We can instead respect oyster life on its own terms. Bekoff and Taylor's argument against eating or otherwise instrumentalising oysters contrasts to Singer's extentionalist argument. By his calculation, while shrimp should probably not be eaten, oysters are fair game.[50]

March 2018
Puebla, Mexico

Last night I started reading Probyn's Eating the Ocean, *which begins with an invitation:* "Imagine a sparkling day on Sydney Harbour... eating creamy Sydney rock oysters and drinking a glass of fine Australian white wine with a light warm salty breeze on your face."[51] *Probyn then encourages the reader to go beneath this pristine scene, to picture the life, forces and interactions that enable this classically bourgeois experience of fine wine, fine dining, fine weather and fine views. This is not just a sexing of food. It is the experience as a whole that is eroticised in the opening passage. Still, the choice of oysters is not accidental. They have a reputation for getting the juices flowing.*

Re-reading Singer's distinction between oysters and shrimp I am taken back to a dinner party shortly after I became vegan. I was in queer company, among anarchists who had squatted in digs close to my flat in East London, in the years before the area became synonymous with trendy cafés, cocktail bars and yes, overpriced vegan junk food. Like so many ageing activists, my dinner mates were on a wide spectrum between vegan and omnivore, many of them eating a wider — or, as in my case, narrower — range of foods than they once had. As so often happens at the dinner table when a vegan eats amongst veggies or omnivores, our discussion turned to the politics of eating. One of our party said that she eats oysters — or would if offered them — because of the common assertion that they are not sentient (I think she cited Singer).

These briny creatures of the sea never wielded their aphrodisiacal powers on me. But seafood certainly was an object of my desire. For some time after I stopped eating all sea creatures I could still feel and taste the salty crunch of shrimp in my mouth. Shrimp was the animal food I missed most. I think it was the associations: memories of eating gambas a la plancha in dirty bars — literally filthy — in Madrid in the late 1980s, peeling off the warm, hard flaked shells and throwing them on the floor amidst the sawdust, cigarette butts and olive pits while drinking small glasses of cold, frothy beer. Many of my early adult memories of food, drink and sex are tied to Madrid, which is where I lived far from home for the first time, and where I came out.

In the end, no shrimp or oysters for me last night. After a day of writing I wandered outside after dusk in search of the veggie taco van advertised on the website Happy Cow. The van was nowhere to be found, but the streets were alive, and I walked down the pedestrian way Cinco de Mayo past strollers, stalls and musicians. I settled for an elote (corn on the cob) with lime, salt and chilli powder. The earnest young guy who sold it to me insisted I choose my own cob and warned me that the powder was hot. I persisted. I went back through the main square filled with balloons, running kids and adults in historical costumes selling street tours, munching on my cob, chilli singeing my lips. At first I regretted not taking the seller's advice to go light on the spice powder, but then I decided to embrace the searing pain as part of the experience. By the time I dropped the naked

cob in the bin at the doorstep of my rented flat I was feeling
surprisingly full and contented.

By arguing against "saying no to fish," Probyn exhibits sincere concern about food sustainability and solidarity with the millions of fishers and their communities that coexist with and depend upon the ocean to live. But though she presents these concerns as a challenge to supposedly simplistic strategies for food production, I am suspicious of the zero-sum game that juxtaposes caring for people and caring for other animals. I admire Probyn's detailed descriptions of the historical and often intricate and complicated relationships among sea critters and human earth-dwellers in different parts of the globe. She writes compellingly about what scientists, fishing communities and consumers can bring to the table for discussions about human-fish worlds.[52] But I am curious at her lack of curiosity about fish. "Considering food through the optic of fish" is not the same as "considering the fish," in the way Wallace considers the lobster.[53] Probyn takes for granted that any attempt to interpret fish feelings must be sentimental and anthropomorphic, the result not of an attempt to understand beings different from ourselves, but a projection of human self-interest onto other animals.

The word "complexity" is repeated time and again on the pages of *Eating the Ocean*, mantra-like. Probyn makes a convincing case that fish and other sea creatures are caught up in human life in complex ways, and that solutions to food sustainability will have to take account of this complexity. Yet the equally repeated claim that most food politics are too "simplistic" is backed up by fewer empirical examples, relying instead on sweeping generalisations about vegans and white, middle-class urbanites obsessed with local, organic produce.[54] This qualification of attempts to create ethical food practices as prone to "simplicity" reflects a pattern I have detected in many arguments against veganism. How did we get to the point where taking into account animals — their lives, feelings, intelligence and relationships to us — can be labelled "simplistic"?

Resisting fish

If I have learned anything by reading and writing about veganism over the past few years, it is that taking animals and their lives seriously complicates everything I thought I knew about power relations and politics. Most of the lessons I have learned come from imaginative and intellectually astute artists, activists and academics who started this thinking work long before I did. By way of keeping with the watery theme that has run through this chapter, I close with a brief discussion of the work of one of those teachers. Dinesh Wadiwel's article "Do Fish Resist?" asks us to reconsider what we think we know about the creatures of the sea and our relationships with them.[55]

Like Probyn, Wadiwel recognises that land animals have received far more attention from those concerned about food ethics than marine creatures. One result is "a somewhat perverse silence in relation to fish welfare." Wadiwel is not indifferent to fish pain. But he prefers to move away from the emphasis in classic animal rights philosophy on the question of animal sentience. He sets out to reframe the question of human-fish relations in terms of power and resistance. Following Foucault, Wadiwel argues that every power relation involves some form of resistance. From this perspective, we can understand fish as actors in their relations with people without having to demonstrate that they "possess capabilities worthy of moral recognition (language, reason, capability for suffering and so on)." Instead of relying on scientists to provide us with definitive proof as to whether fish feel pain, or gathering evidence that individual fish fight back when fishers attempt to capture them (like the lobster who scurries to escape the boiling pot), Wadiwel focuses on the modern human technologies used to control, capture and kill fish for food. He argues that the very existence of violent technologies such as fishhooks, purse seines (large fish traps) and aquaculture is evidence that violence is needed to bring fish under human control.[56] Human-fish interactions have therefore not only been shaped by human needs for sustenance and desires for connections with other beings, but by sea creatures' resistance to our attempts to control their lives and deaths.

Wadiwel defines his research as belonging to the "relational approach" to human-animal studies. This differs from rights–based theories, which emphasise human domination over other animals and downplay the role of other creatures in their engagements with people. Relational approaches emphasise that people can have sincere emotional attachments to other animals, that animals are often active participants in forming bonds with people, and that humans and animals alike can benefit from those relationships. The work of Plumwood and Probyn can be considered relational, because both writers emphasise, in different ways, the interconnections and inter-dependencies among different species. But Wadiwel warns that some relational approaches understate the violent dimension of human-animal relations. He proposes that people should replace our violent and controlling relationships to fish with one that recognises the complexity of marine life on its own terms:

> Fish create worlds we cannot even understand; they defy our imagination. Our primary relationship with fish, at least so far, has been violent and parasitic. We have quite literally fed off their creativity for our

own benefit. Recognising fish resistance might give us different ways to think about how we might relate to fish beyond simply finding new ways to counter their resistance to us.[57]

In the writing of Wadiwel and Plumwood we find an ethics of eating that departs significantly from the classic animal rights and utilitarian arguments that prioritise the question, "Can they suffer?" By putting people back in the food chain as prey, Plumwood rejects the dualistic and extentionalist arguments that have dominated much writing on animal rights and many defences of veganism in the West since the 1970s. She also provides a powerful model of contextual vegetarianism, recognising that Western attitudes towards other animals are not universal and that the West is not the centre of ethics. Wadiwel moves away from mainstream animal rights arguments by proposing that the issue of fish suffering need not be at the heart of the question of how humans should treat fish. Rather than understanding fish and other sea critters as victims of human maltreatment, he sees that they are active participants in their relations with us, and that their resistance to human attacks upon them offers evidence of this. In the accounts of both authors, animals exist in their own right, and not merely to serve the uses of people. If Wadiwel's image of fish as active resisters and creative creatures comes across as a bit mad, that is perhaps an indication of the limitations of our all-too-human imaginations. There are other ways to relate to the earth's bodies of water and their inhabitants. Finding ways that honour the complexity of human-fish relations while relinquishing violent control may require the biggest imaginative plunge of all.

Interlude 1

RAW

I won't kill an animal in order to eat it, but I am no respecter of dead bodies as such...In practice I suspect I should choke on a rissole which I knew might contain bits of Great-Aunt Emily...and I admit I might have to leave rational cannibalism to future generations.

Brigid Brophy, "The Rights of Animals"

In Julia Ducournau's 2016 film *Raw* a female veterinary student transforms from a strict vegetarian to a reluctant if greedy practitioner of anthropophagy or "cannibalism," in the process morphing from a rather uptight, virginal Mummy's girl and teacher's pet to a sexually voracious young woman who seduces her gay male roommate while seeking out human meat.[1] Amidst the critical and popular responses to *Raw*, there emerged a mini debate about whether or not this is a vegan or vegetarian film, a discussion that perplexed the film's director:

When I read reactions stating that this is a vegetarian movie, I get very confused... Her [*Raw's* protagonist, Justine] being vegetarian is just a storytelling tool. If you're going to have a character become a cannibal, it's good to have her be the complete reverse of that at the start of the story.[2]

In response we might say that the intentional establishment of vegetarianism as the "complete reverse" of anthropophagy is precisely what allows for an interpretation of *Raw* as a "vegetarian movie," one that, by presenting anthropophagy as a form of non-or even anti-humanity and monstrosity, highlights the ethical advantages of a plant-based diet. Ducournau's comment notwithstanding, *Raw* does at certain points offer an ethical vegetarian view of the world, inviting comparisons between vulnerable people and vulnerable animals, notably through the vicious hazing rituals undergone by the first-year vet students and the more banal, but often violent, day-to-day activities of the veterinary college. At the same time, by tracing Justine's transition from a strict vegetarian to consumer of human flesh, the film traffics in a series of clichés about Western female vegetarians. Justine is white, bourgeois, feminine, fragile, emaciated, puritanical, ascetic, sexually uninitiated and repressed, obsessively and pathologically controlling her diet in a way ostensibly similar to a bulimic.

The stage is thus set for our protagonist to discover her supposedly repressed animal nature through a coming-of-age story, a hedonistic awakening marked by increased — and increasingly brazen — sexual as well as dietary abandon. Whether we understand this as a process of liberation or oppression would depend on our take on the feminist politics of food, whether we understand vegetarianism as a particularly feminine form of repression and control, or a feminist resistance to the aggressive masculinity of meat-eating.[3] But to zoom in on consumption would be to miss one half of the anthropophagist encounter in *Raw*. Yes, this is a film about eating; but it is also a film about *being eaten*. The representation of people *as prey*, as much as predators, offers, to my view, a more intriguing vegan feminist take on *Raw*.

Justine's first nibble of human meat comes in the form of her sister Alex's finger, which she — Justine — has inadvertently cut off in an attempt to escape a torturous Brazilian wax job. While Justine greedily and messily gobbles up her sister's digit, Alex rises from a post-amputation shock-induced stupor, tears streaming down her face. The sisters' eyes meet. Just as Justine is getting her first taste of human flesh, Alex gets her first taste of what it's like to be eaten. She is discovering what it means to be prey.

Let's recall the work of Val Plumwood, whose ecofeminism was shaped by her near-death experience with a crocodile. Plumwood recalls that just before her boat was overturned and she was dragged underwater, the huge reptile "rushed up alongside the canoe, and its beautiful, flecked golden eyes looked straight into mine."[4] In *Raw*, the predator (Justine) also gazes into the eyes of her prey (Alex). From the perspective of the eater the anthropophagy in *Raw* might be interpreted as a metaphor for flowering female sexuality and desire, or as a reminder that the violence that humans inflict on other animals will eventually come home to roost.[5] But the sisters' eye-to-eye encounter provides an alternative angle, which includes the perspective of the eaten.

In the film the two sisters, Alex and Justine, share the experience of being both prey and predator, but live this out in divergent ways. After the finger-eating scene, Alex tries to become Justine's mentor by showing her younger sibling the art of hunting (the weapon in this case being the unsuspecting human victim's own car). But just as she earlier refused society's pressures to be an omnivore, Justine resists the admonition to become a single-minded consumer of human flesh, especially if it involves murder. And while Alex eventually devours Justine's lover, the film ends with a reminder that it is possible for people to be meat for other people while also being much more. As Justine sits in her parents' kitchen and pokes at the vegetables on her plate, having tried and failed to rebel against her mother (just as she did at the start of the film) her father says to her, slyly: "I'm sure you will find a way, *chérie*." He then opens his shirt to show off the scars of what I presume to be his wife's multiple feasts upon his chest. We never learn whether he, too, is a people-eater. But by giving these final words to Justine's father, *Raw* allows us to imagine a future for our vegetarian anthropophagist heroine in which the humanist fantasy of being predator but never prey gives way to a less anthropocentric world where humans take our place in the food chain.

When I saw *Raw* I was reminded of an essay by Brigid Brophy, in which the late English novelist and animal rights advocate envisions herself eating a dish made from her naturally-deceased Great Aunt Emily. Brophy uses this imagined foray into anthropophagy to remind readers that the crime of what she calls "flesh food" lies not in the fact of eating other animals, but in the arrogance of designating some animals as food and nothing else, thus justifying the violence committed against them.[6] Brophy confesses that her own "irrational prejudice" against anthropophagy, a result of her upbringing, would probably make her pause before consuming human flesh, though "whether through love or repulsion I am not quite sure". But she is confident that such irrationalities will be overcome by future generations. In the tradition of Jonathan Swift's *A Modest Proposal*, Brophy employs satire to highlight the hypocrisy and cruelty of animal agriculture (she was writing in the mid 1960s, shortly after Ruth Harrison's *Animal Machines* carefully documented the outrages of postwar industrial farming in Britain and the subsequent Brambell committee on farm animal welfare).[7] By suggesting that we humans are fair game for the dinner table, Brophy — like Plumwood some years later and like

Raw in a different way — paints people as, but not just as, potential meat.

Chapter 3

SLOW VIOLENCE AND ANIMAL TALES

How can we turn the long emergencies of slow violence into stories dramatic enough to rouse public sentiment and warrant political intervention, these emergencies whose repercussions have given rise to some of the most critical challenges of our time?

Rob Nixon, *Slow Violence and the Environmentalism of the Poor*

While writing this chapter in July 2018 I look out the window and my eyes settle on the flat lawn, yellow and thirsty. Northern Europe is burning. Forest fires rage near the Arctic Circle and Sweden has hit the highest temperatures since record-keeping began in the late eighteenth century. I have just returned to London from a week camping in the fjords near Gothenburg, dipping daily in the salty waters off the rocks to keep cool. The locals are bewildered. A comment by a woman from Stockholm startles and stays with me: farmers are having to kill more of their animals than usual at this time of year because without enough rain, they cannot feed and water them.[1]

Even as we humans complain of the sweat and discomfort, many of us are able to get some respite. Other creatures and plant life suffer the brunt of the uncharacteristically hot weather. But it's the heat that makes the headlines.

Forest fires are fast and they make fast news. In the words of Nigel Clark and Kathryn Yusoff, "Wildfire moves with eye-catching speed, it rages with dramatic intensity, its energetic excitations light up the screen." Clark and Yusoff contrast the rapidity of fire to "painfully drawn out" drought and the largely invisible "chilly realms of retreating ice."[2] The events of summer 2018 bring these elements together — fire, drought and melting artic ice. But still, when it comes to the front page, the flames win hands down.

Fast news and slow violence

Clark and Yusoff's observation that "[t]he scale and complexity of climate change present challenges when it comes to depicting the current planetary predicament in ways that will appeal — starkly, immediately, viscerally — to non-expert audiences" echoes concerns expressed by Rob Nixon in his book *Slow Violence and the Environmentalism of the Poor*.[3] In an age that relies on sensational visuals and riveting tales to capture the imaginations of publics and policy makers — to spur us to action — just how does one tell a good story about "the long emergencies of slow violence"?[4] To the lay observer, these are the largely imperceptible forces behind much of the erosion of the earth and its inhabitants — human, animal and plant — as well as the elements themselves. Turning creeping change into a pressing cause is a highly political matter, and not just because the futures of so much and many depend upon it. It is political because slow violence often has the greatest impact on the most dispossessed human and other beings.

In his search for narratives of slow violence, Nixon focuses on examples of "intersectional environmentalism": grassroots movements that are as attentive to inequalities among people as they are to the wider environment. Nixon contrasts the "environmentalism of the poor" — a term he borrows from the Catalan economist Joan Martínez Alier — with the Western conservationist movements of the mid-twentieth century, which were founded in the colonial tradition and tended to prioritise the preservation of charismatic megafauna.[5] In moving away from an emphasis on vibrant endangered species and their habitats, the "environmentalism of the poor" has something in common with animal rights. Animal advocates have long challenged the idea that conservation should prioritise those species deemed desirable for humankind (the big and the colourful) above concern for the lives of individual animals of *all species*. In fact, animal rights activism has often focused precisely on those species — the ones used in farming and scientific experimentation — that are in no danger of extinction.

Kathryn Gillespie has argued that it may be easier for people in the West to grieve for the lives of chimpanzees and elephants (for example), whose fate we imagine is not in our hands, than to acknowledge our complicity in the suffering of farm animals bred purely for our own ends.[6] She has a point. Yet it is becoming increasingly clear that our collective indifference to the exploitation of certain domesticated animals also has an impact on endangered wild species. A World Wildlife Fund report from 2017 claims that the "UK food supply alone is directly linked to the extinction of an estimated 33 species at home and abroad." On a global level, one of the main threats to wildlife habitats is the clearing of land to grow feed for animals reared on industrial farms.[7] By telling the story of how rising demand for animal products poses a threat to some endangered species, the WWF paper brings home the links between our consumption habits in the West and the fate of wildlife globally. This is an important story. But we also need tales about the animals that people consume directly. When I heard about the Swedish farmers slaughtering their animals in greater numbers than usual I was reminded of the largely invisible impact of environmental destruction on those beings who don't make it into the big narratives. Indeed, the more cows, sheep, pigs and chickens are raised for human consumption, the more difficult it becomes to imagine ways to tell stories about them as individual creatures rather than a huge anonymous mass. How might we find stories that help us better to perceive "the long emergencies of slow violence" that affect different species, including people, without pitting them against one another? What kinds of stories might move us to change? Alongside the big narratives that help to bring everything together, we could tune into smaller tales of everyday encounters. These are the stories that draw out, rather than hammer home, connections among people, animals and the rest of the other-than-human world.

The numbers game

Shortly after my return from the Swedish fjords I got caught up in a Facebook thread started by a friend who was exercised by vegans and vegetarians who "are ok with eating avocados/drinking almond milk/consuming palm oil like there's no tomorrow" but "are silent about social inequality, gentrification, capitalist exploitation or waged labour." In the ensuing online conversation several of us pointed out that many vegans and vegetarians are less-than-silent on issues related to class and economic exploitation. But it was no surprise that avocados, almond milk and palm oil were singled out for attack. The production of such foodstuffs, which commonly feature in foods marketed as "vegan," has devastating impacts on forests, endangered species and water supplies in the southern regions and countries where they are grown.[8]

By accusing vegans of hypocrisy over these products, critics imply that we care more about individual animals, and about the health of individual human beings who can afford to shop at pricey health food stores, than we do about poor people and the rest of the planet. In contrast, some vegans are concerned that, in the era of climate change and a growing human population, a preoccupation with the environment and food security are being given too much air time.[9] The fear seems to be that if the human community manages to resolve the problems of environmental catastrophe and global hunger, we will forget all about the suffering of farm animals. In these competing claims, vegans stand accused of being either too concerned about the environment or not concerned enough. As someone who came to veganism in response both to growing evidence of the negative environmental impact of the meat, egg and dairy industries *and* a growing consciousness about the fate of farm animals, I am puzzled by attempts to pit environmental and animal rights arguments in favour of veganism against one another. This kind of thinking goes against my understanding of contextual ethical veganism. In Sunaura Taylor's words, "for animals to thrive (including human animals), our environment needs to thrive too, which means that the struggle for animals is inseparable from the struggle for the environment more broadly."[10] Surely we can acknowledge complexities and conflict without resorting to zero-sum game playing.

Because of the urgency of climate change and the growing evidence of the role of animal agriculture in contributing to it, for this chapter I wanted to tell tales that provide perspective on these interrelated issues. But the more I looked for connections the more I ran into competitions. I started to get data fatigue. When my mind stopped whirring I recognised that many animal rights and environmentalist arguments share one thing in common: an obsession with counting. How many animal lives can I save by becoming vegan? What percentage of the world's greenhouse gases are produced by animal agriculture? What is the respective impact of industrial and organic farming on the environment? How much meat, dairy and eggs should a healthy person eat? How many years until we reach tipping point? A preoccupation with numbers is part of our increasingly technologised and digitised world. We live in a time when big and small data proliferate, and just about everything — including our bodies, habits and most intimate lives — can be quantified. Understanding the numbers is sometimes sold to us as the key to changing ourselves and the world for the better. There is nothing wrong with using statistics to educate ourselves and others about the urgencies of animal exploitation and environmental destruction, and how changes to our behaviour might help to mitigate these. Campaigns for change should be based on reliable evidence. At a time when so much news seems to be fake news, facts are important. But statistics are more than facts; they tell stories and are open to interpretation. They are always presented through the prism of cultural and social values, and are open to manipulation and selective citation. Without further explanation and contextualisation, statistics cannot provide the basis for effective action for change. And even when the scientific information appears relatively self-explanatory, it cannot provide all the answers. Getting the numbers right will not get us out of all the ethical dilemmas surrounding climate change, animal rights, social justice and food security.

Veganism vs. the Planet?

With the rise of movements promoting food that is healthy for both the planet and human bodies, veganism is increasingly featuring as either part of the solution or part of the problem. Vegan diets in the West are sometimes condemned for being too reliant on the consumption of high-fat, industrially produced fake meats that rely on products such as palm oil. At other times, veganism is associated with expensive foods — like almonds or avocados — with a giant carbon footprint. In the light of these competing images of veganism, we should not be surprised to find counter claims telling us that the most environmentally friendly diets must include some animal products.

An article published in *The Guardian* in late summer 2018, provocatively titled "If You Want to Save the World, Veganism isn't the Answer,"[11] takes as its starting point reports of the recent rapid rise in the number of vegans in the United Kingdom — 3.5 million people, or about seven percent of the population, in early 2018, according to one study, up from just over half a million two years before.[12] Farmer Isabella Tree pounces on news that the main reason for this increase is concern about the environment and sets up her opposing argument: strategic consumption of organic meat is the best bet for protecting the planet. Tree paints vegans as creatures with poor tastebuds and worse knowledge of nutrition and nature. "Rather than being seduced by exhortations to eat more products made from industrially grown soya, maize and grains," she writes, "we should be encouraging sustainable forms of meat and dairy production based on traditional rotational systems, permanent pasture and conservation grazing." Tree further entreats her reader to "question the ethics of driving up demand for crops that require high inputs of fertiliser, fungicides, pesticides and herbicides, while demonising sustainable forms of livestock farming that can restore soils and biodiversity, and sequester carbon."[13] The implication that vegans are responsible for this trend is disingenuous at best, deliberately misleading at worst. As Tree recognises in her book *Wilding: The Return of Nature to a British Farm*, the increase in global soy and maize cultivation is driven first and foremost by the rise in demand for animal feed on intensive farms, which is in turn driven by increased demand for meat, dairy and eggs among people.[14]

Tree's piece is an example of the strategic use of a few select statistics to make a case against veganism that doesn't hold water. In fact, veganism and vegans are a proxy for her main target: intensive animal farming. Recognising that large-scale industrial agriculture is taking a toll on the planet and potentially creating a backlash against meat consumption among some informed consumers, Tree makes the case that there is a better way to eat meat. But when she writes that in order to do one's bit to counter climate change we should all "add the occasional organic, pasture-fed steak to (our) diet," what she really means is that the sale of meat from organic, pasture-fed animals allows farmers such as herself to profit from those animals.[15] The environmental advantages are not sufficient reason for allowing animals to graze. Moreover, the argument — made by Tree and some other proponents of organic farming — that grazing and browsing animals produce fewer greenhouse gases than animals reared on intensive farms has been called into question by researchers. A 2017 report from the University of Oxford concluded that "grazing livestock – even in a best-case scenario – are net contributors to the climate problem, as are all livestock."[16]

When I read Tree pulling out a few carefully chosen numbers to try to make the case that everyone should eat a bit of organic, pasture-fed meat in order to do one's bit to save the world I hear echoes of claims made in the first decade of the twenty-first century by proponents of the American local food movement or "locavorism." In the words of Vasile Stanescu: "The essence of the locavore argument is that because it is harmful to the environment to transport food over long distances (referred to as food miles) people should instead, for primarily environmental reasons, choose to consume only food which is grown or slaughtered locally." In this equation, locally produced meat from small organic farms was assumed to be better for the environment than, say, vegetables flown from abroad. But as Stanescu and a number of others pointed out, the locavores sometimes got their maths wrong. Transportation is just one element of the total environmental impact of any individual food product; one needs to take full account of the overall energy expended in producing it.[17] In some instances it might be less damaging to eat a vegetable from half-way around the world than a steak from a cow raised and slaughtered a few miles from home.[18] This is not to say one should not eat locally-grown vegetables. But a food's environmental impact cannot be determined simply by the distance it has travelled before landing on one's plate.

The consumption of what is sometimes called "happy meat" is not, therefore, as environmentally sustainable as its defenders sometimes claim. Nor does it address the issues of food justice and security, or the exploitation of farm animals. In Stanescu's words, "locally based meat, regardless of its level of popularity, can never constitute more than either a rare and occasional novelty item, or food choices for only a few privileged customers."[19] Proponents of organic meat argue that paying more is the price of providing better welfare for the animals.[20] But while there can be little doubt that animals raised on small farms using traditional grazing methods have better lives than those raised on industrial farms, organic farms may use a range of invasive and painful practices, including tail docking, castration and forced breeding. And the animals' deaths may be just as brutal: some small farms rely on mainstream abattoirs for slaughter.[21]

Ultimately, organic farms in the West treat animals as commodities.[22] They do not exist independently of the larger "animal industrial complex," as Barbara Noske famously called it; they are part of that system.[23] As the philosopher John Sanbonmatsu argues, the growing popularity of local organic meat in countries like the United States and Great Britain should be understood not as an ethical alternative to industrially produced meat but as evidence of the effectiveness of animal rights and environmentalist campaigns in highlighting the abuses of the meat industry.[24] Moreover, if, as Cora Diamond and Chloë Taylor argue, eating animals is one of the main ways that Westerners learn and regularly reaffirm our sense of superiority over other creatures, consuming organic meat will not challenge that way of thinking.[25] Rather than confronting the exploitative nature and environmental consequences of animal agriculture head-on, proponents of organic meat, eggs and dairy offer solutions that enable an elite minority to continue to consume some animal protein while leaving the anthropocentric worldview that promotes the exploitation and commodification of farm animals untouched.

Too many cows?

Debates about the relative advantages of a plant-based diet have heated up in the early twenty-first century in proportion to the publication of scientific studies showing that raising animals for the production of meat, dairy and eggs is a major cause of anthropogenic climate change. A key moment came in 2006 with the publication of the United Nations Food and Agriculture Organisation (FAO) report *Livestock's Long Shadow*, which concluded that animal agriculture "emerges as one of the top two or three most significant contributors to the most serious environmental problems, at every scale from local to global." The authors called for urgent action to reform the industry in the face of spiralling levels of meat-eating.[26]

Livestock's Long Shadow is not a vegan document. It does not call directly for reductions in the human consumption of animal products; nor does it pay much attention to animal welfare. But it makes very clear that the human demand for meat, eggs and dairy depletes natural resources and diminishes the quality of life for people and other animals across the world. The report's soundbite is that animal agriculture is "responsible for 18 percent of greenhouse gas emissions measured in CO_2 equivalent. This is a higher share than transport."[27] There is no way simultaneously to maintain or increase the human consumption of animal products, combat climate change and guarantee global food security — that is, the ability to feed a human population estimated to rise to over nine billion by the middle of this century.[28]

If that last statistic gave you pause, you are not alone. Human population growth has long been cited as a cause or potential cause of world poverty, famine and environmental damage. But the English environmentalist and writer George Monbiot cautions us that calls for population control, especially when made by wealthy Westerners, risk drawing attention away from our own excessive consumption habits and our disproportionate responsibility for climate change by foisting the blame onto people in poorer countries. Monbiot proposes that instead of focussing on the possibly insoluble rise in human numbers, we should turn our attention to a form of overpopulation we can actually do something about: the vertiginous increase in the number of farm animals.[29] While I share Monbiot's wariness of movements for human population control and support his argument that animal agriculture must be abated, I am less convinced by his tactic: pitting one "population crisis" against another. By drawing attention to the environmental damage caused by large numbers of cows, sheep, chickens and pigs, Monbiot unwittingly repeats one of the problems with the population control argument: the offloading of responsibility onto a large and anonymous group of other beings for problems not of their making.

Lumping individual animals together in a mass of numbers, even with the best of intentions, runs counter to contextual ethical veganism, which is based on the premise that all beings are of value in themselves. A similar problem is apparent in the 2014 documentary *Cowspiracy: The Sustainability Secret*, cited by some as partly responsible for the recent rise in the popularity of veganism.[30] Inspired by *Livestock's Long Shadow*, the film drives home the argument that animal agriculture is largely to blame for climate change. A rather clunky and parochial documentary with its fair share of irritating features and inaccuracies, *Cowspiracy* nevertheless makes it difficult for the viewer to avoid the conclusion that there are way too many cows in the world. At the same time, the film encapsulates some of the problems with trying to tell the story of veganism and climate change through a zippy narrative relying on a barrage of statistics.

Cowsipriacy's protagonist and narrator, "average American" Kip Anderson, has an epiphany when he comes across the film *An Inconvenient Truth* (Davis Guggenheim, 2006), featuring former American Vice President Al Gore. Alarmed by Gore's warnings about anthropogenic climate change, our intrepid protagonist becomes a self-confessed OCE (obsessive compulsive environmentalist), cycling and recycling his time away, until he comes across a rogue post on social media about the link between animal agriculture and climate change. How had this super keen climate change warrior not heard about this before? And why are the Big Green NGOs he's been supporting all these years — Greenpeace, the Sierra Club, Oceana — telling him to drive less, turn off his leaky faucets and consume "sustainable fish," while saying nothing about eating fewer hamburgers?

Our host soon discovers that these organisations, along with the American government, are in the pockets of the farming industry. Anderson proceeds on a mission to document proof of this collusion, seeking out specialists willing to go on record with the facts about the multiple environmental evils of animal agriculture.

Cowspiracy's strength lies in its muckraking of environmentalist NGOs and the animal agriculture business, and in its satire of the endless admonitions to the greediest consumers on the planet — "average" Americans — to tweak their lifestyles in minor ways without paying attention to the food they eat. By turning the camera on policymakers who are in denial about the damages caused by animal agriculture, the film makes very clear that there is an enormous resistance among people in power — many farmers, big food companies, supermarket chains, politicians, even some green NGOs — to the rather obvious message that the raising and killing of animals for food on a mass scale is catastrophic for the planet and its inhabitants.

Ultimately, however, the reliance on statistics lets the film down. As the vegan environmentalist Danny Chivers writes, although *Cowspiracy* is full of factually accurate information, it exaggerates the impact of animal agriculture on climate change, taking its headline "'animal agriculture is responsible for 51 per cent of global greenhouse gas emissions" from a single study from 2010, which has since been discredited.[31] The real statistic, claims Chivers, is more like 15% (a bit lower than the 18% cited in *Livestock's Long Shadow* in 2006). Does it matter that *Cowspiracy* gets the numbers wrong? As Chivers says, 15% is still an awful lot. The problem lies in the use of statistics to spin a particular story about how to avert climate change. In Chivers's words, the film "is built on the assumption that persuading Western people to change their lifestyles is the best way to save the world."[32] This argument, he implies, is both individualistic and imperialistic. Furthermore, it fails to take into account that a vegan diet is not necessarily available to many of the people most at risk from the fallout of Western food consumption.

Veganism is not enough

Chivers's gripe is not with veganism *per se*. Rather, he questions the implication that the movement for climate justice can be led by middle-class Westerners. In particular, he objects to such people telling others in the world — especially "poorer Southern and Indigenous peoples...engaged in frontline battles against fossil fuels, local pollution, and — yes — livestock megafarm projects around the world" — that cutting out animal products is the key to saving the planet.[33] Speaking on a 2017 BBC World Service radio programme entitled "Should We All Be Vegetarians?" Jimmy Smith, Director General of the International Livestock Research Institute in Kenya, made a similar point:

> Where you stand on this issue is a function of where you sit. And if you were sitting in the developing world, then, production of meat is a very important source of livelihoods. About a billion people depend on animals, 500 million directly currently couldn't live without them, under current conditions. The issues about nutrition would be considerably worse, because many of these people consume poor diets.[34]

What Smith is saying, in effect, is that there is no universal "we" who can answer the question of whether "we" should all be vegetarians. Joining Smith on the programme were the scientist and health researcher Peter Scarborough and the sociologist and former chair of the Vegan Society Matthew

Cole, who are based in the U.K. Each provided good and, to my view, convincing arguments in favour of a dramatic reduction or total elimination of animal food products from the perspectives of climate change mitigation, human health and animal rights. But it was Smith — who promoted not an end to animal agriculture, but measures to make it more efficient and more fair for people — who kept coming back to the question of geographical, cultural and class context — "where you sit." Smith emphasised the importance of animal food in providing nutrition and protein to some of the poorest people in the world, its central place in local economies, as well as the social and cultural role of animals in many smallholder families and communities.[35]

Smith's observations are not arguments against contextual ethical veganism. He stresses that wealthier people should reduce our consumption of meat and other animal products. But, echoing Chivers, his remarks can be understood as a warning against the universalist pretensions of entreaties to "Go Vegan!"[36] Instead of proposing a global transition to a plant-based diet, contextual ethical veganism recognises that many poor farmers in the world — a majority of them women — continue to rely on animal agriculture for their livelihoods, nutritional needs and social roles.[37] The needs of smallholders in southern countries are rarely considered in campaigns that encourage Western consumers to "save the world," whether by "going vegan" or by eating locally produced organic beef. Yet poor farming communities in the global south are not driving the global rise in demand for meat; nor are they likely to benefit from it. An FAO report from 2013, *Tackling Climate Change through Livestock*, stresses that the projected increase in meat and dairy consumption over the coming decades will come from urban middle-class consumers. Most of this demand will be met by large-scale modern farms "while hundreds of millions of pastoralists and small-holders, who depend on livestock for survival and income, have little access to emerging opportunities for growth."[38] In other words, the consumption of animal products is increasingly both a symbol of class status and a driver of inequality among human beings.

Understanding the ways that animal agriculture affects people, other animals and the rest of the other-than-human world becomes more urgent as the scientific evidence linking animal agriculture to climate change continues to grow. A 2018 study by Joseph Poore and Thomas Nemecek, which draws on an extensive range of data covering much of the world and different types and dimensions of animal agriculture, provides perhaps the most compelling case yet that a dramatic reduction or total elimination in the human consumption of animal products is an essential component of climate change mitigation. The study concludes that even the most environmentally friendly animal products have a higher environmental impact than plant foods. By translating a mass of data into recommendations for change, Poore and Nemecek provide a dense narrative of the violence caused by animal agriculture to the environment. They do not propose that the solution to climate change rests exclusively in the choices of individual consumers. Substantial change in policy is also needed. For example, in order to address affordability at both production and consumption levels, governments, which currently spend billions of dollars annually on agricultural subsidies, will have to reallocate that financial support, and/or provide greater incentives for the production of plant foods for direct human consumption through, for example, credit or tax breaks. But Poore and Nemecek also insist that consumers have a role to play in initiating dietary change. In the United States, for example, "where per capita meat consumption is three times the global average, dietary change has the potential for a far greater effect on food's different emissions, reducing them by 61 to 73%."[39] This is not to say that American consumers have the power to save the world simply by changing their diets. It is to say that transformation of agriculture will require action at different levels: policy, production and consumption.

In chapter 6 of this book I argue that we should be wary of claims that veganism is little more than an individualistic consumer lifestyle. Similarly, I think we should resist suggestions that any attempt to lower our carbon footprints as individual consumers is a harmful diversion from collective political action against the corporate power and neoliberalism driving planetary destruction.[40] One of the many lessons I take from feminism is that if change is to be meaningful and lasting, it needs to recognise the interconnectedness of the individual and the collective, the personal and the political. Of course, "green" lifestyles, like veganism, can be sold to us, just like any other product, under contemporary capitalism. But as I argue in chapter 4, a careful (re)consideration of the wider impacts of our individual consumption habits can help to turn us toward collective action rather than drive us away. For those of us who consume far more than we need, facing up to the consequences of eating animal products can be, in the words of the Indian environmental historian and activist Ramachandra Guha, one way to "internalise the costs of (our) profligate behaviour."[41]

In his 2006 book *How Much Should a Person Consume?*, Guha — following the language of ecologist Madhav Gadgil — divides contemporary Indian society into three socio-economic classes: omnivores (middle and upper class people), ecosystem people (poorer people who rely primarily on local resources) and ecological refugees (people displaced by environmental changes). These groups are distinguished by their respective access, or lack thereof, to power, resources (financial, environmental and socio-political), cultural capital and consumer goods. Guha insists that comprehensive environmental policies must do more than seek to meet the needs of ecosystem people and ecological refugees; they must also seek to redress the overconsumption and "ecological entitlements" that typically accompany higher economic status.[42] Though Guha was writing specifically about India, the spirit of his argument can be expanded to the global context. And although he was not writing specifically about the impact of the consumption of animal products on the environment and economic inequality, his use of the word "omnivore" to name the most profligate consumers is particularly apt for an argument in favour of contextual veganism in the context of what Sunaura Taylor aptly calls "the growing international fetishization of meat as a class signifier."[43] It is by highlighting the links between the inhumane treatment of animals in animal agriculture, the damage it does to the environment and wildlife, and its role in exacerbating inequalities among people — and not by pitting environmental arguments against animal rights *or* by entreating everyone in the world to "Go Vegan!" — that vegan activists in the West can make the most powerful interventions.

The scientific studies and activist and academic arguments cited in this section seek to draw connections in order to propel individual and collective change. By focusing on links that often get lost in the bigger picture, they tell stories about how our behaviour has impacts that we may not be aware of, or prefer to ignore. The calls for Western "omnivores" to internalise the costs of our high consumption, and for Western vegan activists to prioritise coalition-building with people in different parts of the world, echo the work of ecological feminist Val Plumwood, who was also a lover of stories and a great storyteller. Taking heart from Plumwood's writing on women, animals and the environment, I conclude this chapter with some tales that have brought home to me, in different ways, the "long emergencies of slow violence" that sometimes get lost in competing statistics and big narratives about veganism and the environment.

Corn ears, pig tales and chicken bones

In early 2018 I saw the documentary *El Maíz en Tiempos de Guerra* ("Corn in Times of War," Alberto Cortés, Mexico, 2016) in Mexico City. The film tells the story of four Indigenous families from different regions (Chiapas, Jalisco and Oaxaca) who cultivate maize.[44] We follow each family over the course of a year — the full cycle of the annual crop — viewing images of *milpa* (cornfields) and kitchens, and hearing stories about each family's relationship to the grain their people have grown for centuries. *El Maíz en Tiempos de Guerra* is a slow film. There are long silent shots of people of all ages working in the fields, of men and children storing piles of cobs, of women and girls preparing tortillas, of families eating and speaking variously in Tseltal, Ayuujk and Wixárika around the table. Both the stories and images provide a strong sense of the central place of corn in the lives and histories of Indigenous Mexicans. But the film does not represent the families as trapped in an imagined time warp. There are indications of gender and generational conflict, as well as racism, as the families interact among themselves and with other Mexicans.

The "war" of the title refers to some of the twenty-first century threats to the cultivation of maize: the introduction of genetically modified seeds (used in the United States and elsewhere but prohibited by law in Mexico), the spread of tourism, and the appropriation of Indigenous land by the state, industries and drug cartels.[45] The film's protagonists speak of the increasing difficulty of cultivating ancient types of corn, of preserving a spectrum of seeds, colours and flavours in the face of an externally imposed uniformity.

The attentiveness to the life and history of corn in *El Maíz en Tiempos de Guerra* in some ways echoes the work of the Indian ecofeminist Vandana Shiva, who has long defended seeds against the uniformity of genetically modified crops, a struggle she understands as inseparable from food justice.[46] If *El Maíz en Tiempos de Guerra* makes visible the economic and political struggles of Indigenous peoples to safeguard the staple food of the Mexican diet, it also provides a distinct angle on a war that gets substantially more media attention: the violent conflict between state security forces, politicians and drug cartels. This story of the tremendous human cost of organised crime, corruption and violence is told repeatedly in contemporary Mexico, including in any number of documentaries and films, often in sensationalist style. *El Maíz en Tiempos de Guerra* tells another story, of how this war also kills slowly, as Indigenous farmers who are not able to defend their lands are driven from them, their ancient maize crops razed to grow poppies. "Cultivating maize," as the voiceover for the film's trailer puts it, "is a profoundly political act of resistance."

El Maíz en Tiempos de Guerra is not a vegan film. But it documents in detail the slow violence committed against a historically rich and diverse plant, and the losses this brings to connections among people, the land and the past, as well as the dangers for the future. The film invites reflection on the complexity of the relationship between veganism and environmentalism, diet and colonialism, and different kinds of violence. Viewing the film and having conversations with people in Mexico about it, I was struck by the challenges of telling such a story in a country where tales about murder, disappearances and political corruption dominate the news and much of everyday conversation. I was also reminded of Plumwood, who warned against "the insensitivity to non-animal forms of life as beyond moral consideration." By this she did not mean that plants are the same as animals or that human beings should not eat plants. She argued, rather, that plants should not be constructed as a radical other to animal life. Plants, in Plumwood's ecofeminism, are "ethically considerable beings," part of the "continuities of planetary life."[47] Though belonging to a colonial settler community and writing in a European philosophical tradition, Plumwood was particularly attentive to the lessons of Indigenous peoples' relationships to the other-than-human world. In its own way, by foregrounding the intimate relationship of Indigenous Mexicans to corn, *El Maíz en Tiempos de Guerra* tells the story of resistance to food imperialism in the early twenty-first century — an imperialism evident not only in the histories of the Spanish conquest and more recent American and Canadian economic expansion, but also in the slow violence wreaked by the intensification and globalisation of agriculture.

Before the Spanish conquest of the early sixteenth century, the original peoples of what is today Mexico consumed a diet primarily of corn and other plants; there were no large domesticated animals. The conquistadors brought with them horses, sheep, cows and pigs; the pigs proliferated most rapidly.[48] Pork had been a mainstay of the diet among the medieval and early modern Christians of Iberia, and the Spanish passion for pork persists to the present day, as any vegan or vegetarian who has tried to order food in a bar or restaurant in Spain can probably attest. But the news in summer 2018 that for the first time pigs (50 million) outnumbered people (some 46.5 million) in Spain raised alarms. One British newspaper reported that a growing preoccupation about the environmental impact of the pork industry added to existing concerns about food safety and conditions for workers in slaughterhouses, many of them Muslim migrants who do not eat pork.[49]

By drawing together dangers to the environment, animals and people, the Spanish pig story puts the problem of too many pigs in a wider context in which care for animals, people and the planet are connected rather than pitted against one another. It highlights the different but interdependent forms of violence — some slow, some much faster — involved in animal agriculture. The abusive working conditions in abattoirs — including typically low wages and the risk of serious accidents and psychological damage — have been documented in many countries. At least one author has argued that vegans should form alliances with meat-eaters to address the appalling situation of slaughterhouses, which he says pose a threat to human flourishing as well as animal welfare.[50] The tale of too many Spanish pigs is an example of what Plumwood identified as a small story about the environment and its inhabitants, behind which lies much bigger narratives involving often unnamed killers and entire systems of violence.[51] In this case these include: the history of industrial agriculture in Spain and elsewhere; international trade; changes to local, national and international foodways; the popularity of Iberian ham as a national and, increasingly, transnational delicacy; human migration and labour; and racism and religious discrimination.

Rob Nixon defines slow violence as that which "occurs gradually and out of sight, a violence of delayed destruction that is dispersed across time and space, an attritional violence that is typically not viewed as violence at all."[52] The harm done to farm animals and slaughterhouse workers is not slow in the strict sense. Animals reared on intensive farms typically live truncated lives and die fast, brutal deaths that, in the process, may also cause injury to the human workers who kill them. But this violence certainly occurs largely "out of sight." The sleuth work of animal rights and workers' rights activists has gone some way in bringing this brutality to public attention. Some slaughterhouse workers have testified to the demeaning and dangerous conditions in which they labour, and the systematic abuse of animals they are required to carry out as a routine part of the job.[53] Less easy to access is the experience of the animals themselves — except to know, through scientific studies, that they experience pain and fear.[54] There is an ethical problem, however, in relentlessly portraying farm animals as nothing more than suffering victims. This is one of my objections to *Cowspiracy*: by highlighting the problem of too many cows the film represents bovine creatures as an uncountable mass of wretched beings. Images of individual cows (with the exception of shots of a free-range farm) show them labouring under the weight of heavy udders or cramped in pens. These are real images of animal suffering. But the message that there are too many cows and pigs in the world may actually work against building an appreciation among people that those creatures are worthy of ethical consideration. As Sunaura Taylor argues, "animals are too often presented simply as voiceless beings who suffer." Images of "mute" animal suffering may reinforce rather than challenge the belief that farm animals can be exploited by people because they do not have the capacities — such as speech or human-like intelligence — that would grant them equal moral status with people. Put another way, images of farm animal suffering can both exaggerate the differences between those animals and people (some of whom do not speak), and ignore things that we have in common, including emotional awareness, the ability to feel pain, vulnerability and dependency.[55]

The sociologist Erika Cudworth has argued that of all the animals who have close relationships to human beings, those who work on intensive farms have the least liberty. For example, "the pigs in a factory farm may ultimately only be able to exercise agency by growing ill and dying before their industrialized slaughter can reap the benefits."[56] And who is going to record evidence of such lives and deaths? Written or spoken records of human engagement with individual farm animals may be more valuable than sensationalist visual images or alarming statistics. In the following account Kathryn Gillespie records her experience of bearing witness to the lives of cows at an auction:

> I sat and took notes, watching carefully as each animal passed through the ring. As I watched, I saw cows limping, their bodies worn from intensive milk-production and repeated impregnation. I saw cows and calves auctioned off — some together, and some sold to different buyers as mother and calf called to each other across the auction yard. I saw day-old calves with their umbilical cords still attached stumble through on unsteady legs. I saw cows collapse with exhaustion, too weak to stand. I watched as cows, steers, and calves were auctioned by the pound for meat and per head for dairy-production.[57]

By extending interest and compassion to the specific suffering of the cows she watches, Gillespie recognises their pain as something that can be communicated and that people can perceive, even though cows do not "speak" our language.[58] She also acknowledges the difficulty involved in testifying to the experiences of large numbers of animals, whose faces and bodies she is unlikely to remember. Witnessing animal grief is ethically problematic, she argues, if it means leaving the animals behind to meet their fate. It is important to keep this dilemma in mind, even if witnessing can lead to political action against animal agriculture. Gillespie's writing offers the possibility of recognising farm animals as individual beings whose lives are worthy of our care. By giving our attention even to a small number of cows and other animals people can begin to counteract the erasure of those creatures from human consciousness and memory.[59]

My last story is about a different kind of witnessing of animal death, one that highlights, in Nixon's words, the "violence of delayed destruction that is dispersed across time and space."[60] In early 2017 I attended the taping of the BBC World Service programme "Should We All Be Vegetarians?," described above. Amidst all the useful moral debate and statistical evidence, one image remained with me. But when I listened to the radio broadcast some months later I discovered that this detail had been edited out. On the programme, the archaeologist Holly Miller describes to the audience two different chicken bones she is holding in her hands: one from the Tudor era, discovered at an archeological site, and one from a chicken dinner she has eaten some weeks previously. The older bone is longer, harder and more robust; the modern one shorter and spongey. Whereas the Tudor chicken had likely been slaughtered at age two to three, the newer bone was from a typical broiler chicken, much fatter than her ancestors, and likely killed at about thirty days. And here, from my memory, is the anecdote that was edited out of the programme: as Miller held the two bones she reflected that whereas chickens were valued animals in Britain in the past, their remains sometimes found in graves, today the average Londoner is most likely to encounter chicken bones scattered on the pavement outside a fast food shop.[61]

This story of the fate of dead chickens and our relationship to their remains came back to me as I finished writing this book, in the company of a small dog with a feline penchant for sitting on my lap as I wrote. When I took my new canine kin on outings, introducing her to the neighbourhood, I found myself constantly on the lookout for rogue chicken bones, frequently wrenching them from the dog's mouth when I had not been fast enough to stop her from snatching one up. These moments of encounter — me, the sprightly dog and the splintered bones of an anonymous chicken — provided evidence in my very hands of Cudworth's argument that animals raised on industrial farms and pets provide two extremes of contemporary human-animal relations in the West.[62] Perhaps if I did not practice veganism, and if I did not know a bit about the history of industrial chicken farming in England, I would see these small bones as little more than a menace to the health of the dog. But my reading tells me that chickens were the species most affected by the rise of factory farming in postwar Britain, that between the 1950s and 1980s the rearing and slaughter of chickens for meat underwent a process of rapid industrialisation, that human consumption of chickens increased seven times during this period, and that most chickens raised for meat ("broiler" chickens) are still kept in sheds, crammed next to other birds, pumped full of antibiotics and vitamins, and likely to suffer physical and psychological pain.[63] Each time I hold a chicken bone between my fingers I am reminded of how human beings have turned a once admired animal into little more than a machine, a commodity, totally instrumentalised for consumption by humans and, in some cases, our creaturely companions. Walks with my dog have become occasions for brief moments of witnessing, acknowledging and wondering about the life of these anonymous chickens.

Sharing my life with a dog, I have had to return to face the issue of animal agriculture in a more immediate and intimate way than I have for several years, as I consider what I can and cannot do to support the thriving of a small companion — who, in turn, helps me to thrive — in the context of the animal industrial complex. In this regard, although it is wrong to say that I extend my love for all animal others out from my affection for this individual dog, this relationship has helped me to think in new ways, and with greater urgency, about the fate of animals raised for food and other commodities for humans on the one hand, and the animals with whom we keep closest company, on the other hand. Through my interactions with a dog I have come closer to the slow violence committed against farm animals. These experiences have humbled me, reminding me of the ongoing dilemmas involved in ethical contextual veganism, even for someone with a disposable income and access to a wide variety of healthy food. As I weigh the advantages and risks of a vegetarian or vegan diet for my rescue dog, these walks are a reminder that my relationships with other beings are always to some extent beyond my control. Even as I acknowledge my multiple responsibilities — to the dog, myself, other animals, other people and the planet — I will not come up with perfect answers. In this way, my regular encounters with the remains of chickens have prompted me to pause and reflect on veganism not as an aim for perfection, but as a striving for more ethical relationships in a world in which our care for ourselves and the beings we love is so intimately entwined in the lives and deaths of others.

Chapter 4

CARING THROUGH SPECIES

We care for ourselves through the bodies of others. In omnivore societies, human beings are often socialised to believe that we need to use and consume animals in order to attend to our physical, mental and emotional health, and that of our families and communities. This message sometimes comes from those closest to us. But it is also spread by powerful institutions, in the form of scientific studies, government guidelines, the advice of healthcare professionals, media reports, and advertising by food and pharmaceutical companies. This information often tells us that human wellbeing requires the exploitation of animals in agriculture, scientific experimentation, and the manufacture of drugs and other products. This in turn implies that caring for people is fundamentally incompatible with caring for animals, or at least that the needs of people must always come first.

In this chapter and the following, I explore some of the challenges faced by vegans when our commitment to other animals seems to come into conflict with our need to care for ourselves, and with our desires to create and nurture relationships with people. Such challenges are exacerbated by the fact that inequalities among people help to determine the degree to which we have access to the food, medication and clothing we need to survive and thrive. These realities make the struggle to find ethical approaches to caring for ourselves and others all the more complicated, and all the more urgent.

How (not) to grow old as a vegan

Writing in the 1970s and 1980s, the most frequently cited philosophers of animal liberation and animal rights — Peter Singer and Tom Regan, respectively — insisted that moral commitment to other animals should be based on reason. Regan rejected arguments that revealed people's feelings, while Singer exhibited disdain for "animal lovers" who pampered their pets while ignoring the plight of farm animals.[1] In the late twentieth century, some feminist animal advocates challenged what they considered the masculinist and rationalist premises put forth by Regan and Singer, especially their male philosophers' depreciation of supposedly "feminine" sentimentality towards animals. Ecofeminists such as Carol J. Adams and Josephine Donovan proposed instead a responsibility to animals based on a feminist ethic of care.[2]

More recently, the scholar and avowed animal lover Kathy Rudy has proposed a novel approach to human-animal relations, taking as its starting point the everyday emotional ties between people and the creatures with whom we share our lives. In her book *Loving Animals: Toward a New Animal Advocacy*, Rudy eschews what she understands as the "cold, clinical, and sterile" nature of Singer's utilitarianism, and the rationalism that characterises some animal rights discourse and activism. Rudy wants an animal advocacy with heart. "For me," she writes, "the moment of transformation comes by falling in love with a particular animal, and when that happens, a part of my subjectivity shifts and somehow I belong to that animal." Rudy's affective approach is a two-way affair: "loving animals" refers both to people's capacity to love other creatures and the ability of those animals to love us back. By exploring her own and others' intimate relationships with animals, both wild and domesticated, Rudy pushes at the boundaries of popular assumptions about the kinds of liaisons human beings and other creatures can create. In the process she asks us to reconsider what we understand by the very categories "human" and "animal." Her version of human-animal loving refuses to play by the rules of fixed categories of gender and species, and challenges the celebration of romantic relationships between two people as the ultimate form of intimacy.[3]

I am drawn to Rudy's descriptions of the queerness of human-animal kinship. The Singeresque disdain for sentimental animal lovers is no match for the species-border-crossing love Rudy finds with her canine cohabitants. But in Rudy's world and worldview, like that of Western society more broadly, different animals are entitled to different kinds of, and opportunities for, love. Inspired by the American locavore movement, Rudy visits a number of small farms close to her home in the south of the United States to witness the lives of free-ranging animals who are well cared for and guaranteed a "humane" death.[4] She concludes that although these creatures "pay their dues in life with their products and flesh...they would rather have lived and loved and played in the sun and the dirt and the rain, than not be born at all."[5] This strikes me as little more than wishful thinking. As Vasile Stanescu details in a reply to Rudy, local, organic farms engage in a number of invasive practices that are painful for animals.[6] But he has another objection to Rudy's claim that animal advocacy can grow out of mutual love:

> if animals can make the choice to love (or not to love) humans, surely they must also be able to make the choice to love each other? And if animals can love one another (as Rudy herself would seem to argue), humane farming, even if animals are given a name or a little more room, can never truly exist.[7]

Stanescu pinpoints the limitation with the idea that people's attachments to individual domestic animals can lead to an ethical commitment to *all* creatures. There is an echo here of Singer's claim that emotions are an insufficient and inconsistent basis upon which to build animal liberation.[8] But Stanescu's critique differs from Singer's rationalist approach. Instead of dismissing love for animals out of hand, Stanescu proposes that there can only be truly loving human-animal relations if there is also *justice* for animals.[9]

Rudy is not oblivious to the contradictions of loving cats and dogs while consuming farm animals. The mistake she makes is in universalising from her individual and very specific experience of both transpecies relationships and veganism. Her turn to locavorism came in reaction to what she concluded were the inadequacies of the vegan diet for human health and the environment. As argued in the previous chapter, these are important concerns; it is not enough to embrace veganism without considering food justice and sustainability. As the work of Stanescu and a number of other authors discussed in this chapter shows, these should be understood as part of the same struggle.[10] Rudy's tendency to treat food sustainability, environmentalism and veganism as separate issues arises from the particular context in which she experienced veganism. Moreover, notwithstanding her cleverly queer take on companion animals, her vegan story betrays very conservative assumptions about age and womanhood.

In the following excerpt Rudy describes how, following her sudden awareness of the horrors of factory farming, she embarked on her "vegan year":

> I started buying these products in the frozen food section of my grocery store; I thought they tasted pretty good, almost just like real hamburgers and bacon, and I tried

not to let the list of unpronounceable ingredients bother me. As long as they didn't have any meat in them, I ate them. I wrote letters to Morningstar Farms, a subsidiary of Kellogg's, thanking them for their products and for helping me become a real vegan... Sometimes I ate fruits and vegetables, but the logic of the frozen food aisles made the fresh ones seem much less palatable (some of them actually still had dirt on them!), so I bought and ate highly colored boxes and bags of washed, processed, and frozen peas, potatoes, corn, strawberries, and peach slices. Maybe they didn't taste as good as their fresh counterparts, but my taste buds were being retrained by my new food regime and I believed I had to put my own pleasure behind my politics... My food ethic consisted of the simple dictum that no piece of flesh or any other animal products would ever pass my lips. I couldn't really see exactly how my practices were making a difference to real animals, but the growing animal rights movement told me veganism was the only answer, and so I persisted.[11]

As she recounts it, veganism turned Rudy into a consumerist dupe, the vegan equivalent of the global food consumer as represented, according to Elspeth Probyn, by critics of the hamburger mega chain McDonald's. Such activists portray fast food consumers as, in Probyn's words, "basically incapable of action...infantilised members of the McDonald's family... brainwashed, malleable half-subjects, incapable of any decision or responsibility."[12] In Rudy's version, the strings of the all-powerful food industry are pulled not by Ronald McDonald but by his evil McVegan twin. Rudy may well have become addicted to the sugar, corn and salt contained in many vegan prepared foods. But her story says more about the success of transnational corporations in cashing in on vegetarian and vegan markets (and, perhaps more importantly, their success in re-defining what counts as food in the contemporary United States) than it does about veganism and its relationship to animal advocacy. While it is important to have a critical understanding of how we are seduced into different forms of consumption, it is also important, as Probyn rightly argues, to acknowledge our agency in consuming food that may be bad for us, especially when we have access to different kinds of food.

Predictably enough, Rudy soon got sick of, and from, vegan junk food. The remainder of her story reads like the confessions of a recovered addict. Instead of heading back to the fresh fruit aisles, she gave up on veganism and blamed animal rights activists for presenting her with a false choice between a healthy, balanced and environmentally responsible omnivore diet, on one hand, and a deadly food regime full of processed fake meats, on the other:

> My new friends and I were quite satisfied with ourselves. We thought of ourselves as morally pure and were even a bit smug about it. The rest of the world was unenlightened, we thought. We shored up our superiority over vegan potlucks by eating mounds of corn chips and canned salsa and reconstituted corn and soy products of all types. At animal rights conferences, we paid ten dollars for ice-cream bars that were made of soy and corn syrup. When we did eat out with "flesh eaters," we made a big deal about grilling the waitperson about ingredients.[13]

When her doctor told her to stop eating so much soy and corn and start eating more animal products, Rudy felt torn. Eventually, she chose to eat "ethical meat" and animal products produced locally. Rudy acknowledges that she "was the wrong kind of vegan," that she should have done more research on nutrition and recognised the trap of the corporate vegan sales job. But she blames her experience on the lack of attention to nutrition, sustainability and industrial farming in the vegan literature she encountered at the turn of the millennium.[14] In her proposal for an "alternative animal advocacy" Rudy focuses most of her attention not on the ways in which capitalism, including the selling of healthcare as a commodity in the United States, works to constrain her agency and self-care, but on the ostensible moral intolerance of vegans for whom, she implies, the *only* thing in the world that matters is ending the exploitation of animals.

Rudy attributes to vegans — by all accounts a tiny percentage of the American population — astonishing powers of persuasion and political influence.[15] She also insinuates that vegans are naive and intolerant because most are young. "A steady diet of mostly corn and soy mixed with a lot of sugar ravages most middle-aged bodies,"she notes.[16] This may well be true. But I challenge the suggestion that veganism is a youthful fad that people grow out of if they know what's good for them. Rudy's account generalises about the bodies and experiences of middle-aged women from her own limited experience, implying that we all need animal products in order to flourish as we grow older. Obviously there is no such thing as a typical "vegan body." All human beings require different kinds of nutrients in different quantities at different points in our lives, and some of us have food intolerances and allergies. The consumption of animal products may help to fill in some of the gaps, but it certainly cannot magically meet all the nutritional needs of ageing bodies. Most importantly, Rudy misses the opportunity to consider how veganism may provide access to healthier and more ethical food for those millions of Americans who cannot afford the expensive, locally-produced meat, dairy and eggs championed by the locavore movement.

There are alternative ways of envisioning the relationship between caring for the ageing female self, wider human communities and other animals. In her essay "Thinking and Eating at the Same Time: Reflections of a Sistah Vegan," Michelle R. Loyd-Paige recounts how she started to think and eat differently "as the result of a *Kairos* moment." *Kairos* is an ancient Greek word meaning "right or opportune moment" and in Loyd-Paige's faith it is used to describe "the appointed time in the purpose of God." Loyd-Paige's *kairos* moment occurred not in a church or during a moment of conscious prayer or other spiritual reflection, but while queuing at a fast food restaurant to buy some chicken wings. In the midst of this seemingly banal errand, "from out of nowhere, I began wondering what happened to the rest of the bodies of the three chickens it took to create this snack for my husband that I was about to so casually order." The next thing she knew, a series of thoughts and experiences converged: her academic expertise on the inequalities of global food distribution; a recollection of an animal rights message about the methods used in chicken production; the memory of how well she had felt on a recent forty-day spiritual fast in which she had cut out meat and dairy; and "a desire to lead a more authentic life."[17]

Loyd-Paige's description of how she came to understand that her way of eating was out of sync with her commitment to social justice provides a wonderful account of the ways in which caring for ourselves, for our human communities and for animals are connected. Loyd-Paige is acutely aware of the deadly impact on African Americans of poor access to good food. In her words, "I am convinced that eating a meat-based diet — not to mention dairy products, eggs and fish — is not only hazardous to food animals and harmful to the land, but, more important to me, perilous to the health of my people." On an individual level, Loyd-Paige concluded that adopting a vegan diet was the best thing for her body as it entered menopause.[18] Her change of diet — eliminating animal products as she had done during her religious fast, and reintroducing more soy products — was overseen by her doctor, and her story provides an important counterpoint to Rudy's unfortunate encounter with a medical professional who instructed her to start eating animal products again. Different women will require different kinds of foods before, during and after menopause, and soy will not be the answer to all our problems. But by adopting a varied diet consisting largely of locally produced organic fresh fruit and vegetable and fair-trade products, Loyd-Paige offers a version of vegan ethics that incorporates a commitment to sustainability and food justice for human beings and other animals, both close to home and further away.

All the writers in *Sistah Vegan* stress the interconnectedness of: compassion towards other animals; individual bodily, mental and spiritual health; the right of African Americans and other racialised communities in the United States to access good food and healthcare; the ways in which products such as sugar, coffee and chocolate harm both consumers in the West and producers in poorer countries; and the impact of reckless American food consumption on the earth. A. Breeze Harper identifies Black women's commitment to veganism as a practice aimed to "decolonize their bodies" within a wider project of decolonisation.[19] There is a parallel movement among some Mexican Americans promoting a return to pre-Columbian plant-based foods as part of a project to decolonise Mexican American diets.[20] By incorporating women of different classes, sexualities, family circumstance and ages, *Sistah Vegan* acknowledges differences of access to affordable, healthy vegan food while refusing reductive representations of vegans as young, white and thin.[21]

I find *kairos* a useful way of interpreting the often unexpected convergences that can lead to significant and meaningful change on a personal level. My resistance to the idea of veganism as a lifestyle arises in part from the emphasis on the individual and consumer choice. But I am also wary of anti-vegan rhetoric that represents veganism as a conversion stripped of any spiritual meaning or the potential for individual and collective transformation. While I do not share many of Loyd-Paige's experiences or her religious faith, in retrospect the concept of *kairos* helps me better to understand the disparate forces that came together to push me rather quickly and definitively towards veganism some years ago. As the philosopher Amélie Frost Benedikt suggests, *kairos* is not simply a subjective, personal experience of time, to be understood in opposition to objective chronology or clock time. *Kairos* also has an objective dimension because opportunities for action and decision present themselves on a regular basis, even if people do not pick up on them. The ethical dimension of *kairos* involves the individual or collective ability/willingness to act at the right moment: "A concern for *kairos* signals an interest in being 'on time' chronologically speaking, which leads to being 'on time' ethically speaking."22

Similarly to Loyd-Paige's reflection of her *kairos* moment as one in which personal reflection converged with conscious knowledge of wider realities, Benedikt's description of the ethics of *kairos* underscores the political dimension of moments of connection between personal experience and awareness of the objective situation of life beyond the self. My *kairos* moment occurred in late 2013 while I was undertaking an online course on climate change. As someone always vaguely committed to environmentalism but who didn't live a terribly environmentally-friendly life — I cycled and recycled regularly, but also flew an awful lot and ate whatever I fancied — I had decided that I needed to try to understand better the science behind climate change. I saw out the course, though I found the material on computer modelling challenging. At the end of the ten weeks I did one of those online carbon footprint tests, the results of which were frankly alarming — we would need three and a half planets if everyone consumed as much as I did. The course may have had some material on animal agriculture, though I don't remember that part. Regardless, something in me shifted that autumn. Over New Year I passed on partying in favour of a three-day solitary fast, during which I wrote and meditated a lot. I broke the fast with some vegetarian food, and ended the solitude with an icy swim in the women's pond in London's Hampstead Heath on New Year's Day. I started cutting out animal products over the next couple of months. By the time I went on a ten-day silent meditation retreat over Easter I was eating a vegan diet.

My *kairos* moment was not influenced by particular religious teachings, but there was a strong spiritual dimension to it, enhanced by self-education, meditation and careful reflection. Reading the chapters in *Sistah Vegan* reminded me that for some people of different faiths — whether institutional religions or not — veganism is part of a wider set of beliefs and practices. For many years my main contact with vegans was in urban anarchist circles in the U.K. and other parts of Europe in which alternative spiritualities were part of a wider project that incorporated anti-capitalism, environmentalism and veganism with alternative sexual practices and relationships. Whether one takes a consciously spiritual or religious approach to veganism or not, we can understand it as facilitating a practice of mindfulness that is consistent with the teachings of many faiths. In the words of Melissa Santosa:

Veganism cultivates an attention to minute details of food ingredients, clothing labels, and how the things you consume are produced. This mindfulness leads to the deeper investigation of all things you consume, not only as to their material content but also the conditions in which the products are manufactured, their ecological impact, and the standard of living they create for all those on the chain of raw material, manufacturing, selling, buying, and disposing.[23]

Of course, many people cannot afford to pay attention to much more than the price of the products they purchase, and all the authors in *Sistah Vegan* emphasise that vegan foods must be economically accessible in order to be part of a viable project for change. Combined with an awareness of the need for food justice, veganism demands of us a more mindful and care-full being in the world. Although meditation is often associated with tuning out the chaos and tuning into the individual body and soul, mindfulness can also allow one to see the world — the objective realities that surround us — with more clarity, offering opportunities for action and change. Whether and how we seize these moments is part of the ethical dimension of veganism.

I want to close this section with another middle-aged vegan story. While writing this chapter in early 2018 I received an email from a dear friend — like me, a white, middle-aged, middle-class person with a penchant for consuming things that taste and feel good but may not always *be* good for us. This friend was also someone I considered an unreconstructed omnivore, though hardly of the straight, macho variety. His message was a lyrical and poignant description of the end of a recent relationship with a lover with whom he had discovered new aspects of his sexuality. The lost lover was younger and vegan, and after the affair ended my friend continued to practice veganism. A few months later we met over a mezcal margarita and some vegan tacos and quesadillas in a new vegan pub in my neighbourhood. I asked for an update on his love life and food life. His former lover had become a friend, and my friend was still vegan. He felt great in his body and was happily discovering lots of new vegan recipes. He had recently come across a local vegan group and had gone to an event, where he was a good twenty years older than most of the other participants. When one young man asked why he had become vegan, my friend replied: "I was concerned about my health." He was met with some trepidation — vegans, don't you know, should be committed first and foremost to animal rights. But like most enthusiastic vegans they were happy to welcome him to the fold for some vegan beer and junk food.

I love this story not because it is a triumphant tale of a hardcore carnivore conversion to veganism, but because of the way my friend mourned his lover by taking in and preserving her way of eating within his own body, changing it in the process. This tale is an example of the unpredictable and wonderful ways bodies — human and otherwise — can come together through desire, mourning and care. Care of the self does not — should not — preclude care of others, and vice versa. My friend's tale is more an intermingling than a mere hyphenation of sex and food. It reminded me of the best moments of Elspeth Probyn's work, in which eating and sex come together, bringing often unexpected transformations in their wake.[24]

September 2015
London

A restful stay with E in the Welsh countryside on the last bank holiday weekend of the summer. But by Saturday my right eye was getting increasingly red and angry. As soon as I got back to London I headed for Moorfields Eye Hospital. After a few hours in A&E, various nurses and a meeting with the doctor on night duty, I was diagnosed with an autoimmune disease: uveitis. The remedy: a six-week treatment of steroid drops. My first big vegan test beyond the food/clothing sphere, and I have failed miserably – not because I reflected deeply on the dilemma I found myself in ("Your ethics or your eye"), but because it was only yesterday, when the pain and discomfort began to wane, that I even bothered to consider the history of the liquid I was dripping in my eyes several times a day – and to imagine the red, sore, swollen eyes of the animals they likely had been tested on. I vowed to do some research on this. And continued to drip the drops.

Veganism at the edge

If you are going to develop an autoimmune condition — or indeed just about any medical condition, mild or life threatening — London is probably the best place on the planet to be. We have not one but two public eye hospitals as well numerous other specialist hospitals and clinics, community hospitals and General Practitioner surgeries throughout Greater London. As I write in mid-2018, the National Health Service (NHS), established in the postwar period as part of the rollout of the welfare state, is celebrating its 70th anniversary. Amid small doses of nostalgia, a recent junior doctors' strike and a swathe of cuts under yet more government austerity measures, there is still much to be grateful for and to admire. The NHS is the envy of the world in terms of public healthcare. It runs on a colossal budget and thanks to the skills and care of millions of highly trained human practitioners from all over the world. And like all modern medical systems, it relies on a multitude of treatments and drugs developed on the bodies of other animals.

Animal testing has a long history, and animals continue to be used in the contemporary era in a wide range of scientific experiments. Some of these — part of what is known as pure or fundamental research — have the objective of enhancing general scientific knowledge. Others are used in applied research, that is, studies whose aim is to solve specific problems. These include experiments designed to discover more about diseases that affect people and find treatments for them. Animals are also used in research to determine whether new drugs are safe for human testing before being released to wider parts of the population. The testing of drugs on animals before clinical trials using people is a legal requirement in the United Kingdom and European Union. Some animals are used in experiments for medicines and products designed for other animals (for example, in veterinary use). Many medications, whether over-the-counter or prescription, contain animal products, including gelatine and lactose.[25] According to the organisation "Speaking for Research," which defends the use of animals in scientific research, in the U. K. today mice make up the significant majority of animals used in testing (around three quarters); others include fish, rats, birds, dogs, primates and cats.[26]

Animal experimentation is probably the most hotly contested area of animal ethics, and debates about animal testing for medical purposes are particularly fraught. Defenders often point to advances in medicine as evidence that animal testing is necessary for human progress and even survival.[27] In the late twentieth century the American Medical Association (AMA) exploited the emotional stories of people with disabilities in order to promote the message that cures for particular conditions could only be discovered using animal experimentation. A small group of disability activists challenged the AMA's position in the midst of painful divisions within the disability community.[28] In the early twenty-first century a growing community of medical doctors, veterinarians and scientists is challenging claims that human health necessarily benefits from and depends upon the use of animals in scientific research.[29] But the common wisdom that many of our life-saving and life-prolonging medical treatments are the result of scientific advancements enabled by experimentation on animals makes it difficult for many people to envision a world without animal testing. Most can likely imagine — even if many do not desire — a world free from animal foods and clothing. But although we live in an age where patients are increasingly treated as consumers, the majority of us probably conceive of human healthcare as something more than a commodity. Moreover, even in the best public healthcare systems in the world, people's experiences of medical care vary widely. Class, location, migration status, ability, levels of education, language, religious beliefs, gender and sexual identity, race and ethnicity, income level, prior experiences with healthcare systems and specialists — all these and many other factors condition whether and how we access healthcare, and our experiences of the system. When we take animal ethics into account as well, looking at the complexities of contemporary healthcare from a vegan perspective, the world of agriculture and foodways suddenly looks a lot more manageable.

Because of the significant barriers and the high stakes involved in accessing vegan treatment and medication, vegan discussions about healthcare provide valuable insight into how vegan ethics can involve negotiation rather than adhesion to a strict set of rules. As in many areas of alternative healthcare, the internet has proven a valuable resource for those who want to educate ourselves and each other about treatments and medications that avoid or minimise the exploitation of other animals. On vegan forums, users exchange information on which products are "cruelty free" (not tested on animals). Some vegan websites post lists of medications that do not contain animal products, and others provide testimony to the difficulties some vegans encounter when dealing with medical professionals or pharmaceutical companies.[30] In the vegan blogosphere we also encounter stories of the challenges met by vegans in the face of serious illness. I tell the stories below not with the aim of promoting certain forms of treatment over others, but with the conviction that some of the most meaningful conversations around veganism and ethics happen when we are confronted with the most difficult dilemmas.

In April 2015 the London-based blogger Fat Gay Vegan (FGV) — aka Sean O'Callaghan — informed his readers that his friend Indira had been diagnosed with secondary breast cancer of the liver. Indira had asked FGV to post a brief message from her "on the emotional struggle of being a dedicated vegan faced with medication which has undoubtedly been tested on animals."[31] In her message Indira recounts that she had become a vegetarian aged eight and vegan some twenty years later. In her mid-thirties, while pregnant with her second child, she was given a terminal cancer diagnosis:

> Despite losing the weight, I refused to give up my vegan diet. Although initially I was in a lot of pain and was too poorly to think straight, as the disease was becoming more controlled, I became conscious of all the drugs and medicines I was taking to do nothing other than prolong my life. As a vegan, I read labels in everything before it comes anywhere near my mouth. I didn't do that with the drugs. Instead, I took everything that was given to me with very little questions asked about what was in it and whether it was suitable for vegans. I read the medicine

packaging recently and noted there is lactose in several of the tablets I take. I had to undergo chemotherapy too. I am pretty certain these drugs have been tested on animals as their toxicity is so high. Yet, despite this knowledge, I continue to take these medicines as I am scared to die. I have two children, a daughter aged three and a son aged 6 months. Every time I think of leaving them I am overcome with heartbreak so I am fighting to stay alive and the only way I know is to take these medications which clearly are not designed for vegans. Does this make me a bad vegan?[32]

In the comments section following Indira's message the readers replied to Indira by affirming her choices, reminding her that veganism is an ethics of compassion rather than an inflexible regime, writing of their own similar struggles in the face of cancer and other diagnoses, and suggesting complementary treatments. Some readers responded that animal rights activists are better alive than dead; others stressed that the moral obligation for the provision of cruelty-free treatment and medicine lies not with individual patients and their families and friends but with the drug manufacturers.[33] Reading these comments, I was reminded of how much I owe to long-time vegans like Indira: for starting and sharing these conversations, even at the hardest of times; for continuing to ask the questions so many others fail to ask; and for being honest and open about their doubts.

Indira's blog post and the responses to it remind me of the profound importance of Sunaura Taylor's argument that discussions of animal care and veganism can benefit from the perspectives of people living with disabilities. Taylor brings from a disability perspective the fundamental lesson that intra-human and human-animal relations are by definition relations of interdependence. It is both anthropocentric

— and, I would argue, more than a little macho — to equate independence with strength and superiority. Disability activism challenges the idea that to depend on others for care is a form of weakness. Similarly, veganism can expose the myth of adult human independence, recognising, in Taylor's words, "that we are *all* vulnerable beings who will go in and out of dependency," and that a significant part of that dependency involves other species. It is not the case that veganism creates a dilemma about how people can care for ourselves without harming animals. Rather, thinking about illness and medicine in relation to veganism highlights the fact that all beings are dependent on one another for our survival and care.[34]

Cancer guinea pig

> Greetings, and welcome to Cancer Guinea pig...DIY trials from the Smart Lab inc – explorations of health modalities for cancer using myself instead of the mute harmless animals kept in medical laboratories.[35]

In the summer of 2017 I read a Facebook post from a cherished friend: spiritual teacher, alternative health aficionada, DJ, musician, feminist anarchist pathbreaker and queer high fem extraordinaire. The post linked to the blog Cancer Guinea Pig, where for five years my friend had been charting her process of healing breast cancer using mostly naturopathic treatments. The post "Holding it Together in the Darkness" opens with a reference to the early stages of her illness and moves forward to the present day. The words chilled me to the bone and melted my heart, transporting me back to the beginning of our friendship, some months after my friend's diagnosis in April 2004. It was a hot night in June and we were swaying to music at the Women's Anarchist Nuisance

Café (WANC) in a squatted former Chinese restaurant in East London. My friend had been hosting this magical women's caff since the late 1990s. At WANC women came together to watch musical and other performances, exchange skills and stories, and hang out. Cooking and sharing vegan food was the centrepiece of each monthly caff, and the author of Cancer Guinea Pig was one of my first vegan mentors. "Holding it Together in the Darkness" is about memory, voyages, teaching, searing pain and hope. In it my friend shares an especially intense and difficult moment of her journey through self-care and despair. The post situates one particular female human body in a wider universe. "To wish for hope that doesn't acknowledge global pain and suffering is a blindness," she writes.[36]

Cancer Guinea Pig is written in the voice of Calliope — an "anthropomorphic guinea pig" and herbivore *par excellence* — and her human alter ego. The entries are styled with wit and humour around a serious but far-from-morbid subject: non-allopathic treatments for cancer. This is not a remedy blog or instruction manual for how to heal with herbs, sound and spirituality, though there is plenty about all of those things and more. It is a lengthy meditation on the potential dangers of mainstream medical treatment for human and other bodies, and the potential benefits of the alternatives available. Through the posts on Cancer Guinea Pig, the voice of Calliope morphs from the squeaks of a small rodent to the lyrical tones of a full-sized female human and back again. The blog embraces anthropomorphism as a way of reminding readers that guinea pigs are far more than a metaphor for experimentation on human beings. These small rodents have been used in scientific experiments for centuries, ever since Spanish conquerors brought them back to Europe in the 1500s. Their desirability as research subjects derives from their biological similarities to human beings.[37] It was the vegetarian and anti-vivisectionist George Bernard Shaw who first used the term "human guinea pig," in protest against the testing of vaccinations on people in the early twentieth century.[38] By speaking "as" Calliope, the author of the CGP blog challenges species boundaries not by *personifying* the guinea pig in order to tell a tale about human behaviour, but by meditating on the shared experiences of human and other animal bodies. This is not a parable but an ethical exercise, the moral of which is that neither guinea pigs nor people *need* to suffer in the specific ways dictated by allopathic medicine, industrial capitalism and Western science.

The first post, from May 2012, explains:

> A cancer diagnosis is very scary, and there is intense pressure to take aggressive allopathic treatments as the only option. I have decided it is time to set up some record of the last eight years of experimentation on myself, working with cancer and without use of conventional allopathic medicine...My initial criteria for things I have used and tried were:
> - Cheap and locally sourced (if possible).
> - Vegan as far as possible.
>
> The Reasons I chose to use non allopathic modalities were within keeping of my ethics to:
> - Harm none.
> - Not leave toxic residues in the water.
> - Not contribute to the multibillion pharmaceutical industry.[39]

Cancer Guinea Pig is a lesson in do-it-yourself education in the digital age, full of examples of people exchanging stories and advice on how to care for themselves and others over the internet via social media, blogs, YouTube videos and the like. The blog confronts head-on the most difficult dilemmas involved in following a non-conventional cancer treatment: the fear, warnings and judgments of medical specialists, loved ones and wider society, and the challenges of maintaining a strict vegan diet while trying to heal from cancer through naturopathic means. It also details the writer's carefully considered movements around her vegan values and the needs of her own healing body.

In the comments section of the first entry, Cancer Guinea Pig responds to a message from a vegan activist who praises her efforts:

> I did have to bend and bow and let go of some of my principles but they simply taught me more compassion, and a lesson that things are never black and white. And a vegan lifestyle is truly wonderful and something I have been enjoying now for nigh on 25 years.[40]

A few months later, in the post "The Carrot or a Stick," Calliope expands on her experience of giving up, temporarily, her vegan diet while trying to adopt the right cancer-countering food regime. I cite this story at length because for me it encapsulates some of the complexities of practising contextual ethical veganism:

> After bean sprouts, and trying to go raw but just getting cold and grumpy inside I decided to try metabolic typing and blood group diet. I sent off the blood sample, I can't remember how I did it, but it came back with the earth shattering information that I was blood group O, the original meat eater, and to optimize my immune system meat was required. Oh ironies of irony for a herbivorous guinea-pig. Furthermore I was told that in order to find out how fast my metabolism was I would have to go on a controlled diet of meat three times a day.

I decided to leave the metabolic typing but to follow the blood group diet – thus breaking my codes, ethics and preferences and try and eat meat either from organic health food shops, or straight from the organic farmers market and cooked at friends houses as a more ecofriendly alternative to chemotherapy.

It took me a year.

To get my head around it.

[...]

I also knew that I needed to eat digestive enzymes that came from ox bile or something like that and that if I was going to work with this cancer using alternative methods I had to let something go. I had to make a trade. I spent many times imagining a chicken running across my path and me wringing its neck. Whilst thanking it and blessing it. Getting my head around the fact that it is not the action it is the intent.

A year of envisioning chicken running in front of me, at random times, and me wringing their necks, in deep gratitude for the sacrifice.

A proper mindfuck and the first of many during the last eight years.

So a year or so after I decided to eat meat I nervously trotted off to Fresh and Wild in Stoke Newington. I had arranged a meet up for the meat up with an old friend, ostensibly for moral support, though he was barely able to stifle his incredulity that I was going to eat meat in front of him, which worked well with my contrarian nature. I chose a chicken breast cooked in lemon, eyed it suspiciously for a while as it lay on the plate in front of me, and then the next minute I had eaten it. It had been relatively painless. And I felt great.

I went to my parents and requested organic steak. I ate it with quick relish. They were dumbfounded.

For three months I ate meat once or twice a week and my body liked it. It was weird. I would find myself standing at the counter of some posh organic food deli/place as I surveyed the dishes available. The beautiful colours of the vegetarian dishes would leave me cold, whilst the chicken/lamb or beef casserole would sing a song of loud joyous affirmation. It was like my third eye had opened and become a magnet. A magnet for meat. After about three months, I was once again eating a warmish chicken breast in a health food shop when all of a sudden I just felt cold dead flesh in my mouth and in-between my teeth, and knew this no longer felt right. And I stopped.

That was quite a few years ago now, but the experience had quite a profound effect on me. I love having a vegan diet, but I am no longer so adamant about it. I will eat the occasional egg if it feels right, or a bit of sheep's cheese but I guess I am lucky that after 25 years vegan food is my default and preference, my programmed recipe databank. This interlude taught me an invaluable lesson though. A lesson to not stand in judgement of people doing things that I didn't think were right. A lesson in the fact that maybe it is never the action, but the intent and context of the action. A lesson that by creating a positive vibe and love for the informed choices we make we can influence and inspire hundred times more than if we wittingly make others feel bad for their lifestyle choices.

I will conclude this lengthy epistle by affirming that as a guinea pig I will take the carrot over the stick any day – though if I was a dog...[41]

Calliope recounts her brief conversion into a "meat magnet" with humour and humility, inviting compassion and empathy (yes, those same emotions that vegans encourage all humans to have towards other animals). She tells us not only how her body reacted to the meat she was eating, but also how the experience taught her to be a less judgemental vegan: "Life changing dances with the 'enemy' that simply widened my capacity for and understanding of compassion."[42] Calliope's tale echoes a story, recounted by Sunaura Taylor, about the disability rights activist and vegan Dona Spring. In the last years of her life, when her body rejected plant protein, Spring began to eat some seafood. Rather than interpreting this decision "as evidence that holding on to one's animal ethics position is impossible or romantic," Taylor stresses that Spring "mobilized the dilemmas and contradictions she lived into powerful activism." From Spring's experience we learn that "some people may be politically vegan … but unable to sustain themselves on vegan food."[43] This, too, should be part of our understanding of contextual ethical veganism.

Thinking about veganism in relation to illness and disability also challenges modern Western ideas about time and progress. Calliope the guinea pig reflects that pressures to be on time can warp our ways of understanding the passage of years and the meanings of our lives. A "normal" life is one lived to the beats of heterosexual marriage, biological reproduction and traditional family life. Chronic illness disrupts this fantasy of the average healthy life:

> You see the thing is this cancer business has occupied so much of my prime time. From 38-52 years of age already. Sometimes it makes me feel left behind my peers in terms of success, work and earnings, mortgage and kids… though tbh I have lived in queer femme time most of my days where the conventional markers of

life don't create my dawns and dusks and achievement rungs.[44]

In this excerpt I hear an echo of Taylor's reflection that *all* bodies, human and other-than-human, whether defined as able or disabled, "are subjected to the oppression of ableism ... what it means to be independent, how to measure productivity and efficiency, what is normal, and even what is natural." According to Taylor, "Disability fosters a different sense of pacing, of progress, sometimes even of life span."[45] The implication is that we can *all* learn from these differences. The experiences of people — and other animals — living with disabilities and illness have much to teach those of us who identify as abled about our perceptions of time. Similarly, and without in any way glamorising the realities of cancer, *Cancer Guinea Pig* challenges conventional understandings of people with cancer as abnormal, questioning as well popular understandings of progress as healthy and desirable, for people as well as animals:

> there is something to be said for stepping outside of the treadmill of linear post-industrial time organisation, and reclaiming time for your body's temporal creativity is a vital antidote to the thing known as medical time. Medical time, with its absolute and unquestionable linear progression of illness. The body has its own natural cycliclar [sic] operating system, and – if yours is anything like mine – is fluid, multidimensional and also prone to randomness. And this can be harnessed and worked with as a tactic to help our bodies restore themselves to health.[46]

Reading *Cancer Guinea Pig* on healing outside medical time, to the rhythms of queer fem time sustained by a largely vegan diet and care for other beings, I am reminded of Melissa Santosa's observation, cited above, that "Veganism cultivates an attention to minute details." Another way of putting this is that veganism takes time. *Cancer Guinea Pig*'s blog, Taylor's theorisation of animals and disability, and the writings of other vegans grappling with care for their bodies and those of others are reminders that thinking about care across species is a crucial part of the process of educating ourselves about the interconnections among different forms of care, and the range of ways in which we depend upon other creatures. Yet negotiating the practical, ethical and emotional dimensions of caring for ourselves involves much more than careful consideration, self-education and conversation. It also requires dealing with and, in many cases, struggling against, the formidable powers of governments, large industries — be they agricultural, food manufacturers or pharmaceutical — and the medical and scientific establishments. These institutions wield significant ideological and financial power. We cannot care for ourselves or others in total isolation from them. As Brian Luke argues, "All of us, whether vivisector or vegan, have been subject to mechanisms undercutting sympathy for animals." Practicing care for animals therefore involves a significant break with dominant and institutionalised forms of anthropocentrism.[47] Different people will use the often competing and sometimes bewildering information about the use of animals in scientific research and medicine in different ways. Contextual ethical veganism is not about rules for how and whether to use practices that rely on animal research or products. Rather, it requires of us that we inform ourselves and share our knowledge with others. It means challenging the message that the instrumentalisation of other animals is always justifiable in the name of human progress.[48] It means understanding that different people will practise veganism in different ways and at different speeds.[49] And it asks that we support those who are seeking and putting into practice alternatives that recognise and honour the interdependence of self-care and our commitment to others.

Chapter 5

CREATURES WE WEAR

If food drips with memory, connecting us to the past as it passes through our bodies, clothing wraps us in history even as it makes a statement — bold or muted, conscious or unconscious — about who we are and what we want in the here and now. Yet when it comes to talk of the vegan revolution, food always seems to come first. In much writing on veganism, the refusal to wear clothing made from animals — fur, leather, wool, silk — is mentioned as an afterthought, if at all. But after eating, dressing is probably people's most regular and intimate relationship with dead animals. What we wear, like what we eat, is closely connected to our bodies. Items of clothing, though, tend to be more permanent than foodstuffs. The combination of durability and visibility makes attire a more immediately identifiable marker of identity. With clothing we wear our wealth or poverty, politics, beliefs, desires and tastes on our sleeves, and just about everywhere else. But clothing invites mistaken identities as much as intended ones. It conceals as much as it reveals.

For vegans clothing holds many possibilities for political pronouncement, whether through t-shirts, hats or other paraphernalia presenting the bearer as proudly *VEGAN*, or in the style of a particular subculture with which veganism is readily identified. But the biggest clothing issue for vegan politics is the fact that many fabrics are made of or with animal products. The threads we wear are knitted and knotted into so many issues related to animal and human lives and livelihoods that they cannot simply be unravelled by an animal rights sweatshirt or fake leather sandals bought at the annual VegFest. In this day of mass-produced synthetic clothing, eco-chic and online vegan shoe stores, the question is less whether you can find items free of animal products and more whether you can afford them. Some vegans may wear second-hand leather or wool (though, interestingly, probably not fur). And even when we don't sport clothes made with real animals, animals are not necessarily absent from our wardrobes. Many of the vegans I know — myself included — wear imitations of them in one way or another. What are some the issues involved in challenging or giving up the use of real animal skins? What does it mean for vegans to wear false hides instead? And why do some of us wear representations of animals on or close to our skin in different forms? In this chapter I explore these questions with reference to my own experiences and observations of (fake) fur, tattoos and leather in the queer subcultures I am most familiar with. To wear or not to wear animals is, I suggest, a question intimately tied to our relationships to other creatures, other people and our (sexual) selves.

The ugliness of fur and anti-fur

Fur is entangled in long histories of intra-human as well as human-animal relations. For millennia it has played a key role in the economies and cultures of many peoples, including some Indigenous communities. Fur also has an important place in the history of global trade and European imperialism. For centuries, fur clothing and accessories have been used as markers of human identity, including class, race and gender. In Europe, fur clothing and accessories have long been associated with wealth and power, as well as sexuality.[1] Once the preserve of the rich, in Britain during the first half of the twentieth century fur became an increasingly desirable female fashion item, part of a dream of class mobility. By the 1950s a fur coat — preferably mink — was, in the words of historian Carol Dyhouse, "the height of luxury, the ultimate object of desire, a defining quality of femininity, tantamount to a secondary sexual characteristic." The meanings and associations attached to fur changed as the industry diversified, and as the use of different animals came and went out of fashion. According to Dyhouse, the use of fur was already in decline before animal rights activists began their campaigns against it in the 1960s and 1970s. Fur's fall from grace wasn't all about fashion. In the second half of the twentieth century the development of central heating, along with rising costs of production, made fur coats less attractive, a vanity item with little practical purpose. And by the 1960s younger women were less interested in what some saw as a symbol of an outdated brand of femininity.[2] This association with a bygone era may help to explain the reappearance of real fur in contemporary vintage clothing shops, such as the ones that now proliferate in my East London neighbourhood.

By the latter part of the twentieth century fur had a new look, or new looks. "Fun furs" came in a variety of colours, sometimes in outfits made in an "animal style," complete with tails.[3] It was in this period that fur also came increasingly under attack. In Britain, animal advocates had, since at least the early twentieth century, campaigned against women wearing fur.[4] By the latter part of the century conservationists began to ring alarm bells over the fur industry's impact on endangered species. In the United States anti-fur campaigners targeted the sale of pelts from leopards, tigers and other large cats.[5] In Canada, during the late twentieth and early twenty-first centuries, environmentalists and animal advocates joined forces with celebrities, loudly and visibly calling for a boycott of seal skins. Although the vast majority of Canadian seals were killed by non-Indigenous commercial hunters, the seal hunt protest became a flashpoint for debates about animal rights and Indigenous cultural and economic rights. Inuit seal hunters and their allies accused anti-sealing protesters of cultural insensitivity and even imperialism.[6] Furthermore, for some Inuit communities, the boycott of seal skins had devastating social and cultural as well as economic impacts.[7] The Canadian legal scholar Maneesha Deckha insists that criticisms of the seal hunt were not necessarily imperialist. But she argues that a response to the hunt that took seriously anti-colonial critique as well as concerns for animals and the environment would require that the "final ethical assessments...come only after a process of attentive listening and consideration of divergent perspectives characterized by mindfulness of Canada's colonial legacy."[8] In contrast, according to the anthropologist George Wenzel, in the late twentieth century seal hunt protesters often spoke from a universalist position that ignored both colonial history and Inuit traditions.[9] As a result, the seal protest and the boycott of seal pelts became an example of an animal advocacy that prioritised the rights of other-than-human animals above all other considerations, including the rights of people.

By the time the European Economic Community banned the import of commercially hunted seal skins in 1983, fur was increasingly being sourced from fur farms, which had their origins in Canada and the United States in the late nineteenth and early twentieth centuries.[10] While conservationists were primarily concerned about species protection, by the 1980s and 1990s animal rights groups like People for the Ethical Protection of Animals (PETA) increasingly criticised the maltreatment of animals on fur farms.[11] In 2000 fur farming was banned in the United Kingdom, though it continues in Canada, the U.S. and much of the world in the early twenty-first century. PETA's protests against fur, like their animal rights campaigns generally, have often been provocative and explicit.[12] Their trademark anti–fur slogan — "I'd rather go naked than wear fur" — is still trotted out today, emblazoned on posters over photographs of the bodies of nude female celebrities.[13] Some feminist critics have expressed dismay at PETA's use of this kind of soft porn imagery. But it was in the U.K. that perhaps the most explicitly misogynist anti-fur propaganda was in full view. In the 1980s, in Julia Emberley's words: "[d]emonized images of fur-clad women dominated the media landscape of the metropolis of London." Billboards and posters paid for by the anti-fur organisation Lynx made provocative visual and written comparisons between "dumb animals" and dumb women, between the "poor bitches" who died to make fur coats and the "rich bitches" who wore them.[14]

These admittedly truncated accounts of fur fashion and anti-fur protests are not meant to represent the full histories of a complex industry and trade, or the controversies surrounding them. I tell these particular tales because they are ones I have long been familiar with and they have shaped my views. Writing about vegansim and animal skins brings back memories of hearing about the contentious campaign against the seal hunt when I lived in Montreal in the early 1990s, a twenty-something MA student canvassing, alongside lots of other mostly non-Indigenous young people, to raise money for Greenpeace, the Canadian-founded environmental NGO that had played a major role early in the protest.[15] I have a vaguer recollection of studying reproductions of the London anti-fur billboards in a Women's Studies class at the University of Toronto a few years earlier. The racist and sexist character of some anti-fur campaigns colour my thinking about the politics of fur and the anti-fur movement. They caution me against making generalisations about who benefits from the use of fur and who wins when hunting animals for their skins is halted, and fur is replaced by other fabrics. They remind me that the tactics and language used by animal advocates in the past have sometimes harmed and alienated people, and that this damage may still be discernible today. These are histories that stick, as indelible as the thick red paint that anti-fur protesters so love to spray on the fur coats of "rich bitches."

Faux fashion

The furry history of animals, people and power is transferred and transformed in the transition from real to fake fur. Erica Fudge writes that fake fur is "[c]aught somewhere between fashion and ethics — the desire for the symbolic power of fur, but the refusal of the death of the animal."[16] However, the ethical distinction between wearing real and fake fur is not so easy to draw. While the popularity of faux fur was certainly boosted by the anti-fur campaigns of the past fifty years, the fabric had been around since the early part of the twentieth century.[17] At that time faux fur — sometimes made with another animal product, wool — was largely marketed as a cheaper alternative. But by the middle of the century some faux fur was being deliberately made to look fake. A *New York Times* article from 1950 declared that "frankly fun" fur, often "dyed in fanciful colours and made with exaggerated markings," had been made "not only to imitate the animal kingdom, but poke fun at it."[18]

So what if we take into account the fact that for some people fake fur is attractive not because it conceals its counterfeit nature through successful imitation, but because it is so obviously fake? I for one have never bought real fur, but I have a substantial collection of faux fur jackets, as well as tops, scarves, tights and trousers stamped with animal prints, in my wardrobe. The coats especially come out when I want to glam up. My fake fur is visibly so — usually "leopard," "lion," "tiger," "zebra" or bright pink, blue or purple — and obviously synthetic to the touch. Much of the fake fur I see around me similarly mimics the skin of imaginary or "exotic" animals, especially leopard, with all the imperialist history implied by those associations. When Black female celebrities like Mel B and Little Kim wear leopard skin they draw the viewer's attention to racist associations of Black women with nature and animality, and challenge the equation of glamour and sophistication with white femininity. As a white woman wearing fake leopard print, am I reinforcing racist tropes and trivialising imperial violence against people and animals alike? Am I "poking fun" at the "animal kingdom"? I do not ask these questions rhetorically. I don't think there are straightforward answers. I want to stress that just because no animal has been harmed in the production of my faux fur coat, it is not an unambiguous example of ethical fashion. Fake fur is not entirely free from the fraught histories of the human use of real animal pelts. Yet in the move from real to fake these are shaken up. When it is ostentatiously fake, faux fur allows the wearer to nod to these histories while performing new identities in ways that can be subversive. From this angle, one way of understanding the ethics and aesthetics of fake fur is in the tradition of camp.

In her iconic essay "Notes on Camp," first published in 1964, Susan Sontag writes that "the essence of camp is its love of the unnatural: of artifice and exaggeration." In her list of "items which are part of the canon of Camp" Sontag includes an example from fashion: "women's clothing from the twenties (feather boas, fringed and beaded dresses, etc.)."[19] Boas may make the list because, even when they are made of real feathers, they are often dyed in exaggeratedly bold colours or jet black, giving them an air of dramatisation.

The flapper herself carries connotations of fun and frivolity, and camp in turn always has an element of the playful. It inhabits the realm of irony.[20] This is the point at which fake fur and queer drag meet — in the realm of irony and over-the-top performance.

May 2018
London

As I reread Sontag's "Notes on Camp," a memory takes shape. It starts with a bright image of a long-lost pair of green, fake snakeskin shoes-heeled, strapped, toeless and clunky. And a faux fur stole, boldly but poorly imitating a now-forgotten species. It's around 2003 and I am walking with a friend from the bus stop to a pub near Farringdon. It's the early years of Club Wotever, now a fixture on the London queer club and bar scene. In those days Wotever was a high camp event, the punters as dressed to kill as the performers. As I walked — nay, stomped — along in my fake snakeskin heels my friend chuckled:"You walk like a drag queen." Of course. High fem is drag. There is nothing real about it, even when the person performing — in this case a younger, wobbly me — identifies as a woman. The give-away may in fact be that I was and remain so spectacularly crap at walking in heels. Someone with another gender identity might have tried harder to promenade with "feminine" grace. For this particular high fem outing, performed very shabbily on the streets of London, I was dressed from head to toe in pretend animal skin.

My personal attraction to fake fur stems from a desire to impersonate, with tongue firmly in cheek, the glamour associated with over-the-top femme-fatale-era femininity, while snubbing the notion that there is anything "natural" about either feminine fashion or sexuality. And though I started wearing faux fur long before I practised veganism, this is where my queer sensibility crosses paths with critiques of anthropocentrism. According to Steve Baker, one of the ways human beings create and recreate our sense of superiority over other animals is through visual images that associate animals with nature. Some animal representations, for example those that place animals in the wild, can help keep people at a distance, reinforcing our sense of uniqueness and difference from other species by keeping us safely in the realm of culture. But when images of animal bodies are dislodged from human ideals of nature, we may more easily be able to identify other creatures as part of the same world we inhabit. Even the most anthropomorphised and kitsch representations of animals — such as fluffy toy bunnies — may be more valuable for getting people to think in different ways about human-animal relations than ostensibly authentic images of wild animals.[21]

Fake fur, like furry animal toys, is "awkward, problematic, and provisional."[22] Wearing it does not necessarily represent an attempt to access the social status associated with real animal pelts without the expense and violence. Faux fur has its own history, and its own problems. Wearing it does not constitute a direct intervention into the causes of species conservation or animal rights. It has also raised objections for its use of environmentally unsustainable synthetics.[23] But when worn with a sense of irony, fake fur can signal a recognition that our relationship with animals always involves a dimension of desire and fantasy. I wear my faux fur fashion in the spirit of queer camp, and as a protest against the tyrannies of "the natural."

Totems and tattoos

Another place where animal symbolism is increasingly visible in the early twenty-first century is on the skin of human bodies. Animal tattoos are perhaps best understood as modern totems.[24] Like the faux leopard scarf or deep purple shag coat, they reference animals without pretending a direct connection to a once-living creature. In this regard, while not in themselves vegan, animal tattoos invite reflection on the different dimensions of human relations to other species. If you do an internet search for "vegan tattoos" you are likely to come up with two themes: recommendations on where to find tattoo artists who use vegan-friendly ink and aftercare ointments, and images of tattoos that showcase the wearer's commitment to veganism.[25] Among the latter are clear political statements: the word "vegan," or images and words that reference cruelty to animals or animal liberation.[26] Some people proudly advertise on their bodies the delights of the plant-based diet (bizarrely, tofu and carrots seem to be favourites).[27] Others among us have chosen animal images that mix the personal and political.

In the process of writing about animal images I came increasingly to see that my middle-aged queer fem identity had been constructed in part through the wearing of fake furs and animal tattoos — including the large graphic moth on my upper back. A moth may not be an obvious totem. It is often represented as a poor cousin to the butterfly. As Lepidoptera go, butterflies are more readily used as symbols of metamorphosis, the transition from humble caterpillar to brightly coloured, fully-fledged, winged creature. I associate butterflies with the stunning golden monarchs of my childhood. For my tattoo, I wanted something less colourful, and less regal. A being who signalled the excitement of flight, but also the mundane. We share our living spaces with moths, but often seek to be rid of them. Moths are frequently classified as pests, the insects that wreak havoc in the home by getting caught in our lamps or munching on our clothes. Yet moths, like all insects, are vital to our ecosystems, interrelating in important ways with other animals as well as plants.[28] I was aware of moths as complex beings in their own right, but did not seek to replicate one on my body by having it try to look too real. I imagined my totem as part animal, part machine.

My cyborg moth was many years in the making, cocooned in my imagination during a time of intense change and uncertainty in my life. During this period of my mid-40s, I was surrounded by people with dashing tats, astonishing gifts of creativity and wild senses of adventure. At the time, I thought of the moth-in-my-mind as a deeply personal expression of renaissance, and even as I write now the vivid possibilities of those years spark again. When I visualised the being that would soon spread across my back it was the wings, stretching out magisterially across my shoulder blades, that I pictured. When I finally found my ideal tattooist I was surprised that I had never thought about the creature's body. We are often seduced by wings, their flapping evasiveness and vibrant colours; they symbolise a freedom to which we mere human mortals do not have ready access. To be called Icarus today usually comes with a stern warning against hubris. But the Icarian fantasy of flying and flaming sustained and propelled me through those troubled times. The French anthropologist Claude Lévi-Strauss famously argued that animals are common totemic figures because "they are good to think with."[29] But we might say that they are also good to feel with. Today I think of my moth as a healing metaphor in the sense understood by Gloria Anzaldúa, inked on my skin but also working in and through my body.[30]

By wearing fake fur or tattoos we can acknowledge the

many ways in which animals inhabit our imaginations, while recognising that they are not ours to use for our own ends. Although I did not make much of it at the time, the moth tattoo was born in the same months I started practising veganism. Since then I have mostly thought of my moth as a private vision, one I let out on occasion to air and share with others, but whose nurturance is ultimately up to me. Today I realise she took shape through ongoing interactions — emotional, intellectual, political, cultural, erotic — with a much wider community. I cannot now picture those years without bright creatures, inked in colour or stark black lines, dancing on beautiful queer bodies before my eyes. Tattoos are one of the ways in which we present ourselves to others. My moth, like the other tattoos I wear, is less a shield than another skin, not unlike my favourite fake fur. I think of these different animal images as layers between my skin and my surroundings, helping me move in the world, and the world in me.

Mourning leather

I started to think about the issues involved in wearing and giving up different kinds of animal skin a few years ago after reading an article by Niels van Doorn, "The Fabric of our Memories: Leather, Kinship, and Queer Material History." I was both moved and troubled by the author's account of how a small group in Baltimore's queer community use leather as a material that "mediates between intimate experience and collective memory."[31] Moved, because this is a story of a marginalised community whose members have experienced multiple forms of loss, violence and exclusion, including HIV/AIDS, poverty and racism; and because I have my own history in queer leather communities. Troubled, because I am acutely aware of the violence that lurks behind the word leather.

Leather has been used by human beings for millennia. Originally made from the hides of animals hunted for food, it has been employed in different cultures for clothing, footwear, shelter, parchment and military materials, among other things. Today, leather is made predominantly from the skins of animals raised and slaughtered for meat. The leather industry and some consumers claim that the production and use of the fabric is a form of recycling or waste management, arguing that it is a by-product of the beef and dairy industries (most leather sold today is made from the skin of dead cows), which would be thrown away if not put to other use.[32] According to Jennifer Farley Gordon and Colleen Hill, the argument that animal parts worn by people — including leather, fur and feathers — are by-products of meat production has been used to justify their use since at least the nineteenth century.[33] But the skins and feathers of animals reared for food are not given away; they are sold, like other parts of the slaughtered bodies of farm animals, for profit. Today, leather is among the most widely-sold commodities globally.[34] For these reasons, some vegans have proposed that it is better to understand leather as one co-product of a wider industry that relies on the commodification of animals.[35] While there is a growth in demand for "eco leather," the industrial tanning methods used in the production of most leather sold today are highly toxic and damaging to the environment as well as the health of the human workers who produce the leather.[36]

The history of leather production is absent from van Doorn's account of the Baltimore queer leather community. The tension at the heart of his investigation — one that neither he nor the leather people he interviewed confront directly — is that the collective memory, sexual intimacy and care binding their community together are made possible by previous acts of unacknowledged violence against other animals.[37] Reading van Doorn's article got me thinking about what it means to stop using animal products in circumstances where they play an important role in bringing people together, especially when those people belong to marginalised groups. While I reject the idea that veganism is a sacrifice, I began to see that in some cases giving up the use of animal products might involve a dual process of mourning: for the animals who have died for our convenience *and* for the kinds of attachments their dead bodies have allowed us to form with other people. Many vegans experience our commitment as a form of joy, a validation of the lives of other creatures; veganism may also bring with it the exciting discovery of new communities of like-minded people. Yet the vast majority of us were raised and continue to live in cultures in which animal products are used in all sorts of ways, including a range of rituals, formal and informal, at the heart of our human communities. These are things that we need to say goodbye to when we start practising veganism.

Ceasing to use animal skins as clothing or other items is not the same as giving up meat, eggs and dairy. The human body relates to leather and food in divergent ways. Whereas food goes in and is absorbed or expelled as waste, leather is typically more enduring. Through its contact with the body's skin, leather passes through a more gradual process of change. Like food, it has its own smell, touch, colour, even taste. It can carry the physical traces of live bodies — human and other animal — with whom it has come into contact. Unlike washable fabrics such as cotton or polyester, leather absorbs, stores and transmits body fluids and smells. As porous matter, leather can literally soak up pieces of the past. Therefore, ceasing to use or wear leather may mean losing physical traces of other bodies, including those of people who have died. As van Doorn argues, leather holds community and individuals together, "creating a measure of continuity and cohesion in its frequently ruptured history" through shared sexual practices, alternative forms of kinship and mutual care.[38]

September 2018
Berlin

Last night at a club I sat with a small group in the common area watching as a young person polished, with enormous care and dedication, a pair of very old leather boots. The wearer gazed down attentively as the boot blacker did their job, interrupting occasionally to give advice on the proper form of brushing, polishing and finishing. As we watched, enraptured by this intimate scene, several people, exchanged stories about boot-blacking and leather codes, including memories of former partners. As these stories were aired it was as if those people had joined us in that space.

The experience described here evoked for me intense feelings of belonging — to this small, treasured group of queers with whom I shared an intimate experience just by my presence, as well as to a much longer tradition of lesbian and queer subcultures — and also of alienation. This simultaneous sense of belonging and not-belonging is part of the queer condition in a heteronormative society. It is also an all-too-familiar experience in queer spaces for people with non-normative bodies, be they racialized, trans, fat, older or disabled. But in the boot-blacking scene my intertwined feelings of belonging and alienation were not brought on by a sense that *my body* felt out of place. While moved by my participation in a moment of immediate intimacy and collective memory, I felt displaced as a silent witness to the violence of leather.

This ambivalence has become an integral part of my queer

vegan life, including my reading of queer history. Van Doorn's moving rendition of a Baltimore leather bar in the early twenty-first century reminded me of Gayle Rubin's chapter "The Catacombs: A Temple of the Butthole." Rubin's piece is an exquisitely detailed and lyrical description of a gay men's fist-fucking club set up in 1970s San Francisco by a man as a gift to his lover. The club, in the basement of a house, was situated in a neighbourhood where "[a]t night, leathermen owned those streets, prowling easily among the bars, sex clubs, bathhouses, and back alleys."[39] Rubin gives us a tour of every twist and turn, nook and cranny of the small club space. Her description pays careful attention to the ambience as well as the intense sexual and emotional relationships among its patrons. She tells us about the club's pre-history in the gay male leather scene in the postwar years of the United States, as well the legacy it left after it closed.

Steve, the Catacombs owner, had "a profound sense of the history of his community." When he died suddenly of a heart attack in 1981 and the original club was shut down, his lover Fred recreated the Catacombs in a new venue. The eventual closure of the second Catacombs in 1984 — in the early years of AIDS and the pernicious moralism that accompanied it — "occasioned" in Rubin's words, "a deluge of mourning." One thing that facilitated the closure of the Catacombs, other sex clubs and gay male bathhouses was a lack of awareness of, or interest in, "the losses involved" in the disappearance of these spaces. Rubin does not paint the Catacombs in nostalgic terms as an ideal space free of conflict and drama. But, she stresses, "it was a sexually organised environment where people treated each other with mutual respect." One of the club's legacies was "a very deep love for the physical body." And although most of the patrons were men and "its focus was on the male body, the Catacombs gave me [Rubin] a greater appreciation for my own, female body."[40] I, in turn, have a deep appreciation for Rubin's assessment of the loss and lessons of the Catacombs. She reminds us of the value of spaces where queer people of different gender identities and body types can learn to appreciate and love our own bodies, and those of others.

I first encountered leatherdykes at the Michigan Womyn's Music Festival in the late 1980s. Those tall, butch dykes striding around the woods and fields in chaps with bare breasts scared and thrilled me in equal measure. They seemed so tough and unattainable to a twenty-something not-yet-out middle-class white girl from small-city southern Ontario. Some years later, while living in Spain, I bought my first pair of leather trousers, smooth and sleek. Leather was hot among the young gay people I was hanging out with in the early 1990s. Over the following years I would inhabit lesbian and queer communities where the wearing of leather was common. Although I did not experience the passing down of leather from earlier generations the way van Doorn's informants did, I learned to be a queer fem by inhabiting and playing with leather. Although I no longer wear or use the fabric, I can remember the smell and feel of the real animal skin, and memories of these sensations can quickly transport me to the queer spaces of my past.

Along with her description of the inside of The Catacombs, Rubin gives us a glimpse of the animal skin worn and used in the club: the tight leather shorts with removable codpiece worn by the club's owner, Steve; the harnesses, arm bands and assorted paraphernalia used by otherwise naked patrons; the slings for fisting in the back of the club, most hand made by Steve himself.[41] We get an impression of leather as a fabric that brought people together, through sex and other activities. In his writing about the Baltimore leather scene van Doorn goes further, endowing leather with significant power. He describes it as "a shape-shifting fabric that organizes kinship relations, induces sexual desire/pleasure, and accumulates history as it is passed on between leathermen." Leather is "a thing that *wants things*." It "calls upon" and "makes demands" of its owner/wearer.[42] For the leather people interviewed by van Doorn, the material's ability to act is attributed to its status as the skin of a previously living animal. Leather has life, a history, DNA. The leather folk of Baltimore use it to forge relationships and identities. Leather is a kind of a modern-day totem.[43]

Missing from the writing of van Doorn and Rubin are the stories of the anonymous animals killed to produce leather. The people interviewed by van Doorn show an intense interest in the history of the leather they wear and use. But this interest begins at a particular point in the past, *after* the animal has been slaughtered and the skin cured and manufactured into an item — all by human workers who are also anonymous — to be purchased and worn or used by other people. In this way, the animals involved in the production of leather become "absent," and along with them any question of human ethical obligation towards them.[44] This absence of consideration for the lives and experiences of other animals contrasts to the careful codes of respect, safe sexual conduct and consent that often govern relations among people in queer sex spaces, whether formed around leather or not. Yet as Gary Steiner argues, we should not assume that animals give their consent to be instrumentalised or killed, even in situations where the use of their bodies may be of value to human beings.[45] This is all the more true, I believe, when the people who benefit from an animal's death have not had any relationship to that animal when she or he was alive.

The value accorded to leather in some queer sexual subcultures derives from its association with a particular postwar gay history (as detailed by Rubin) and its status as an animal skin (as described by van Doorn). Although queer leather scenes also feature other fabrics — including rubber and latex — leather continues to have a pride of place. Of course, fake leather is increasingly available. But it does not come without problems. The production of cheaper fake leather often involves the use of petroleum products. Today there is a range of more environmentally friendly versions. For example, my own fake leather boots are made from micro-fibres that breathe. They are sturdy and many people have remarked how attractive and real they look. But they were not cheap. There is an irony, write Gordon and Hill, in the production of high quality, durable and eco-friendly fake leather. Manufacturers of these products often focus on expensive "investment pieces, purposefully made to last, in much the same way that high quality wool or fur pieces have long been touted as lifetime purchases."[46] In addition to carrying this mark of exclusivity, because quality fake leather aims to pass for real, it may actually affirm the aesthetic and fetishistic attraction of leather, rather than challenge it.

Because, as the stories of van Doorn and Rubin detail, leather is associated in some queer communities with a sense of belonging to a longer tradition, memories of people now gone, and the gift of sexual pleasure in the face of discrimination, discontinuing the use of leather may mean learning to hold onto these connections while giving up the fabric that helped to bind them. Ceasing to use leather, in other words, involves a dual process of mourning. Although the things mourned — the lives of anonymous animals, on one hand, and the practices/communities and people associated with leather, on the other — are not the same, the emotional processes involved in these different kinds of mourning should not be dismissed or underestimated.

Recognising the lives of dead animals as worthy of mourning could help to disrupt what Chloë Taylor identifies as a Western ethics that "prescribes using the bodies of dead animals so that their deaths are not for nothing." In this ethos, wasting is interpreted as "the ultimate act of disrespect to the dead." The understanding of leather as a by-product of meat is part of a logic that justifies, even encourages, the killing of animals so long as their body parts — and the more parts, the better — are put to use for human ends. This logic stands in contrast to the dominant Western ethics regarding the mourning of people, in which the sanctity of the human body requires precisely that we *do not* use it after death. Val Plumwood, who believed that people should take our full place in the food chain by being available to other animals as prey, was buried in a cardboard coffin so that her remains could become food for the critters of the earth. This gesture was a final rejection of the human/animal dualism against which Plumwood had fought so passionately in life.[47] In a similar fashion, according to Taylor, "[t]o dignify a nonhuman animal's corpse" — through, for example, some form of ritual — "rather than to use it," would not only rupture the utilitarian logic upon which the production and sale of leather rests, but would also "confuse" the species boundary between people and other animals.[48]

Queer leather communities are often constructed around rituals. Why not use our creativity and imagination to invent scenes in which we say goodbye to leather and our dependence on the instrumentalisation of other animals, and to welcome new rituals into our erotic lives? Alternative queer communities already provide examples of the creative use of alternative vegan fetish items. I have a plethora of memories of these discoveries: Queeruption and other queer anarchist gatherings, in assorted squats, where young queer punks taught each other how to make wristbands and constraints from bicycle tires; the delight of finding a forgotten hand-made rubber whip at the London Fetish Festival many years ago, carrying it with me wherever I went for years; the sadness of misplacing it some years ago and hoping that whoever picked it up would delight in it as I had; ordering my first ever proper faux leather flogger from a kinky couple up north and collecting it in anonymous brown paper wrapping from my work pigeon hole just a few days before a play party; and attending that party with a date who was one of many young queers who don't seem to be very interested in leather, preferring sports gear and other fetish wear. All traditions are invented, after all; we work through by remembering and mourning but also taking pleasure in the new.

When I started practicing veganism, like many neophytes I focused rather obsessively on diet and ignored, or at least did not prioritise, clothing or shoes. I had lots of leather in my closet, including many vintage leather jackets and a range of fetish costumes. Gradually I stopped wearing the jackets, and started buying fake leather boots. Then one day, in a rush of shame verging on mania, I packed up all my leather jackets, trousers and skirts and hauled them off to the charity shop — even the precious leather trousers I had bought in Spain shortly after I had first come out almost thirty years before. I regret that haste now. In getting rid of my treasured leather so unceremoniously I forsook the opportunity to find ways to mourn the animals whose lives had been taken in order for me to wear their skin; and I denied myself the opportunity to mourn properly my own queer leather history — to remember consciously, to honour, so that I could work through, the memory of countless sexy, kinky and more banal encounters I had experienced in those skins. I refuse to see those processes as separate. Giving up animal skins, like giving up animal food, should not be merely a practical process, or one filled with shame. It should honour the histories associated with those products, as well as the histories of the animals themselves.

If we want to avoid the moralistic tone that does sometimes

characterise vegan rhetoric, we might need to acknowledge that we have all benefitted and probably experienced pleasure, even if indirectly, from the use of animal products, including as clothing. Giving up the use of animal products in societies that rely overwhelmingly on them is difficult. It will be more difficult — for a whole range of reasons including economic, cultural and emotional — for some people than for others. We should not envision such giving up as a form of self-sacrifice. It does, however, involve a loss. To acknowledge this is to acknowledge the constant presence of the past in our lives. When we give up using animal products we do not break free from the histories of violence behind them. Nor do we give up our desire for animals. For these reasons, ceasing to wear or otherwise consume the bodies of dead animals does not get us out of all the ethical issues that surround the multiple uses of animals in human cultures.

Over the course of writing this chapter I have concluded that a non-anthropocentric approach to wearing animals should challenge the association of animals with "nature" and acknowledge that animals always form part of a culture which we humans also inhabit. For me this means resisting the temptation to reproduce and wear perfect replicas of real fur or hides. Some have argued that wearing fake leather can prove to the world that vegan fashion can "kick ass" without killing animals.[49] But I am concerned that real-looking fake leather may ultimately affirm our society's deadly attraction to dead animals without fully challenging the ideology or economic interests that propel the demand for real animal skin. This is especially true in contexts in which leather — real or fake — is produced, sold and bought just like any other commodity. We would be better, I believe, to acknowledge that animals are often present in our lives in symbolic form, that animal symbols are part of our human-animal histories and our individual and collective imaginations, and that we sometimes want to honour these by decorating our bodies with these symbols. We can do this without trying to replicate nature or the "real thing." The longing for animal skins — whether as totems, fetishes or just plain fancy — reminds us how much we owe to other creatures, and how contradictory our relationship to them is, and always will be. By inhabiting those contradictions we might wear images of other animals in such a way that acknowledges our attachments to them, as well as our debts.

Interdule 2

CARNAGE

Being vegan is similar in feeling to being in a science fiction story.

Joshua Schuster, "The Vegan and the Sovereign"

In his 2017 mockumentary *Carnage: Swallowing the Past*, the comedian and filmmaker Simon Amstell conjures up an imaginary future in order to highlight the injustices of present-day atrocities against animals. *Carnage* opens with a group of youths lounging peacefully in a field in the year 2067.[1] Britain has become a nation of plant-eaters and these young people have never consumed animals. Nor do they know much about this aspect of their country's history. Collective memory of "carnism" has been repressed, and some older folks are concerned that the guilt and shame associated with eating meat, cheese and dairy has not been properly worked through. With the aid of a mild-mannered psychotherapist, a few learned specialists and some recovering omnivores, the director journeys into Britain's pre-vegan past.

It all starts in November 1944, with the publication of the first issue of *The Vegan News*. Through a series of images from bona fide TV footage, *Carnage* condenses the contemporary history of the meat, dairy and egg industries and their advocates, making them look outrageously decadent and preposterous, as well as brutal. When meat rationing is lifted after World War Two the country fast-tracks into a flesh frenzy: in 1956 the fur-clad celebrity cook Fanny Cradock roasts, saws and serves up a small pig in front of a packed middle-class audience at London's Royal Albert Hall; the 70s sees Ronald McDonald and his buddies peddling fatty processed meats shaped like toys to kids; and in 1990, during the BSE crisis, the British agriculture minister goes before the cameras, force-feeding his four-year-old daughter a possibly contaminated hamburger. These scenes of over-the-top carnism are spliced with the odd clip of earnest vegans in drab clothes eating mushy brown and grey food. Even by the last decade of the twentieth century, the voiceover tells us, "the vegans were still ridiculous, and rarely allowed on television."

But as the new millennium rolls in, bringing foot-and- mouth disease and growing concern about climate change, the tide begins to turn. In this new era of concern about human and environmental health "[m]iddle-class people felt concerned that they could be eating the same unhealthy, unethical food as poor people, and so were delighted when the white man [TV chef] Gordon Ramsay showed them how they could eat free-range animals." Vegans soon have their own celebrities, helping plant-eating transition from moralising to sexy. But it isn't until the outbreak of Super Swine Flu in 2021, killing tens of thousands of humans and other species and pushing the National Health Service to the brink of collapse, that things start to get serious. The vegan movement is on the rise, direct action replaced by naked vegans dancing in supermarket aisles to block the sale of cheese and sausages. There is the predictable backlash from alt-right-type angry white men, culminating in the murder and subsequent consumption of the world's favourite vegan by a member of the Great British Meat League. Just a decade later the government passes the 2035 Animal Rights Law, criminalising the breeding, killing and consumption of all animals: "Empathy, climate change and the improvements in nut cheese could no longer be ignored."

Carnage rewrites history not by making stuff up but by reminding us that how and what we remember always depends on our present priorities. "When we think of the year 1944," the film's narrator solemnly reminds us, "we tend to think of the establishment of the world's first Vegan Society. But 1944 was also a time of human war." It is by hinting at the violence that mass meat consumption does to *all* animals, including humans, rather than insisting on direct comparisons between animal agriculture and slavery or genocide, that *Carnage* brings trans-species trauma into the frame. Unlike the predictable and sensationalist tactics of the People for the Ethical Treatment of Animals (PETA), the film gets away with this message because it is relentlessly clever and often hilarious. Thus, for example, the determination to acknowledge the painful past of animal agriculture becomes the occasion for poking fun at white new-age hippiness. The mockumentary's hero, Troye King Jones, is a young black man who evolves from angry activist to mature vegan spokesperson when he falls in love with the world's first celebrity vegan chef, Freddy Jayashanka, who makes plant-based cooking look "totally radical, despite having been around for two thousand, five hundred years." The present-day of *Carnage* is a posthuman world. The young people at the beginning of the film have never known animals as anything but kin, but they are able to visit and confront their culture's speciesist past through a multi-sensory time machine. People are cyborgs and animals "speak" through special technology that allows humans to hear their thoughts and emotions. It is the revelations of this interspecies communication ("I am not a cheese factory; I am a goat") that sound the death knell of meat culture once and for all.

One of the many pleasures of watching *Carnage* is its queerness. But like veganism, sexual politics is ripe for send up. The heroes are a gay couple, but the gender-fluid, polyamorous future looks more fluffy than sexy. Near the end of the film there's a shot of a woman in a dark alley lifting her blouse as a man leans down towards her breast. One of the film's expert talking heads, white middle-aged academic Maude Polikoff, shrugs at the scene and responds, "I don't know what you want me to say." In a film less dependent on parody one might get away with interpreting the image of women selling their breastmilk on the back streets to men as a warning about a future when animals are free but women are still sex slaves. But Polikoff's message is less clear; she is a former dancer (possibly glamour model) whose interview blends ecofeminist-type assertions about the parallels between sexism and speciesism with the unapologetic objectification and commodification of male vegans.

In conversations I've had with others about *Carnage*, some vegans have objected to the film's usage of real footage of animal abuse — miserably cramped conditions on industrial farms, butchering, meat grinding and the barbecuing and copious consumption by humans of greasy dead animals. These scenes are distressing and revolting, but they strike me as necessary. Without them the film would descend into slapstick. The vegan one-liners and the clips from early twenty-first-century television (like the fat phobia of anti-obesity reality shows or the pompous male celebrity chefs trying to save the world through "ethical" meat-eating) would lose their irony, and their political punch. Without the violence the film wouldn't make sense. By showing us this violence through the eyes of those who have rejected and distanced themselves from it, and providing other images of human-animal relations in an imagined future, *Carnage* avoids reifying veganism through its association with the bloodied bodies of animals.

Joshua Schuster argues that "Being a vegan means living in a partially alternate world that has a science fiction feel because it involves continual cognitive estrangement from social norms. Vegans must find a way to form a speculative life that bridges this world with a future world of animal justice."[2] *Carnage* offers such a bridge. Not because it provides a realistic image of what the future will look like, but because it reminds us that by remembering the past and inhabiting the present in new ways we can make opportunities for change.

Chapter 6

DANGERS AND PLEASURES

Veganism doesn't solve all the world's problems, but it can offer a springboard into rethinking human-animal relationships, help resist the objectification of animals' lives, and interrupt the idea that animals exist for us.

Lauren Corman
"Capitalism, Veganism, and the Animal Industrial Complex"

The new pink pound

In the late twentieth century, with the increased emergence of gays and lesbians into the social mainstream, commentators in the United Kingdom started talking about the pink pound. LGBTQ people were identified as a potential niche market to be targeted by brands and companies producing gay-friendly goods and services. By the turn of the millennium, the rise of the pink pound and the accompanying corporatisation of LGBTQ life — most visible at annual Gay Pride marches, where corporate logos increasingly outnumbered rainbow flags — were coming under attack from activists and academics alike. The post-Seattle anti-capitalist movement had a queer contingent and a whole subfield of queer theory was dedicated to critiquing queer neoliberalism. I experienced my own mid-30s activist renaissance among the queer anarchist collectives of London, helping to organise colourful anti-pride carnivals, do-it-yourself fundraisers and squat parties where we cooked vegan meals with food salvaged from skips outside supermarkets and health food stores.

Fast-forward a few years, and by the second decade of the millennium the green pound is the new pink pound.[1] As veganism experiences a surge in popularity, often identified with clean eating, the word vegan has become a logo. Like many previous capitalist revolutions, this one started in the United States of America, where big animal rights NGOs such as People for the Ethical Treatment of Animals (PETA) urge people to "Go Vegan!" Quick on the uptake, in my increasingly trendy neighbourhood in East London food shops and restaurants plaster VEGAN in their windows. Friends invite me to establishments that scream *vegan* on their menus and I pay a fortune for avocado on toast. If vegan is just another brand, I am its target consumer: white, female, middle-class, urban dweller.

As the vegan brand spreads, veganism becomes a flashpoint for debates about contemporary socio-economic and political developments, including neoliberalism, gentrification and the rise of the far right. Images of holier-than-thou purists are joined in the mainstream media by happy, healthy, hip mostly white vegan shoppers. Can — and should — vegans resist the association of "vegan" with consumerism? And what about the rise of "white veganism," and accusations of vegan imperialism, racism and even white supremacy? In this chapter I argue that these phenomena, while real, should not make us cynical about veganism. They are reasons for thinking more critically about how veganism is framed and understood. Countering the more dangerous aspects of vegan consumerism, especially its class and cultural exclusivity, means challenging bad arguments in favour of and against veganism, and recognising and celebrating vegan communities beyond the white Western mainstream.

Vegan mainstreaming

Since the mid-2010s the blogosphere has come alive with posts from animal rights advocates concerned about the "mainstreaming" of veganism.[2] The editors of a recent academic volume dedicated to "critical perspectives" on veganism ask "whether the trend towards normalization strengthens or detracts from the radical impetus of veganism as a politics."[3] A key concern among critics of mainstreaming and normalisation is the rise of "vegan consumerism," defined by Tara Lomax

> in terms of plant-based diets that obscure the complexity of other ethical choices on the basis of marketability, campaigns (and fundraisers) that encourage non-vegan multi-national brands to provide vegan options (despite a plethora of other unethical and animal exploitative products), or even the demand that vegans deserve "faux" versions of every animal-based product they once enjoyed (regardless of need).[4]

Critics of vegan mainstreaming argue that this trend is not necessarily good for other creatures and should not be confused with the movement for justice for animals. Wayne Hsiung, for example, warns: "don't let the trappings of vegan consumerism distract you from our central message and goal: not a vegan consumertopia but a world where every animal is safe and happy and free."[5] Others go further. Vegan consumerism is not just a distraction; it actually harms animals. This is because "vegan" brands reinforce the idea that *all* food is a commodity, including that which is made from animal products.[6] In this understanding, animals themselves are still imagined as things (just things you don't eat instead of things you do eat). The dangers of buying into vegan branding are further evidenced by the fact that goods marketed as vegan are not necessarily manufactured by vegan firms. According to the blogger Adamas, "Veganism is now sold to people in the form of products (sometimes explicitly labeled "vegan") by the very corporations ... that exist and profit off the exploitation of animals."[7] Ultimately, critics argue, vegan consumerism focuses not on the needs of animals but on those of people.[8] And if it is unlikely to end the exploitation of animals, the vegan consumerist trend may also narrow the number of people who can eat ethically by equating veganism with expensive, wholesome foods available only in upscale neighbourhoods.

The critique of vegan consumerism has led some to reconsider the very usage of the words veganism and vegan.[9] The understanding of veganism as a small-scale boycott of animal products that leaves the economic status quo intact has come under attack, as have the rather grand claims made by some animal rights organisations and vegan food outlets regarding the number of animal lives ostensibly saved every time someone orders a plant-based dish.[10] As for the word vegan, Kelly Atlas argues that "the label is counter-productive" because it coopts animals as commodities into the economic status quo rather than challenging capitalism.[11] Asked whether animal rights activists should use the word vegan, philosopher John Sanbonmatsu responds that while it is "rather unavoidable... at least in the context of eating," the word vegan has become too closely associated with food preferences and lifestyle. Veganism is, moreover, "a weak substitute or placeholder for the broader theme of animal liberation or animal rights."[12] In other words, through its connection with consumerism, veganism risks becoming depoliticised.

Vegan killjoys and other provocateurs

If the enthusiastic vegan consumer is easily portrayed as a happy-go-lucky character who cares more about following the latest lifestyle trend than justice for animals, the vegan animal rights activist is sometimes painted in broad strokes as a single-minded moralising crusader. We have seen versions of this caricature in previous chapters; she is the vegan who boycotts animal products with the zeal of a religious convert, oblivious to all other political causes, including the environment and the rights of other people. In her 1965 *Sunday Times* article, "The Rights of Animals," Brigid Brophy penned an early and witty response to popular perceptions of animal advocates. She had become used to being condescendingly treated as "a sentimentalist; probably a killjoy; a person with no grasp on economic realities; a twee anthropomorphist... and, *par excellence,* a crank." In response, Brophy asked, "[w]hich, in fact, kills more joy: the killjoy who would deprive you of your joy in eating a steak, which is just one of the joys open to you, or the kill-animal who puts an end to all the animal's joys along with its life?"[13]

In the early twenty-first century, a number of vegan writers have reclaimed the figure of the vegan killjoy.[14] They turn the table on stereotype of vegans as moralistic and holier-than-thou, taking inspiration from Sara Ahmed's figure of the feminist killjoy. Challenging the idea that feminists are bad because we make others feel bad, Ahmed celebrates the feminist killjoy as someone who refuses to stay silent in the face of sexism, racism and other forms of oppression.[15] Although the feminist killjoy has a reputation for being a big-mouth shit disturber, it is her very existence that makes others squirm. Like the feminist, the vegan arrives at the table with the killjoy stigma already attached to her. She doesn't have to open her mouth to be accused of ruining others' dinner.[16] The very act of refraining from eating a certain dish can be interpreted as a negative commentary on others' eating choices. When vegans are expected to sit in silence at the table while others devour meat, eggs, cheese and fish, the implication is that the ethics of eating are a personal matter, not to be brought up in public. But in a society in which so much of our socialising is done around eating, being vegan becomes a public affair whether we like it or not. One of the great ironies of veganism is that a commitment which for us is a "yes" manifests itself in most day-to-day encounters as a "no." A life-affirming decision becomes something negative: "I can't eat that," "No thanks," etc. And, in reply, one is "ungrateful," "snobby," "picky." Or my favourite: "You'd eat meat if you were starving and there was nothing else to eat." Most of us would eat human flesh under such circumstances, but no one seems perturbed that I don't eat other people on a regular basis.

The vegan killjoy is a seductive figure. She provides a compelling comeback to the tedious accusation that vegans believe ourselves superior to omnivores and have perfect solutions to the world's woes. By reclaiming some of the pleasures of old-fashioned pissed-off politics, the vegan killjoy makes me feel at home in a prickly kind of way. And by bringing a concept developed in relation to feminist and anti-racist politics to animal rights activism, the vegan killjoy highlights the common ground between our movements. As James Stanescu argues, veganism offers the opportunity to create new communities with other killjoys. In our new-found company we may also find ourselves killing the joy of other vegans, for example, when they use sexist or racist language.[17] But the discomfort sometimes faced by vegans in omnivore spaces notwithstanding, the model of the killjoy carries a danger in the context of animal rights. Returning to the work of Carol J. Adams, we might say that understanding the vegan as a killjoy risks reinforcing the animal as an "absent referent" by focusing attention on the eating habit of the human vegan rather than the animal being eaten.[18] I may feel anger and pain at the exploitation of other animals, but I am not the one who has suffered directly. In the words of Patricia MacCormack, "Any focus on the vegan rather than the operation (i.e. veganism) is independent of ethics."[19]

Like the feminist killjoy, the vegan killjoy does not have to be a humourless figure. I envision her as part of a loose collective of animal allies, some deliberately taking on the role of sourpuss, while others turn to wit, irony and even flirtation in our quest to turn encounters with other people into moments that may prompt them to see animals in new ways.

January 2017
London

On the tube with S, talking about mammograms. The topic comes up in the course of a rather more sexy conversation about domination and submission, and my memory that a mutual friend had recently commented that she does not find mammograms remotely a turn-on, not a pain she could get into. S then recounts the story of her first mammogram: after being tugged and prodded for awhile, she finally declared to the nurse: "This is my body. These are my breasts. I am not a cow —" As the final sentence comes out of her mouth, her eyes meet mine. I am doing my best Amy Winehouse imitation, raising my eyebrows, twisting my mouth in a posture indicating a mixture of exaggerated interest and "What a load of bollocks." In response I am greeted with a startled look of realisation: "And even if I were..."

This exchange with a new lover who was trying to get used to my vegan ways was not really a killjoy moment. My interjection into our shared tales about the struggle for the autonomy of our female human bodies and desires made room for the other-than-human, changing the story in the process, bringing a smile to both our faces. I think of it as my vegan tease moment.

Vegan imperialism?

October 2014
London

Last night, for the first time, I felt the force of missing out when I found myself the lone vegan at an omnivorous event. It was J's 50ᵗʰ birthday. There was food. And food. And more food. Food was the centrepiece of the evening. Mad cooking in the open-plan kitchen all night, plate after plate brought to the table to awe and words of wonder from the guests. Each dish was lovingly labeled with its name and ingredients. The variety of cuisines reflected the international origins of many of the partygoers, who devoured the food with relish and appreciation. People licked their lips and fingers, piled plates high and went back for more. Eating was also the theme of conversation for much of the night. I was witnessing the wonders of shared food, the ways it connects people — to their cultures and histories, the cultures and histories of others, and to one another, through taste and talk.

I had a bowl of salad, a piece of bread and some peanuts. I had eaten dinner beforehand, anticipating that my options would be limited. What I had not foreseen was feeling at a loss for how to join in the merriment of eating. I didn't feel regret at my vegan commitment, but I did feel regret at missing out on a tantalising collective ritual. I had no desire to interrupt and play the killjoy. As I watched people so evidently enormously enjoying themselves, exchanging stories about where their recipes and ingredients had come from and praising the cooks, I asked myself: Who would I be to deny them these pleasures? This was a food orgy. And since I couldn't fully partake of the pleasure of the voyeur, I ended up playing the vegan wallflower.

The killjoy is at her best when up against the formidable forces of unambiguous oppression. But her kick-ass powers may be drained when she is called upon to disrupt the happiness of loved ones. At my friend's rowdy and hedonistic party I did not want to step in and dampen others' fun. I doubted anyway that this would have been an effective strategy. Instead, I had the strange sensation of being firm in my convictions, and of those convictions distancing me from people delighting in something I no longer take joy in: the eating of food made from dead animals. The killjoy experience is one of challenging how others define pleasure. It is refusing to partake in something that should not be pleasurable for anyone: the racist joke, the sexist comment, the homophobic remark. When I hear those things I have one of two reactions: either "that person's an asshole" or "that person needs to be educated." When I see people delighting in eating what I can only assume to the omnivore pallet is delicious food, recounting memories of home, grandparents or travel, bonding over recipes, I do not think: "Those people are assholes." I don't really even think: "Those people need to be educated." Mostly I think: "The task of overcoming animal exploitation and global climate change is overwhelming because it asks people to give up too much: too much history, too much memory, too much community, too much joy." I cannot kill that joy. I would feel no satisfaction, score no political victory in doing so even if I could. I would feel like the asshole.

There is another important dimension to this story: the

people and food at my friend's birthday party were from all over the world, in some cases from countries that had been colonised by European powers and/or regions with recent histories of war and displacement. This helps to explain my mixed feelings. Food brings people together; it is saturated with longing and sometimes painful memories of family, community and loss. Even if we recognise that all food traditions, like traditions generally, are invented and subject to change, the call to abandon the use of foods that may be associated with a community's identity and history, including attempts to (re)construct links in the face of violence and adversity, might be interpreted as disrespect for a collective's connection to previous generations. It should come as no surprise, then, that veganism sometimes becomes a flashpoint for debates about ethnicity and class, even accusations of elitism, imperialism and racism.

The philosopher Cathryn Bailey has argued that the relationship between vegetarianism, gender, class and race is complex and mutable. In the Western context the historical association of meat-eating with men of the upper classes means that for some people eating animal protein may be part of an aspiration to class mobility, or gender and racial equality. Conversely, holding on to particular foodstuffs can be a manifestation of cultural memory. An example is the popularity among some contemporary African Americans of "soul food," reminiscent of the food eaten by slaves, made from animal parts and vegetables rejected by white slave-owning families.[20] This example is evidence of the powerful role food can play in nurturing connections to forebears. Similarly, for families with histories of war, famine and genocide, protein in particular may be associated with survival and the transmission of transgenerational memory.

A contextual ethical veganism requires that we recognise the different histories and meanings attached to killing and eating animals.[21] For this reason, it is important not to make universalist declarations that align certain traditions or identities exclusively with either meat-eating or plant-eating. Maneesha Deckha has argued that the largely white ecofeminist movement in the United States has tended to privilege gender over other human identities, including race and culture, in ways that help to associate feminist animal advocacy with white middle-class women. Deckha calls for a postcolonial approach to feminist animal ethics, one that is truly intersectional, while recognising the diversity of all culinary traditions. She warns, for example, that the charge that vegetarianism and veganism are by definition elitist and ethnocentric are tenuous and based on selective evidence.

> The elitist and ethnocentric characterization of vegetarianism/veganism obscures the reality that in many parts of the globe, it is more expensive to lead a nonvegetarian lifestyle than a vegetarian lifestyle, with animal flesh marked as a luxury item or indulgence ...and ignore the richness of non-Western flesh-free food traditions and ideologies of nonviolence toward all living beings.[22]

The practice of vegetarianism and veganism among followers of certain Asian religions — for example, Jainism, Hinduism and Buddhism — is relatively well known outside that region. Perhaps less familiar to many people of European descent is the variety of cultures that depended on largely plant-based diets in the Americas before the Spanish Conquest of 1492. As noted in chapter three, before the arrival of the Spanish conquerors there were no large domesticated animals in what is today North America. The familiar association of North American Indigenous peoples with hunting, fishing and meat eating may reflect the racial stereotypes of popular culture, as well as a tendency for non-Indigenous people to treat the category "Indigenous" in the singular, ignoring the differences among distinct communities. The Choctaw writer Rita Laws argues that the stereotype of "the Plains Indian" as "killer of buffalo, dressed in quill-decorated buckskin, elaborately feathered headdress, and leather moccasins, living in an animal skin teepee, master of the dog and horse, and stranger to vegetables" is a colonial invention that reflects neither the long history of people of the Plains, nor the variety of cultures among the original peoples of the Americas. Before the forced removal of Indigenous people from most of their lands in the south of the United States during the Trail of Tears of the 1830s and 1840s, the Choctaw ate a diet consisting mostly of corn, pumpkin and beans, and their clothing and homes were also made from plants and wood. In the late twentieth-century Choctaw continued to cook vegetarian dishes for many of their ceremonies.[23]

Of course other pre-Conquest peoples did hunt and fish, and some continue to do so. The Indigenous writer Tanya Talaga notes that in what is today Canada the transition to a non-traditional diet has had a devastating effect on the health of many Indigenous people. In many small communities of the Nishnawbe Aski Nation in northern Ontario most of the goods sold in local stores are imported and expensive, forcing residents to rely on the cheapest food, which is often processed. This in turn contributes to high rates of diabetes, heart disease and dental problems. In the face of poverty, food insecurity, racism and poor health, some Indigenous people from northern parts of Canada and the United States advocate a return to fish, game, wild berries and wild rice as part of a project to decolonise their diets.[24] Others propose that there is room for a plant-based regime within Indigenous traditions. Margaret Robinson, a scholar from the Mi'kmaq Nation in northeastern North America, argues that veganism can be practised as part of an animal advocacy based on principles of respect towards other creatures and part of a commitment to anti-colonialism, feminism and a defence of food justice. Robinson recognises and honours the centrality of meat and fish to the diets and legends of the Mi'kmaq, as well as the role of the ritual killing of animals in the construction of Mi'kmaq identity. At the same time, she stresses that identity is not fixed:

> The context in which this identity develops has changed significantly since the arrival of the European colonialists. Meat, as a symbol of patriarchy shared with colonizing forces, arguably binds us to white colonial culture to a greater degree than practices such as veganism which, although overwhelmingly white itself, is far from hegemonic.[25]

Robinson cautions white omnivores against trying to "bond with Aboriginal people over meat-eating" by "projecting white imperialism onto vegans." Whereas in European Christian tradition "the othering of animal life [is what] makes meat- eating psychologically comfortable," Mi'kmaq stories reflect "a model of creation in which animals are portrayed as our siblings." Drawing on these legends, Robinson advocates an "ecofeminist exegesis of Mi'kmaq legends [that] enables us to frame veganism as a spiritual practice that recognizes that humans and other animals possess a shared personhood."[26] The writings of Laws, Talaga, Robinson and other Indigenous activists serve as a reminder that contextual ethical veganism must recognise the divergent histories and contemporary contexts of different Indigenous peoples, acknowledging that traditions are open to change and new meanings, and that legacies of racism and colonialism can be met with different forms of resistance.

White veganism

In the of summer 2017 a young black man, Rashan Charles, died while being arrested by police in East London, not far from where I live. After his death, protests were held in the neighbourhood to demand explanations and justice for Charles and his family. During one protest, which was heavily policed, the windows of a local vegan restaurant were damaged. The next day, the restaurant's social media account shared a post associating the (unidentified) people responsible for the window damage with "animals," adding that "all life matters." By reposting this implicit comparison of Black Britons to animals, and in its inappropriate appropriation of the widely-recognised name of the anti-racist movement Black Lives Matter, the eatery promoted a version of veganism that was both racially exclusive and racist.[27]

In response to this set of events, some commentators made reference to the problem of white veganism: the practice of veganism by people who are more concerned about the lives of other animals than the lives of Black people.[28] During the latter half of the 2010s the expression "white veganism" has increasingly appeared in English-language posts on social media from the U.S., Canada and the U.K., part of a critique of the racial exclusivity of mainstream veganism.[29] Critics emphasise the role of the media in representing veganism as little more than a celebrity trend or consumer lifestyle available first and foremost to wealthy whites. As London journalist Miranda Larbi observes, mainstream veganism is often hailed as something new and fashionable, hiding much longer histories of plant-based diets among peoples in many parts of the world, including Asia and the Caribbean.[30]

Veganism can also become a flashpoint in wider debates about class, race and urban regeneration. In her response to the racist tweets following the murder of Charles, Heather

Barrett pointed out that the restaurant in question is located in a neighbourhood "rife with gentrification."[31] When certain neighbourhoods are targeted by government and industry for "regeneration" in order to make them more prosperous and attractive to middle- and upper-class residents and businesses, services run by and for working-class and migrant communities — who may have longer histories in the area — can be put out of business. Or, as in the case of my local corner shop, they might re-brand and diversify in order to cater to a wealthier clientele. Gentrification does not, as a rule, bring with it a slick row of exclusively vegan shops, cafés and restaurants. Nevertheless, the label "vegan" is more visible in the process of *embourgeoisement* because non–vegan establishments and goods do not have to be advertised (they are taken for granted as the norm). I often hear people living in East London say that the boom in vegan stores and products is a symbol of gentrification and class exclusion. But this assertion hides a more complicated reality. Yes, my corner shop now stocks more brands of non-dairy milk than I can count. Yet the expensive vintage shops sell real fur, and most of the swanky new eateries are a carnivore's wet dream.

In contemporary London, as in many places, the relationship between veganism, class, gender, race and regeneration is far from straightforward. The histories, identities and circumstances that shape people's eating patterns do not always line up in ways that are predictable or permanent. This does not make them less fraught. As Bailey writes: "whether one is a meat eater or a vegetarian would not carry such visceral moral and emotional impact if it were not experienced as deeply entwined with the production and reproduction of identity."[32] She reflects on her own experience of these in a brief story about a family holiday:

On a rare trip home last year for Thanksgiving, to the white working-class town where I grew up, I arrived early enough to help with meal preparations. I watched as my sister patiently opened one can after another: green beans, cream of mushroom soup, crunchy fried onions. Having long since fled the processed, pre-packaged fast food world of my childhood (and the overweight I associate with it), I was shocked that this continued to be my sister's idea of cooking. Clearly, my reaction reflected more than an aversion to sodium and preservatives. Like most people, my sense of who I am is connected both to the foodways I have left behind and to those I have embraced. Gone are the slabs of processed cheese, white bread, and heaps of tuna casserole from my childhood. In their place are organic yoghurt, fresh greens, tofu and a passion for Indian food, usually in measured portions.[33]

If, on a personal level, the acquisition of a new diet reflects Bailey's transition from a working-class girlhood to middle-class adult academic life, collectively she interprets her experience as part of a process whereby white, middle-class Americans increasingly construct their identities through the fetishisation of healthy and "ethnic" foods. While her sister continues to feed her family from tins, Bailey and her colleagues drive long distances to find Thai, Indian and Ethiopian restaurants. Her vegetarian diet is an expression not only of her feminism, but of a collective "special" whiteness.[34]

Bailey's point is not that eating different foods from those that one grew up with, or becoming vegetarian, are *de facto* elitist activities. Contextual vegetarianism, she argues, is not about condescendingly allowing less privileged people to eat (some) animal products, but about acknowledging the different cultural and economic contexts in which animals are eaten. At the same time, when considering the place of identity in debates about vegetarianism, we should not overemphasise the deeply embedded cultural importance of meat-eating to contemporary culinary cultures; habit, convenience and/or apathy also play a role.[35] So, of course, do factors largely beyond our control, including price, variety and availability. Even when we do feel a strong attachment to a certain practice as part of our collective identities, this is not necessarily a reason to continue it. As Rasmus Simonsen reminds us, the meat of today is not the meat of yesterday; it is produced in different ways, just as the farm animals made into meat are not raised in the same way as those eaten by our forebears.[36] We should not underestimate the desire to connect with the past when we eat certain foods; but we may also find ways to honour that desire without seeking totally to replicate the diets of our ancestors. And there are other ways of thinking about food in relation to the future — not just as a continuation of past relations, but as a way of experiencing and expressing an invitation to see ourselves in new ways.[37] A sense of the possibilities of the new is one of the potential pleasures of adopting a vegan diet.

At their best, critiques of vegan mainstreaming and white veganism point to the limitations and even dangers of veganism when practised as a lifestyle choice rather than an ethical and political commitment. These critiques demonstrate that selling veganism as a brand to privileged consumers risks reinforcing inequalities and injustices among people, including class hierarchies, racism and sexism, while reproducing anthropocentrism by defining animals as commodities. But there is also a danger with these critiques; they sometimes have a moralising ring to them. They implicitly divide the world into "good vegans" (intersectional and anti-capitalist) and "bad vegans" (consumerist and bourgeois).

The reality is rarely so simple. And we should be wary of making judgements about what people eat. Vegan fast food may make veganism more available to people who are not able to cook from raw ingredients — for example, some people with disabilities.[38] I am privileged to be able to cook, and to have access to a kitchen and affordable fresh produce at my local market. And I do sometimes cringe at the increased commercialisation of veganism around me. But I also enjoy indulging in the occasional £1 vegan sausage roll from the iconic British bakery chain Gregg's, and the convenience of buying vegan cheese at my corner shop, while supporting not-for-profit and collectively-run vegan initiatives.[39] There is no getting out of consumerism altogether. That's why contextual ethical veganism needs critiques of vegan consumerism that recognise the challenges it poses, but also acknowledge the necessities, pleasures and political potentials of alternative forms of consumption.

More dreaded comparisons

Researching the sections above on vegan imperialism and white veganism, I became increasingly aware of the central role played by the internet and social media in shaping contemporary representations of veganism as the preserve of the white middle class. On Facebook I sometimes see posts of videos from animal rights organisations that highlight the poor animal welfare practices in southern countries, implying that "we" in the West are more enlightened.[40] Vegan bloggers denounce the proliferation of memes comparing factory farming, slavery and the Holocaust.[41] In chapter 1 I argued that the meanings of such comparisons are not fixed, and depend upon context: how they are made, circulated and received. Although social media is diverse and can be used in radical and anti-oppressive ways, it does not as a rule offer the opportunity for detailed historical and political contexualisation. Slavery and Holocaust comparisons are particularly dangerous given recent evidence from the United States and Europe that some white supremacists and neo-Nazis are preaching the virtues of veganism.[42]

The historical relationship between National Socialism, vegetarianism and care for animals is complicated, to put it mildly. The rumour that Hitler was a vegetarian has circulated in and around animal rights circles for some time, though its veracity is in dispute.[43] While of historical interest, from the perspective of constructing an anti-racist veganism, the question of whether or not Hitler ate meat is a distraction. The more urgent political question, to my mind, is how certain present-day representations of veganism may lend themselves to white supremacist arguments. It is not enough for anti-racist vegans to point out that the historical evidence of Hitler's vegetarianism is ambiguous. The far right is not known for its commitment to evidence-based activism. We have a responsibility to ensure that the language we use to promote veganism does not reproduce racist tropes. A particular problem is the association of veganism with purity, sacrifice and rigid morality. The presenters of the American podcast *The Vegan Vanguard* argue that some members of the American "alt-right" have been attracted to language that links vegetarianism with "moral rectitude and fighting degeneracy."[44] Similarly, cultural theorist Alexis de Coning cites evidence that parts of the alt-right have appropriated the Nazi expression *Blut und Boden.* "By romanticizing white people's inherent connection to the land and nature," she writes, "'blood and soil'... underscores notions of racial purity and nobility. Dietary commitments, then, become a means to prove one's racial superiority."[45]Arguments that understand veganism as a form of sacrifice, bodily purity or moral righteousness, and/or portray compassion for animals as a sign of "civilisation," may lend themselves to white supremacist defences of veganism. This is not to say that people who define veganism in terms of moral and physical purity are *ipso facto* fascists. But anyone who takes anti-racism seriously should be wary of repeating such claims.

The far right is not united on the issue of veganism. While some neo-Nazis promote it as part of a project of white racial purity, others align themselves with longer traditions that associate meat and dairy consumption with strength, masculinity and European superiority.[46] Some members of the U.S. alt-right circulate "White Power Milk" memes on social media and use the term "soy boy" to ridicule progressive men by associating them with plant-eating, femininity and Asian cultures. These tropes have long histories, and their contemporary resonance demonstrates the ongoing relevance of the argument, made by Carol J. Adams almost thirty years ago, that in the U.S. mainstream masculinity is constructed, in part, through associations with meat-eating and the derision of femininity and vegetarianism.[47]

Because the meanings of food and food traditions are never fixed, they are available to multiple meanings. The divergent dietary rhetorics of far-right supporters are evidence of the movement's heterogeneity and pragmatism, its ability to incorporate disparate messages to suit particular contexts and priorities. These competing celebrations of veganism and meat-eating caution against attempts to discredit veganism by picking and choosing examples of how it can be mobilised politically. Moreover, while it is relatively easy to spot far-right nationalist arguments — especially when their racist memes are picked up by the mainstream press on a regular basis — there are many more banal ways in which claims of national superiority are made with reference to the production and consumption of animal products.[48] When veganism is in the news in the U.K. today, it is not uncommon to hear defences of the meat, dairy and egg industries based on the claim that "we" have higher animal welfare standards than most of the world.[49] Such arguments may stop short of explicitly declaring that "real Brits" eat meat and dairy, but they certainly align animal agriculture and the consumption of animal foods with a defence of proper modern Britishness.

Omnivores often seem to be more interested in discrediting veganism through select examples of its apparent inconsistencies and hypocrisies than in analysing the political meanings and impacts of their own consumption habits. But those of us who practice veganism also have work to do. The embrace of veganism by some members of the far right warns us of the dangers of making grand claims for it as a progressive or radical political movement. There is a useful parallel between the problem of neo-fascist veganism and the phenomenon of homonationalism. As defined by a number of anti-racist queer activists and scholars, homonationalism refers to the alignment of LGBTQ rights with nationalism, and white Christian nationalism in particular.[50] In practice, the concept has been used to critique claims, especially in the post-September 2001 era, that gay and lesbian rights are unique to, indeed a defining feature of, Western secular liberal democracies, and that non-Western and especially Muslim states, people and cultures are by definition homophobic. Indictments of homonationalism are not, of course, indictments of same-sex practices or queer identities. Rather, they call attention to the dangers of aligning claims to LGBTQ rights with celebrations of Western secularism and liberalism. Similarly, critiques of neo-fascist veganism should focus on arguments that associate veganism with moral and physical purity and so-called "civilised societies," ignore extra-European traditions of animal ethics and plant-based diets, and separate animal rights from struggles against the oppression of human beings.

Towards the end of his life, the philosopher Jacques Derrida responded to those who used the "famous vegetarianism of Hitler" to challenge human compassion for other creatures:

> This caricature of an indictment goes more or less like this: "Oh, you're forgetting that the Nazis, and Hitler in particular, were in a way zoophiles! So loving animals means hating or humiliating humans! Compassion for animals doesn't exclude Nazi cruelty; it's even its first symptom!" The argument strikes me as crudely fallacious. Who can take this parody of a syllogism seriously even for a second? And where would it lead us? To redouble our cruelty to animals in order to prove our irreproachable humanism?[51]

Following Derrida, we could say that the question is not whether there is evidence of zoophilia among the Nazis, or whether veganism can be used for racist ends, but what we are to make of such uses. What we surely are *not* to make of them is an argument against animal advocacy and veganism. Instead they should become the occasion for serious reflection on the complex ways that eating has been shaped historically both by intra-human power relations and competing cultural identities, and how we might make the world a better place for animals while staying alert to the dangers of perpetuating other forms of oppression.

The global vegan

While I was growing up in a small city in Southern Ontario, Canada, in the 1970s, tacos were one of my favourite foods. My mother often made them for my birthday. We would buy a taco-making kit that included corn tortillas that were crispy and had to be heated in the oven before eating, as well as a (very mild) spice packet that was added to ground beef cooked in sliced onion and a mild salsa (sauce). The latter was dribbled over the "tacos" once they were filled with the cooked meat, chopped tomatoes, lettuce and grated orange cheddar cheese. Today I recognise that these crunchy, mild and fat-filled little parcels have little to do with tacos served in Mexico. In fact, they were a home-cooked version of the fast food tacos created by Mexican Americans in the years after World War Two, which later spread across the United States and Canada as part of the growing consumerist trend towards convenient and "ethnic" foods.[52]

When I travelled to Mexico as an adult I quickly learned that tacos, a ubiquitous street food dished out on corners from small stalls, are made with soft tortilla shells, served with different kinds of meat, and topped with various vegetable condiments and an array of (mostly hot) salsas. On later trips, I was delighted to discover that there was a whole range of vegan taco stalls and small restaurants in Mexico City serving tacos made with seitan or tofu. These are typically located in trendy middle-class areas where hotels and flats rented to tourists proliferate. Whenever arriving at a new place in Mexico I would look it up on the Happy Cow website and locate my local veggie taco stand or restaurant.[53] As pleasurable as these discoveries were, I knew that if I followed the Happy Cow trail for too long I would eventually, and literally, get sick of fake meats and fatty foods. The website did throw up the odd family-run restaurant frequented mostly by Mexicans, where salads, beans, rice, root vegetables and cactus were available. But my greatest source of disappointment was not being able to eat these staples of the Mexican diet in most local eateries, where rice and beans are typically cooked in chicken or pork broth.

I have sometimes heard it said of middle-class vegan tourists that we are ungrateful if we turn down animal-based food while travelling. This jibe was famously made by the late television chef Anthony Bourdain, who accused vegans and vegetarians of being "rude" for refusing to accept the generosity of hosts who share their food.[54] The vegan philosopher Gary Steiner would probably reply that the "vegan imperative" requires that we set aside our concerns about what others think, including the "social niceties" of refusing a dinner invitation.[55] Bourdain and Steiner each have a point; but each viewpoint is limited. They present both the vegan traveller and the host as inflexible, the encounter between them conditioned by a difference that can only be bridged by drastic measures: the vegan either goes without food or eats animal products. Such scenarios leave no room for negotiation or the possibility of mutual understanding across difference.[56] It is true that for an outsider of economic means to turn down food prepared by a host with limited resources, or not to show appreciation for the work or gesture of welcoming that may go into cooking, can be an act of arrogance. But eating away from home need not give rise to extremes of outright refusal or silent conformity to a (possibly imagined) meat-eating norm. One alternative might be to inform oneself in advance of the plant-based foods that are available in a particular place, communicating these options beforehand to one's host, or taking them along to share with others. The London blogger Fat Gay Vegan has a few inspirational stories in which taking a "firm and friendly" approach with non-vegan hosts can work wonders.[57] Such a tactic would acknowledge differences among people without assuming in advance that host cultures are static and one-dimensional. Approaching travel and eating as a process of ongoing negotiation would also enable us to include other animals as subjects worthy of ethical consideration in our travel encounters.[58]

The charge that vegans are rude or culturally insensitive

when we do not eat meat, dairy and eggs while travelling is an example of what some vegans call the "Gotcha!" moment: when a non-vegan tries to identify all the potential contradictions or hypocrisies of practising veganism. The travel "Gotcha!" moment reflects an omnivore fantasy: that by eating everything they are offered, omnivore travellers are participating in authentic local culture. This fails to take into account the extent to which the tourist industry helps to determine what food is sold as "authentic" in the first place. This point is made by the geographers Gino Jafet Quintero Venegas and Álvaro López López in their study of the consumption by tourists of *cabrito* (kid meat) in the northern Mexican city of Monterrey. *Cabrito* is often marketed as the typical local dish of Monterrey, even though the historical delicacy is expensive and inaccessible to most of the city's inhabitants. This is an example of what the authors call the "widespread practice" of marketing animal-based dishes in popular Mexican tourist destinations. When tourists in Monterrey seek out *cabrito* they swallow the sales job that this is part of the "authentic Mexican experience." According to Quintero Venegas and López López, because tourists often suspend their everyday habits and even their ethics while travelling, abiding by the injunction "when in Rome," they may not concern themselves with the question of the welfare of the goats (treated in a way comparable to veal calves in Europe). At the same time, travellers partake of a custom that reinforces gender as well as class hierarchies. One meme satirising critics of *cabrito* shows an effeminate man applying lipstick next to the words, "I don't eat *cabrito* because of the ugly way in which they are slaughtered," thus associating the consumption of *cabrito* with proper, red-blooded masculinity.[59]

This is one example of the role of new media in creating a mystique around certain meat-based dishes marketed to tourists. But internet information directed at vegan travellers can also help to spread the message that meat-eating is the norm in many parts of the world. Tourist websites, while enormously helpful to people who can afford to travel, can be bad for cultural and historical narratives. I happily acknowledge and admire vegan bloggers for helping to establish veganism as a viable and desirable practice, even in the meatiest regions of Europe.[60] But vegan travel blogs sometimes imply that vegan tourists are heroic adventurers, seeking out lost plant-based treasures among the meat-eating masses, or bringing the gift of veganism to previously unenlightened peoples. In an age when every tourist with access to the internet can set up their own travel blog, vegan adventure tales can cover up other histories of plant-eating that may not go by the name vegan.

Thinking about vegan travel can lead to extremes: to an endless supply of tips on where to find plant-based foods abroad, on one hand, or a moralistic singling out of vegan tourists for imposing our diets on the rest of the world, on the other. Instead, I suggest that the challenges and pleasures of vegan travel could offer a starting point for meditating more critically on the role the tourist industry plays in shaping the eating experiences we travellers seek out. For vegans who can afford to travel abroad, a good place to start is by learning about the array of cuisines and other cultural traditions from local sources rather than relying on other tourists (even when they present themselves as experts). This may require some effort, especially with language barriers; but practising contextual ethical veganism means taking the time to understand the impacts of our movements and habits on the places we visit.

On my last trip to Mexico City, in early 2018, I attended a large academic conference about animals, where I met a number of Mexican vegan or "anti–speciesist" activists. These people were involved in various projects, from anti-bullfighting campaigns and protecting feral cat colonies, to protesting against slaughterhouses and promoting vegan eating based on pre-Hispanic foods. This last is understood as an important political project combining animal rights with food justice and anti-colonialism. As David M. Peña-Guzman notes, the history of imperialism is still evident in contemporary eating habits, "in the diets of modern day Mexicans who regularly opt for the food of the colonizers, be it the food of the first colonizers (the rice, beef, and pork of the Spanish) or the second (the McDonalds, Burger Kings, and Starbucks of the Americans)." Peña-Guzman calls this legacy "[t]he dinner table as colonial and neo-colonial re-enactment."[61] One project resisting this reenactment is El Molcajete — which takes its name from the Spanish word for mortar and pestle — set up by the Mexican anti-speciesist organisation FaunAcción (Animal Action).[62] I was fortunate to attend the inauguration of the El Molcajete food van in January 2018, where I was served vegan *tamales* — a dish made from corn meal normally stuffed with meat, vegetables and/or cheese — and *pambazo*, a popular sandwich-like street food. El Molcajete was not, however, established to meet the desires of middle-class vegans attending international conferences. Its remit is to repopularise the use of Pre-Columbian Mexican foods — corn, beans, squashes, cactus — as part of a political struggle against animal abuse, poor human health and economic inequalities, through free and accessible cooking classes, pop-up food book libraries, food samples and artwork aimed primarily at Mexico City's poorest communities.[63]

Projects like El Molcajete give the lie to the idea that the popular Mexican diet is based on meat, eggs and cheese, and that veganism is for tourists only. In an echo of Margaret Robinson's argument about Mi'kmaq food culture in what is today Canada, Mexican animal rights activists insist that in many cases it is meat-eating, not veganism, that is colonial. They remind us, like Rita Laws, that before the arrival of the Europeans their ancestors consumed a predominantly plant-based diet.[64] I want to give the final words of this chapter to my friend Wotko/Gerardo Tristan, one of the founders of FaunAcción and El Molcajete. Over a home-cooked vegan taco dinner with a small group of friends at the Black Cat, London's oldest vegan café, Wotko recounted how, over the course of many years, he had come to connect his compassion for animals with his Indigenous heritage and queer identity. It is a fitting tale to end this chapter on the challenges and pleasures of practicing veganism within and beyond the mainstream Western context.

> I was born in the northern Mexican city of Monterrey. My father, José Tristán, an Indigenous man from the Nahuatl people, emigrated from Real de Catorce in central Mexico looking to improve his own and his family's fortunes. There he met Guadalupe Alvarado, who would become his wife and my mother. José worked at a number of odd jobs until his big break: a position at the Nylon plant in Monterrey, where he would become one of the leaders of a successful strike, for which the company eventually blacklisted him. For her part, my mother was the leader of an important land occupation movement, out of which grew the Canteras neighbourhood where I was born. The occupation was severely repressed by the state, and my mother was imprisoned for two months. During that time the women of the neighbourhood looked after me and breastfed me collectively.
>
> My happiest memories are of the kitchen, surrounded by the smell of freshly made tortillas, the sounds of the mortar and pestle, and the stories of my mother and

sisters. My father and brothers tried to get me out of the kitchen so I didn't turn into a *joto* (fag). But there I stayed until I was nine. That's where I learned to read and write, and improve my Spanish. That's also where I learned that I liked the long hair and makeup my sisters wore. And I loved going with my mother on her daily rounds to feed the dogs, cats, horses and donkeys in the neighbourhood. That's when she instilled in me a respect for all animals.

In those years, the only information I got about my cultural identity came from the food cooked by the women in the neighbourhood: *nixtamal* and tortillas, cactus, chiles, *chayotes*, *quelites*, black beans, mushrooms. The people who cooked the same dishes with the same ingredients as we did were also Nahuatl people, many of them from the same village or area as my father.

When I was seven my father, out of work after being blacklisted, brought a pig home. It was my job to care for her. Some months later the pig gave birth to twelve piglets, whom I adored. I played with them and took them for walks. But when the piglets turned four months a van came for them. I protested and struggled, but they were taken away. I was inconsolable. That event earned me the reputation of a famous *joto* who cried for pigs. That's when the harassment started at school. I went back to the kitchen, the only place I felt safe, happy and at peace. There I did my first three years of school. But when I turned nine my father and brothers finally succeeded in getting me out of the kitchen.

Going back to school was brutal. The other kids made fun of me in the schoolyard because I never ate meat or hamburgers or sandwiches, only tortillas. They bullied me, calling me a *joto* and an "Indian." "What else can a dirty Indian eat?" "Bean-head!" "He has a cactus on his forehead!" I quickly realised that if I wanted to survive I would need to change my image and learn to act as a good Mexican and macho, speaking Spanish and eating *cabrito* (kid). By the time I turned ten I was totally accepted by the badass kids. I stayed on that road until I was twenty-seven.

On January 1 1994 news broke that the Zapatista National Liberation Army (EZLN) had seized part of the state of Chiapas in southern Mexico. The Zapatistas presented a series of demands for autonomy, self-government and recognition. This was the same day that NAFTA, the free trade agreement between Mexico, the United States and Canada, came into force; the Zapatista struggle became a pioneer in the global anticapitalist movement.

The words of Subcomandante Marcos, the Zapatista spokesperson, resonated strongly with me: "If you want to know who's behind these balaclavas, just look in the mirror." I felt the urgent need to go to Chiapas. I arrived in the city of San Cristóbal de las Casas in February 1994 to support the "Peace Belt." After the conversations between the Zapatistas and the Mexican government in late February and early March, I decided to stay and join the movement to support the Indigenous communities fighting for their rights. The first visit we made to the communities followed a wildfire. Once we got permission to go we discovered that three of the villages had been destroyed; the scene was heartbreaking. Arriving at one of the remaining villages we encountered more heartbreak: exhausted women and children being cared for after fighting the flames for two days with shovels, buckets and bare hands.

I spoke to a woman with four children. She told me that they had lost their house and were staying with her mother while it was rebuilt. I said I was sorry and offered to help in the construction. This was her reply: "I feel sad about losing the shack, but I'm so happy the fire stopped before it reached the place where the birds live. They are more important to me than the house; I don't know what I would have done if the fire had reached them." At the time I didn't understand her response, but it left me speechless. After that conversation I wouldn't be the same again.

The events I'm sharing here led me to rediscover myself as an Indian, as gay and as an ally of animals. The smell of freshly made tortillas has returned to my kitchen, along with many memories. I'm happy and proud to share this food and stories with my friends and family. Now I understand the words of [Nobel Peace Prize winner] Rigoberta Menchú Tum: "We only trust people who eat the same food that we eat."[65]

Conclusion

DOING VEGANISM

October 2014
London

This morning as I was writing an entry in my "Vegan Papers," thinking through the tricks and trickiness of negotiating non-vegan spaces, I suddenly remembered the joy of my first encounters, while in Bilbao a few months ago, with vegan strangers: bars serving inventive plant-based pintxos, *an Argentine-Uruguayan bakery selling vegan empanadas in the heart of the Old Town, the generous hippy in the vegetarian shoe store who drew me a map of all the vegan-friendly places in the neighbourhood, sitting in the street eating vegan* tortilla de patatas *while reading an issue of a Spanish animal rights journal borrowed from a nearby store run by the anti-bullfighting campaign, and having a stranger come up to me, asking, excited: "Where did you get that magazine? I'm vegan!" The sense of belonging and connection.*

This memory of being newly vegan in a familiar city, where I had once forged friendships over plates of creamy croquettes, is sprinkled — like the story of meeting Wotko and the others who run El Molcajete in Mexico City — with the pleasures of new relationships forged through veganism. Too often veganism is presented in the negative, as a rigid regime that requires giving up a whole range of sumptuous and nutritious foodstuffs. Vegans are portrayed as austere and uptight, losing out in the taste game in the name of a strict and humourless adherence to a greater cause. As I write this conclusion in early 2019, veganism is in the news more than ever. "Veganuary" — the initiative, started in 2014, to encourage people to give up animal products for the first month of the year — has just come to an end. BBC Radio 4 invites listeners to call into a talk show to answer the question "Are you sticking to a vegan diet?" For those who answer affirmatively, the follow-up is usually along the lines: what do you find most difficult, or what do you miss the most?[1] I do not want to dismiss attempts to understand the vegan turn, or to belittle the enthusiasm and generosity of vegans eager to give advice on how to negotiate the practicalities of making healthy and affordable plant-based meals. But in all the fuss over Veganuary, veganism is once again presented exclusively as a diet. And though many callers to the show speak of the joys of minimising animal exploitation and feeling in better health, and even if programmes such as this address important questions about the accessibility of veganism to people of different incomes and the potential impact of a shift to plant-based diets on farming and farmers, the questions posed to those practising veganism come back, time and again, to the challenges, the problems and the supposed hypocrisies.

The framing of veganism as a sacrifice reflects a dominant worldview in much of the West today that associates pleasure with abandon and abundance. This demonstrates a profound level of denial and lack of imagination in the face of evidence that climate change mitigation will necessitate a massive shift in habits and lifestyle on the part of *all* the world's wealthiest consumers. The practice of veganism pushes back against the neoliberal truism that links enjoyment to excess and instant gratification. Cutting down and being patient are often associated in consumer capitalist culture with exercising willpower, giving in to parental-type discipline; these concepts have a ring of the Pollyanna and puritanical. But what about the joys of anticipation and holding back, the delights of indulging in restraint? Or of finding other ways of fun and fulfilment that don't rely on overconsumption and the exploitation of other animals, people and the planet? The ethical practice of veganism allows us to rethink what we understand by pleasure and to reshape our identities in ways that seek both to recognise the material limitations of the earth's resources and fully to acknowledge our kinship with other animals.

Coming to veganism at the relatively late age of forty-seven was a humbling experience. It reminded me that ethical and political commitments are always a process. It helped me not only to practice greater compassion towards other animals but also to have greater tolerance for other people. We come to consciousness in different ways, at different times. This realisation has prompted me to try (even if not always with shining success!) to be less judgemental of others who may not share my priorities, even while I remain committed to education, struggle and critique. I began writing this book in 2015, a year or so after I started practicing veganism, because I was frustrated by what I saw as a limited understanding of the sexual politics of veganism in much writing on the topic. Since then, I have engaged with an expanse of queer and feminist writing about veganism which has inspired me to think in new ways about this ethical commitment and political movement of ours. I have also come across many arguments against veganism. The least convincing of these are those that either dismiss the ethical premise — a recognition that we have responsibilities to other-than-human animals — out of hand for avowedly anthropocentric reasons, or those that rest on limited and stereotypical images of vegans — as purist and puritanical, hypocritical or moralistic. But there are also sound arguments against veganism — or at least, against a certain *kind* of vegan practice. Those are the arguments that stress, like many vegans do, that entreaties to "Go Vegan!" can be elitist and imperialist, and that veganism should always be practiced as part of a wider social justice project that takes into account differences and power relations among people. These are not arguments against veganism *per se*, but against the universalist discourse that has at times dominated defences and representations of veganism.

The recent rise in interest in veganism is something to be celebrated and taken as an inspiration. Yes, we can critique grandiose claims about veganism saving the planet; and we should reject a vegan consumerism accessible only to the wealthy. But no one who takes anti-capitalism or environmentalism seriously can afford to ignore the destructiveness of animal agriculture, or any of the global industries and institutions that rely on the mass exploitation of other-than-human animals as well as human workers. We should also remember that veganism is, at its heart, an expression of an ethical commitment of non-violence against all creatures, not merely a pragmatic tool for mitigating climate change. But we should not assume that when vegans claim that fears of climate change are behind their commitment to avoiding animal products this precludes or is even in competition with a commitment to other animals. Caring for animals is not in a zero-sum competition with caring for ourselves or the rest of the planet.

Veganism is not the answer to all our problems. It will mean different things to different people. Those who have experienced violence, or whose ancestors were treated like "animals" as they were enslaved or murdered, have good reason to fear a loss of human status, as do all women, trans, non-binary and disabled people. These fears may make people wary of claims that human beings are animals and that we are not superior to other species. People whose livelihoods rely on animal agriculture do not have the same relationship to farm animals as consumers who buy meat at the supermarket or from niche organic butchers. Indigenous communities whose traditional diets include wild meat, eggs and fish might continue to practice sustainable forms of hunting and fishing in the face of food imperialism and the imposition of diets reliant on unhealthy, unsustainable farming methods and processing. People with certain health conditions or disabilities may practise veganism while not sticking to a strict vegan diet. Some economically privileged people may have well-considered reasons for consuming animal products. Practicing contextual ethical veganism means accepting and respecting that the context in which people eat, work, dress, and care for ourselves and others varies greatly.

Veganism in the West today is one response — though certainly not the only one — to an arrogant and fatal anthropocentrism, and to the deadly ideology of unconstrained economic growth that is killing so many people, and so much of the other-than-human world, including other animals. It is not a distraction from, or a replacement for, other ethical commitments, relationships and political struggles. Contextual ethical veganism complements and strengthens critiques of individualism and neoliberalism, feminist, queer and anti-racist struggle, anarchist and socialist calls for new forms of collective action and living, and campaigns against climate catastrophe. We can be involved in other political and social movements and cherished communities, acknowledge our commonalities and differences with other people and other animals. We can have our histories, our unstable identities, our desires, our pleasures, our memories. We can live with our imperfections and our ambivalence. We can do these things, and, in our own different and always imperfect ways, we can also do veganism.

ACKNOWLEDGEMENTS

This book grew out of a pair of personal and political passions: a long-standing commitment to sex-positive feminism, and a newer enthusiasm for the practice of veganism. Over the course of writing, these passions have been reaffirmed. I have also enjoyed and benefitted from the generosity of time, intellect and spirit of many others.

Some years ago I went for dinner with my friend Clare Hemmings to talk about feminism, citation practices and the sexual politics of veganism. The ideas that emerged from that conversation initiated the process of putting together this book. I am deeply grateful to Clare for helping get me started, and for many ensuing conversations and much laughter. She also read parts of the book manuscript and has helped to shape it with her sharp insights on feminist theory, ambivalence and the ethics of eating.

This book would not have come to be as it is is without the encouragement and support of D-M Withers and Hammer-On Press. I have loved publishing with an independent press and am thrilled to have the book on the Hammer-On list. D-M has provided just the right balance of schedule pressure, editorial acumen, patience, encouragement and exciting conversations about the text. Thanks a million.

Tamara Schreiber, Chloë Taylor and Anna Davin each read the whole manuscript in its final stages and gave invaluable feedback. My collaboration with Tamara has spanned friendship, family and countless flights of fancy. I have learned so much from her boundless imagination, sharp mind and talents as a writer. "Thank you" doesn't quite sum it up. Chloë has been a more recent, and largely virtual, interlocutor, generously sharing her time and knowledge about feminism, veganism, philosophy and animal studies, as well as tales of cats, travel and Mexican food. She was one of my early inspirations in the newish academic field of feminist animal studies. I feel very fortunate to have had her support, and especially grateful to her for helping me sharpen a number of arguments in the preceding pages. Anna came to the work with her expert editorial skills and her political wits about her. I have benefited from her warmth, friendship, radical historian's insight and matchless story-telling skills, as well as her cooking and hospitality, for well over twenty years. Anna, her partner Henry and their extended family have been a home from home for me in London; their regular dinner evenings have long sustained me with merriment, conversation and love.

A number of other people read chapters, but their contribution to this project goes far beyond their reading skills. Caroline Smart has been a friend, fellow queer fem and role model for a long time. It was at her magical Women's Anarchist Nuisance Café (WANC) that I learned how to cook — well, kind of — and share vegan food. We have shared many wonderful conversations about veganism and so much more over the years. More recently, Nydia Swaby has inspired me with her energy and thoughts on veganism and fugitive feminism, and introduced me to Café Van Gogh, London's finest vegan joint south of the river. Justin Edwards has been around for almost as long as I can remember, confidante, fellow traveller and partier par excellence. It's such a gift that we eventually ended up in the same place. Annabelle Mooney and Clare Bielby have been huge supporters of my work and I have learned so much from them and theirs, as well as enjoying laughter over food and dancing. Ayesha Taylor rocks in many ways; she helps to keep me young, on my political toes and always smiling. Carole Sweeney is a wonderful writer, scholar and dear dear friend. I owe so much to her and the other LG team members, Jackie Clarke and Nicky Marsh. My travels with them have made the bumps of the past two decades both easier to ride and infinitely more fun. Wendy Mitchell has brought joy and wisdom into my life for over thirty years. I can't think of where I would be without her. My thanks and love to all of you.

During the period I was writing this book I had the enormous privilege and pleasure to be part of the editorial collective of the journal *Feminist Review*. *FR* has been an unsurpassed intellectual home. My writing and ideas have been nurtured and — I hope — improved through my ongoing exchanges with Aisha Gill, Avtar Brah, Gina Heathcote, Ioana Szeman, Irene Gedalof, Joanna Pares Hoare, Kyoung Kim, Nadje Al-Ali, Navtej Purewal, Nydia Swaby, Rutvica Andrijasevic, Sadie Wearing, Sita Balani and Yasmin Gunaratnam. Huge thanks and love to you all.

In January 2018 I attended the Minding Animals conference in Mexico City, where I found a welcome and welcoming community of scholars and activists working in the area of animal studies. A number of encounters there influenced my thinking on veganism and this book. In particular I'm grateful for conversations with Jess Ison, Dinesh Wadiwel and Jeff Sebo.

In Mexico City I also met the wonderful people at FaunAcción (Animal Action) and El Molcajete whose work I discuss in chapter 6 of this book. Thanks to Nut López for sharing the cat colonies with me, to Marianna Arrellano Corbello for conversations over vegan food, and to Wotko/ Gerardo Tristan for his unsurpassed energy, enthusiasm and encouragement. My growing friendship with Gerardo has been one of the gifts of working on the themes of veganism and animal rights over this past year, and I was delighted that he could visit London in September 2018 as part of his tour of Europe to promote links between animal rights in Mexico, the U.S. and Europe. The moving and marvellous story of how he started to make links between veganism and his queer and Indigenous identities is reproduced in very short form at the end of chapter 6.

My family is mostly over the sea but never far from my thoughts. They sustain me in more ways than I can think of, let alone name. Thanks and love especially to my mother, Mimi, and my brother, Matthew. Helping my committedly carnivore younger sibling celebrate his fiftieth birthday at a vegan diner in Toronto, followed by an exhibition on "The Anthropocene," was one of the highlights of 2018. And to Moira Middleton: as close to family as one can get. I try never to forget how fortunate I am to have a true life friend.

Special hugs, love and thanks to my dearests: Raf Benato, Taylor Hynes, Bernardo Santarelli and Christian Tecchio. You amaze me and keep me alive.

And to chosen kin, near and far: Antonia Bystram, Lola Vega, Dorothy Atcheson, Linda Royles, Angela Fong, Leti Sabsay, Ceci Sosa, Izaskun Aranbarri, Idoia Campo, Máryori Bello, Emily Paradis, Sarah Fowlie, Lucille Power, Stuart Coxe, An Te Liu, Ellis Slack, Arantxa Elizondo, Maria James.

I can't possibly do justice to all the other friends who have supported me over the past few years, and helped in their own ways to push this book along. But I do want to thank and name them: Alvaro Martínez, Alyoxsa Tudor, Andrea García, Andrew Wareham, Dana Rubin, Eric Jacobson, Hannah Caller, Hector Alejandro, Helena López, Isabel Santaolalla, Jenny Bunker, Jen Parker-Starbuck, John Tosh, Josh Abrams, Kes Sternchen, Liz Dore, Lucy Van de Wiel,

Mandie Iveson, Marta García Morcillo, Meg Arnot, Nadia Valman, Nina Power, Pauline Barrie, Sarah Gartland, Sotiris Lamprou.

Zhora came along at a rather inconvenient time, skewing my writing schedule and opening my imagination. Not only did she make it into one of the stories in the book; her name will forever remind me of a tale that did not: that of the replicant snake dancer, the first to die at the hands of Harrison Ford in the original *Blade Runner* movie. The execution is a brutal moment of misogyny and anthropocentrism. When I finally pulled the strings of her life together, decades after seeing the film for the first time, I knew she was a character who deserved to be remembered. One day I may write more about her. For now, I smile inside each time I introduce the dog I keep company with to the strangers we meet in the park, knowing she is named after a vegan android erotic dancer who wears an animoid python around her neck. Stories of veganism, sex and politics get around in all kinds of ways.

NOTES

Introduction

1   Olivia Petter, "Number of Vegans in the UK Soars to 3.5 million, Survey Finds," *Independent*, April 3, 2018, https://www.independent.co.uk/life-style/food-and-drink/vegans-uk-rise-popularity-plant-based-diets-veganism-figures-survey-compare-the-market-a8286471.html.

2   John Parker, "The Year of the Vegan," *The World in 2019*, https://worldin2019.economist.com/theyearofthevegan?utm_source=412&utm_medium=COM.

3   For a brief summary, see Erika Cudworth, *Social Lives with Other Animals: Tales of Sex, Death and Love* (Basingstoke: Palgrave, 2011), 117–19.

4   Ruth Harrison, *Animal Machines* (Wallingford: CABI, 2013 [1964]); Peter Singer, *Animal Liberation: A New Ethics for Our Treatment of Animals* (New York: Discus/Avon Books, 1977 [1975]).

5   Marion Stamp-Dawkins, *Animal Suffering* (London: Chapman & Hall, 1980); Jacky Turner, *Stop — Look — Listen: Recognising the Sentience of Farm Animals* (Petersfield: Compassion in World Farming Trust, 2003).

6   Petter, "Number of Vegans in the UK Soars to 3.5 Million."

7   See also Melanie Joy and Jens Tuider, "Foreword," in *Critical Perspectives on Veganism*, eds. Jodey Castricano and Rasmus R. Simonsen (Basingstoke: Palgrave MacMillan, 2016), v–vi; Jodey Castricano and Rasmus Rahbek Simonsen, "Introduction: Food for Thought," in *Critical Perspectives on Veganism*, eds. Jodey Castricano and Rasmus R. Simonsen (Basingstoke: Palgrave MacMillan, 2016), 1–2; and Sean O'Callaghan, *Fat Gay Vegan: Eat, Drink and Live Like You Give a Shit* (New York: Nourish, 2018), Electronic Book, 44.0–48.0.

8 "Call You and Yours: Are you Sticking to a Vegan Diet?" BBC Radio 4, February 5, 2019, https://www.bbc.co.uk/programmes/m0002bn2. This comment was followed by clips from three online films, including two discussed in this book: Kip Anderson and Keegan Kuhn, *Cowspiracy: The Sustainability Secret* (United States, 2014) and Simon Amstell, *Carnage: Swallowing the Past* (United Kingdom, 2017). See this book, chapter 3 and interlude 2 respectively.

9 See this book, chapters 3 and 6.

10 See this book, chapter 6.

11 See, for example, Castricano and Simonsen, eds., *Critical Perspectives on Veganism*; Nathan Stephens Griffin, *Understanding Veganism: Biography and Identity* (Basingstoke: Palgrave MacMillan, 2016); Laura Wright, *The Vegan Studies Project* (Athens: University of Georgia Press, 2015).

12 Deane Curtin, "Toward an Ecological Ethic of Care," *Hypatia* 6, no. 1 (1991): 68–71.

13 Jovan Parry and Annie Potts, "Vegan Sexuality: Challenging Heteronormative Masculinity through Meat-free Sex," *Feminism & Psychology* 20, no. 1 (2010): 53–72. See also Ellen Jaffe Jones, Joel Kahn, Beverly Lynn Bennett, *Vegan Sex* (Summertown, TN: Healthy Living Publications, 2018).

14 The American animal rights organisation People for the Ethical Treatment of Animals (PETA) holds an annual "Hottest Vegan" contest. See Chelsea Ritschel, "PETA Announces 2018 UK Hottest Vegan Finalists," *Independent*, July 30, 2018, https://www.independent.co.uk/life-style/peta-hottest-vegan-competition-finalists-vote-2018-a8470411.html.

15 See this book, chapter 2.

16 Carol J. Adams, *The Sexual Politics of Meat: A Feminist-Vegetarian Critical Theory* (New York: Continuum 2000

[1990]). For a critique of the anti-pornography arguments in *The Sexual Politics of Meat*, see Carrie Hamilton, "Sex, Work, Meat: The Feminist Politics of Veganism," *Feminist Review* 114 (2016): 112–29 and this book, chapter 1.

17 For example, A. Breeze Harper, ed., *Sistah Vegan: Black Female Vegans Speak on Food, Identity, Health, and Society* (New York: Lantern Books, 2010); David M. Peña-Guzmán, "Anti-Colonial Food Politics: A Case Study In Action From Mexico," *faunalytics*, October 24, 2018, https://faunalytics. org/anti-colonial-food-politics-a-case-study-in-action-from-mexico/; Rasmus R. Simonsen, "A Queer Vegan Manifesto," *Journal for Critical Animal Studies* 10, no. 3 (2012): 51–81; Chloë Taylor, "Foucault and the Ethics of Eating," *Foucault Studies* 9 (2010): 71–88.

18 Carol S. Vance, ed., *Pleasure and Danger: Exploring Female Sexuality* (London: Pandora Press, 1992).

19 Simonsen, "Queer Vegan Manifesto," 57, 65.

20 Jeff Sebo, "Multi-Issue Food Activism," in *The Oxford Handbook of Food Ethics*, eds. Anne Barnhill, Mark Budolfson and Tyler Doggett (Oxford: Oxford University Press, 2018), 401. See also Kimberlé Crenshaw, "Demarginalizing the Intersection of Race and Sex: A Black Feminist Critique of Antidiscrimination Doctrine, Feminist Theory and Antiracist Politics," *University of Chicago Legal Forum* 1 (1989): 139–67.

21 "History," *The Vegan Society*, https://www.vegansociety. com/about-us/history.

22 Leah Leneman, "No Animal Food: The Road to Veganism in Britain, 1909-1944," *Society & Animals* 7, no. 3 (1999): 219–28. See also Leah Leneman, "The Awakened Instinct: Vegetarianism and the Women's Suffrage Movement in Britain," *Women's History Review* 6 no. 2 (1997): 271–87 and Leela Gandhi, *Affective Communities: Anti-colonial*

Thought, Fin-de-siecle Radicalism, and the Politics of Friendship (Durham: Duke University Press, 2006).

23 See for example, oral history interviews with different animal rights and animal welfare activists, British Library Sound Archive, Animal Welfare Collection.

24 Singer, *Animal Liberation* (1977 [1975]).

25 The term "speciesism" was first used by Richard Ryder in 1970 to describe what he understood as the irrational moral distinction human beings draw between ourselves and other species. Richard D. Ryder, "Speciesism Again: the Original Leaflet," https://web.archive.org/web/20121114004403/ http://www.criticalsocietyjournal.org.uk/Archives_ files/1.%20Speciesism%20Again.pdf.

26 Singer, *Animal Liberation* (1977 [1975]), 164; Peter Singer, "A Case for Veganism," *Free Inquiry* 27, no. 3 (2007): 18–19.

27 For example, Singer, *Animal Liberation* (1977 [1975]), 78. For an excellent engagement with Singer's arguments on human disability, see Sunaura Taylor, *Beasts of Burden: Animal and Disability Liberation* (New York: New Press, 2017), 123–48.

28 For example, Josephine Donovan and Carol J. Adams, eds., *Beyond Animal Rights: A Feminist Caring Ethic for the Treatment of Animals* (New York: Continuum, 1996).

29 Tom Regan, *The Case for Animal Rights* (London: Routledge & Kegan Paul), 1983.

30 See this book, chapter 5.

31 A. Breeze Harper, "Introduction: The Birth of the Sistah Vegan Project" in *The Sistah Vegan Project: Black Female Vegans Speak on Food, Identity, Health, and Society*, ed. A. Breeze Harper (New York: Lantern Books, 2010), 18; Miranda Larbi, "Please Don't Forget that Veganism Hasn't Always Been a White, Middle-Class Thing," *Metro*, January 14, 2018, https://metro.co.uk/2018/01/14/

please-dont-forget-veganism-hasnt-always-white-middle-class-thing-7228027/.

32 See this book, chapters 5 and 6.

33 See this book, chapter 6.

34 Layli Phillips, "Veganism and Ecofeminism," in *The Sistah Vegan Project: Black Female Vegans Speak on Food, Identity, Health, and Society*, ed. A. Breeze Harper (New York: Lantern Books, 2010), 19; Anat Pick, "Turning to Animals between Love and Law," *New Formations* 76 (2012): 68–85.

35 Adamas "A Critique of Consumption-Centred Veganism," *H.E.A.L.T.H: Humans, Earth, and Animals Living Together Harmoniously*, June 3, 2011, http://eco-health.blogspot. com/2011/06/crtique-of-consumption-centered.html; Robert C. Jones, "Veganisms," in *Critical Perspectives on Veganism*, eds. Jodey Castricano and Rasmus R. Simonsen (Basingstoke: Palgrave MacMillan, 2016), 15–39; Griffin, *Understanding Veganism*, 4; Joshua Schuster, "The Vegan and the Sovereign," in *Critical Perspectives on Veganism*, eds. Jodey Castricano and Rasmus R. Simonsen (Basingstoke: Palgrave MacMillan, 2016), 210; Simonsen, "Queer Vegan Manifesto," 69, note xiii; Richard Twine, "Vegan Killjoys at the Table: Contesting Happiness and Negotiating Relationships with Food Practices," *Societies* 4, no. 4 (2014): 624; Dinesh Joseph Wadiwel, *The War Against Animals* (Leiden: Brill Rodopi, 2015), 278.

36 See Roland Barthes, *Mythologies* (New York: Random House, 1983).

37 Cora Diamond, "Eating Meat and Eating People," *Philosophy* 53, no. 206 (1978): 469.

38 Gary L. Francione, "Veganism as a Moral Imperative," *Animal Rights: The Abolitionist Approach* May 12, 2016, https://www. abolitionistapproach.com/veganism-moral-imperative/.

39 See Gary Steiner, *Animals and the Limits of Postmodernism* (New York: Columbia University Press, 2013), 227.

40 Lori Gruen, "Facing Death and Practicing Grief," in *Ecofeminism: Feminist Intersections with Other Animals and the Earth*, eds. Carol J. Adams and Lori Gruen (New York: Bloomsbury, 2014), 127–41.

41 Taylor, *Beasts of Burden*, 163.

42 Wright, *Vegan Studies Project*, 1, 2.

43 Wright, *Vegan Studies Project*, 6.

44 Taylor, "Foucault and the Ethics of Eating," 75.

45 Wadiwel, *War Against Animals*, 280.

46 Taylor, "Foucault and the Ethics of Eating," 88.

47 "Back to-Business, [etc]," *Cancer Guinea Pig*, October 10, 2016 https://cancerguineapig.com/2016/10/10/back-to-business-reflaxing-not-chillaxing/

48 For example, Griffin, *Understanding Veganism*; Harper, *Sistah Vegan*; O'Callaghan, *Fat Gay Vegan*; Simonsen, "A Queer Vegan Manifesto"; *Vegan Voices of Color*, https://veganvoicesofcolor.org; Taylor, *Beasts of Burden*; Wright, *Vegan Studies Project*.

49 On Christianity and veganism, see Robert Wayner, "The Christian Basis for Veganism," *Free from Harm*, October 1, 2014, https://freefromharm.org/veganism/christian-basis-veganism/. For a a strict animal rights argument against pet ownership, which also considers the issue of vegans homing rescue animals, see Gary L. Francione, "Pets: The Inherent Problems of Domestication," *Animal Rights: The Abolitionist Approach*, July 31, 2012, https://freefromharm.org/veganism/christian-basis-veganism/'. On veganism and the stigmatisation of female bodies and eating, see Wright, *Vegan Studies Project*.

Chapter 1
Dreaded comparations and other stories

1   Mirha-Soleil Ross, "Yapping Out Loud for Animals and Prostitutes!" Interview with Nadja Lubiw, ANIMAL VOICES Radio, CIUT 89.5 FM, Toronto, April 27, 2002. Transcript available at https://kersplebedeb.com/posts/yap_int-2/. No page numbers.

2   See, for example, Anat Pick, "Turning to Animals Between Love and Law," *New Formations* 76 (2012): 68–85; James Stanescu, "Species Trouble: Judith Butler, Mourning, and the Precarious Lives of Animals," *Hypatia* 27, no. 1 (2012): 567–82; Chloë Taylor, "The Precarious Lives of Animals: Butler, Coetzee, and Animal Ethics," *Philosophy Today* 52, no. 1 (2008): 60–73; Sunaura Taylor, *Beasts of Burden: Animal and Disability Liberation* (New York: New Press, 2017).

3   Carol J. Adams, *The Sexual Politics of Meat: A Feminist-Vegetarian Critical Theory* (New York: Continuum 2000 [1990]), 23.

4   For example, Julia Twigg, "Vegetarianism and the Meanings of Meat," in *The Sociology of Food and Eating: Essays on the Sociological Significance of Food,* ed. Anne Murcott (Aldershot: Gower, 1983), 18–30.

5   Jovan Parry, "Gender and Slaughter in Popular Gastronomy," *Feminism & Psychology* 20, no. 3 (2010): 381–96.

6   Kelly Struthers Montford, "The 'Present Referent': Nonhuman Animal Sacrifice and the Constitution of Dominant Albertan Identity," *PhaenEx* 8, no. 2 (2013): 105–34.

7   Adams, *Sexual Politics of Meat*, 21.

8   Carrie Hamilton, "Sex, Work, Meat: The Feminist Politics of Veganism," *Feminist Review* 114 (2016): 112–29.

9   Cited in Stuart Hall, "Gramsci's Relevance for the Study of

Race and Ethnicity," *Journal of Communication Enquiry* 10, no. 5 (1986): 26. See also Stuart Hall and Alan O'Shea, "Common-sense Neoliberalism," *Soundings* 53, (2013): 1–18.

10 Andrea Dworkin, *Pornography: Men Possessing Women* (New York: Putnam, 1981); Catharine MacKinnon, *Toward a Feminist Theory of the State* (Cambridge, MA: Harvard University Press, 1989).

11 For example, Carol S. Vance, ed., *Pleasure and Danger: Exploring Female Sexuality* (London: Pandora Press, 1992).

12 These tendencies become more pronounced in Adams's later work, in particular *The Pornography of Meat* (New York: Continuum, 2003), which employs a loose comparison between images from pornography and sexualised images from American meat advertising in the late twentieth century. See Hamilton, "Sex, Work, Meat."

13 Ross, "Yapping Out Loud!"

14 The titles for this chapter and this section are taken from Marjorie Spiegel, *The Dreaded Comparison: Human and Animal Slavery* (New York: Mirror Books, 1997).

15 Joanna Bourke, *What it Means to be Human: Reflections from 1791 to the Present* (London: Virago, 2011), 165–68; Spiegel, *Dreaded Comparison*, 107.

16 Coral Lansbury, *The Old Brown Dog: Women, Workers, and Vivisection in Edwardian England* (Madison: University of Wisconsin Press, 1985), 84–87.

17 Peter Singer, *Animal liberation* (New York: Discus/Avon Books, 1977 [1975]), xii.

18 For examples of these kinds of responses, see Christopher-Sebastian McJetters, "Slavery. It's Still a Thing," *Vegan Publishers*, June 11, 2014, http://veganpublishers.com/slavery-its-still-a-thing-christopher-sebastian-mcjetters/; A. Breeze Harper, "Introduction: The Birth of the Sistah Vegan Project," in *Sistah Vegan: Black Female Vegans Speak on*

Food, Identity, Health, and Society, ed. A. Breeze Harper (New York: Lantern Books, 2010), xiii.

19 See this book, chapter 6.

20 McJetters, "Slavery. It's Still a Thing."

21 Harper, "Introduction," xiii.

22 See for example, d. grace, "Vegetarianism and the PETA incident," *[meory] me. theory. together.,* April 16, 2006, http://barelyesoteric.blogspot.com/2006/04/vegetarianism-peta-incident.html. For further description of the travelling exhibit and media reactions to it, see Claire Jean Kim, "Moral Extensionism or Racist Exploitation? The Use of Holocaust and Slavery Analogies in the Animal Liberation Movement," *New Political Science* 33, no. 3, (2011): 311, 323.

23 Kim, "Moral Extensionism or Racist Exploitation?," 313.

24 Harper, "Introduction," xiv.

25 Harper, "Introduction," xiv.

26 Spiegel, *Dreaded Comparison,* 30.

27 Charles Patterson, *Eternal Treblinka: Our Treatment of Animals and the Holocaust* (New York: Lantern Books, 2002).

28 Gary Steiner, "Animal, Vegetable, Miserable," *The New York Times,* November 22, 2009.

29 Kim, "Moral Extensionism or Racist Exploitation?," 315.

30 Isaac Bashevis Singer, "The Letter Writer," in *Collected Stories* (London: Penguin Classics, 2011), 250–76.

31 Gary Steiner, *Animals and the Limits of Postmodernism* (New York: Columbia University Press, 2013), 204.

32 Harper, "Introduction," xiv.

33 Steiner, *Animals,* 204; emphasis added.

34 d. grace, "Vegetarianism and the PETA incident."

35 Hilda Kean, *Animal Rights: Politics and Social Change in Britain since 1800* (London: Reaktion Books, 1998), 214.

36 Bourke, *What it Means to be Human*, 184.
37 Kim, "Moral Extensionism or Racist Exploitation?," 313.
38 My thanks to Chloë Taylor for helping me to articulate this point.
39 For the United Nations definition of genocide, see "Genocide," United Nations Office on the Prevention of Genocide and the Responsibility to Protect, http://www.un.org/en/genocideprevention/genocide.html.
40 Kim, "Moral Extensionism or Racist Exploitation?," 325.
41 See this book, chapter 3.
42 Kean, *Animal Rights*, 30, 207.
43 Steve Baker, *Picturing the Beast: Animals, Identity, and Representation* (Chicago: University of Illinois Press, 2001 [1993]), 187–88, 221.
44 Baker, *Picturing the Beast*, 232.
45 Mirha-Soleil Ross, "Shaking Things Up: Queer Rights/Animal Rights." Interview with Claudette Vaughn," *Vegan Voice* (September-November 2003), http://www.satyamag.com/oct03/ross.html.
46 Ross, "Yapping Out Loud!" The live show of *Yapping out Loud* ran in Toronto and New York between 2001 and 2004, and a film version was subsequently shown at festivals. Ross, "Shaking Things Up"; Trish Salah, "What's all the Yap about? Reading Mirha-Soleil Ross's Performance of Activist Pedagogy," *Canadian Theatre Review* 130 (2007): 70, note 2.
47 Ross, "Yapping Out Loud!"
48 Gloria Anzaldúa, "Metaphors in the Tradition of the Shaman," in *The Gloria Anzaldúa Reader* (Durham: Duke University Press, 2009), 121.
49 Anzaldúa, "Metaphors in the Tradition of the Shaman," 122.

Chapter 2
Eating and being eaten

1   Val Plumwood, "Being Prey" (2011 [1999]); https://
     kurungabaa.wordpress.com/2011/01/18/being-prey-by-
     val-plumwood/. No page numbers. All the quotations in this
     section refer to this text, unless otherwise stated.
2   Carol J. Adams, *The Sexual Politics of Meat: A Feminist-
     Vegetarian Critical Theory* (New York: Continuum 2000
     [1990]). See also this book, chapter 1.
3   Val Plumwood, "Integrating Ethical Frameworks for Animals,
     Humans, and Nature: A Critical Feminist Eco-Socialist
     Analysis," *Ethics and the Environment* 5, no. 2 (2000):
     288–99; Val Plumwood, "Ecofeminism," in *Encyclopedia
     of Feminist Theories*, ed. Lorraine Code (London: Routldege,
     2000), 151–52.
4   Plumwood, "Ecofeminism," 151–52.
5   Plumwood, "Being Prey."
6   Matthew Calarco, "Being Toward Meat: Anthropocentrism,
     Indistinction, and Veganism," *Dialectical Anthropology* 38,
     no. 4 (2014): 425. Emphasis in original.
7   Val Plumwood, *Feminism and the Mastery of Nature* (London:
     Routledge, 1993); Val Plumwood, *Environmental Culture:
     The Ecological Crisis of Reason* (London: Routledge, 2002),
     155.
8   In earlier work, Plumwood wrote about "ontological
     vegetarianism." See Plumwood, "Integrating Ethical
     Frameworks." In this chapter I cite a later text which uses
     the same arguments developed earlier against "ontological
     vegetarianism" but refers specifically to "ontological
     veganism." Plumwood, "Animals and Ecology: Towards a
     Better Integration" (Australian National University Digital
     Collection: Working/Technical Paper, 2003), https://core.
     ac.uk/download/pdf/156617082.pdf. No page numbers.

9 Plumwood, "Animals and Ecology."

10 See this book, chapter 1.

11 Plumwood, "Animals and Ecology."

12 Plumwood, "Integrating Ethical Frameworks," 294.

13 For example, Andrew Smith, *A Critique of the Moral Defense of Vegetarianism* (Basingstoke: Palgrave MacMillan, 2016). For a summary of contemporary developments in "plant studies" see Greta Gaard, *Critical Ecofeminism* (Lanham: Lexington Books, 2017), 27–45.

14 Plumwood, *Environmental Culture*, 154–55.

15 Plumwood, "Being Prey."

16 Deane Curtin, "Toward an Ecological Ethic of Care," *Hypatia* 6, no. 1 (1991): 68–71. See also this book, Introduction.

17 Plumwood, "Animals and Ecology."

18 Singer stated in *Animal Liberation* that "the absolute minimum" moral commitment required of anyone who wanted to go beyond their own "narrow self-interest" was the refusal to eat all factory-farmed meat. Singer, *Animal Liberation* (1977 [1975]), 175.

19 Plumwood, "Integrating Ethical Frameworks," 289.

20 Matthew Cole, "Asceticism and Hedonism in Research Discourses of Veg*anism," *British Food Journal* 110, no. 7 (2008): 706–16.

21 Plumwood, "Integrating Ethical Frameworks," 291.

22 Cora Diamond, "Eating Meat and Eating People," *Philosophy* 53, no. 206 (1978): 470.

23 Plumwood, "Integrating Ethical Frameworks," 289.

24 Elspeth Probyn, *Carnal Appetites: FoodSexIdentities* (London: Routledge, 2000), 14.

25 Chloë Taylor, "Foucault and the Ethics of Eating," *Foucault Studies* 9 (2010), 79.

26 Probyn, *Carnal Appetites*, 55.

27 Singer, *Animal Liberation* (1977 [1975]), 181.

28 Probyn, *Carnal Appetites*, 68.

29 See Cole, "Asceticism and Hedonism."

30 Probyn, *Carnal Appetites*, 60.

31 Jovan Parry and Annie Potts, "Vegan Sexuality: Challenging Heteronormative Masculinity through Meat-free Sex," *Feminism & Psychology* 20, no. 1 (2010): 53–72.

32 Elspeth Probyn, *Eating the Ocean* (Durham: Duke University Press, 2016), 42.

33 Probyn, *Eating the Ocean*, 2.

34 Camilo Mora *et al.* "How Many Species Are There on Earth and in the Ocean?" *PLOS: Biology* 9, no. 8 (2011), https://www.ncbi.nlm.nih.gov/pmc/articles/PMC3160336/.

35 Probyn, *Eating the Ocean*, 5–6, 10, 3.

36 Elspeth Probyn, "Swimming with Tuna: Human-Ocean Entanglements," *Australian Humanities Review* 51 (2011): 99.

37 Gary Steiner, *Animals and the Limits of Postmodernism* (New York: Columbia University Press, 2013), 21.

38 Probyn, *Eating the Ocean*, 25.

39 David Foster Wallace, "Consider the Lobster," *Gourmet* (August 2004): 56.

40 Wallace, "Consider the Lobster," 62, 64.

41 Brian Luke, "Taming Ourselves or Going Feral? Towards a Nonpatriarchal Metaethic of Animal Liberation," in *Animals and Women: Feminist Theoretical Explorations*, eds. Carol J. Adams and Josephine Donovan (Durham: Duke University Press, 1995), 314.

42 Wallace, "Consider the Lobster," 64.

43 Probyn, *Eating the Ocean*, 25.

44 Singer, *Animal Liberation* (1977 [1975]), 178.

45 Singer, *Animal Liberation* (1977 [1975]), 178–79.

46 Probyn, *Eating the Ocean*, 25–26.

47 Singer, *Animal Liberation* (1977 [1975]), ix–x. Or as he puts it later in the book, "kindly ladies who are dotty about cats" (203). For Singer, such women and their pets are the

concern of populist and largely ineffective "animal welfare" movements which are not "founded on basic principles of justice and morality."

48 Taylor, *Beasts of Burden*, 80.

49 For example, Singer, *Animal Liberation* (1977 [1975]), 78.

50 Taylor, *Beasts of Burden*, 80–81. See also Mark Bekoff, "Vegans Shouldn't Eat Oysters, and if You do You're Not Vegan, So..." *Huffington Post*, June 10, 2010, https://www.huffingtonpost.com/marc-bekoff/vegans-shouldnt-eat-oyste_b_605786.html. By 1990 Singer had concluded that there was enough evidence to indicate that molluscs (oysters, clams, mussels, scallops, and the like) experience enough pain to convince him to stop eating them. Singer, *Animal Liberation,* Revised Edition (London: The Bodley Head, 2015 [1990]), 174.

51 Probyn, *Eating the Ocean*, 1.

52 Probyn, *Eating the Ocean*, 8.

53 Probyn, *Eating the Ocean*, 3.

54 Probyn, *Eating the Ocean*, 3. See also this book, chapter 4.

55 Dinesh Joseph Wadiwel, "Do Fish Resist?" *Cultural Studies Review* 22, no. 1 (2016): 196–242.

56 Wadiwel, "Do Fish Resist?" 199, 200–201, 202.

57 Wadiwel, "Do Fish Resist?" 222.

Interlude 1
Raw

1 Julia Ducournau, *Raw* (France-Belgium, 2016). According to Gananath Obeyesekere, the literary critic Peter Hulme suggests "that we make a distinction between cannibalism, which is essentially a fantasy that the Other is going to eat us, and anthropophagy, which is the actual consumption of human flesh." Obeyesekere, *Cannibal Talk: The Man-Eating Myth and Human Sacrifice in the South Seas* (Berkeley and

LA: University of California Press 2005), 14. In this definition cannibalism describes not the human consumption of human flesh *per se*, but the paranoia of the white settler in the face of the "savage" native. "Anthropophagy" is derived from Ancient Greek and was revived in Europe in the early modern period. Although not necessarily free from the Eurocentric associations of "cannibalism", it is less sensationalist and less commonly used in contemporary English. I use "anthropophagy" in order to signal the problems that come with uncritical use instead of "cannibalism" in popular culture, including in "cannibal films" such as *Raw*.

2   Kaleem Aftab, "Director Julia Ducournau on her Cannibal Film *Raw*: 'I asked my actor, what do you think in principle about shoving your hand up a cow's arse?'" *Independent* April 5, 2017; https://www.independent.co.uk/arts-entertainment/films/features/julia-ducournau-raw-a7666871.html.

3   See this book, chapters 1 and 2.

4   Val Plumwood, "Being Prey" (1999). See also this book, chapter 2.

5   Rick, "Human and Non-human Horror Cinema," *Luddite Robot*, August 4 2016, https://ludditerobot.com/vegan-horror/human-nonhuman-horror-cinema/.

6   Brigid Brophy, "The Rights of Animals," in *Animal Rights: A Historical Anthology*, eds. Andrew Linzey and Paul Barry Clarke, (New York: Columbia University Press, 2004 [1990]), 157–58. On "flesh food," see Brigid Brophy, "In Pursuit of a Fantasy," in *Animals, Men and Morals: An Enquiry into the Maltreatment of Non-Humans*, eds. Stanley and Rosalind Godlovitch and John Harris (London: Victor Gollancz Ltd, 1971), 131.

7   Ruth Harrison, *Animal Machines* (Wallingford, CABI, 2013 [1964]); F. W. Rogers Brambell, *Report of the Technical Committee to Enquire into the Welfare of Animals kept under Intensive Livestock Husbandry Systems* (London: Her Majesty's Stationery Office, [1965]).

Chapter 3
Slow violence and animal tales

1   See also "Sweden Heatwave: Hottest July in (at least) 260 Years," *The Local*, July 28, 2018, https://www.thelocal. se/20180723/sweden-heatwave-hottest-july-in-at-least-260-years; Christina Anderson and Alan Cowell, "Heat Wave Scorches Sweden as Wildfires Rage in the Arctic Circle," *New York Times*, July 19, 2018, https://www.nytimes. com/2018/07/19/world/europe/heat-wave-sweden-fires. html.

2   Nigel Clark and Kathryn Yusoff, "Queer Fire: Ecology, Combustion and Pyrosexual Desire," *Feminist Review* 118 (2018): 8.

3   Clark and Yusoff, "Queer Fire," 8; Rob Nixon, *Slow Violence and the Environmentalism of the Poor* (Cambridge, MA: Harvard University Press, 2011).

4   Nixon, *Slow Violence*, 3.

5   Nixon, *Slow Violence*, 138–9.

6   Kathryn Gillespie,"Witnessing Animal Others: Bearing Witness, Grief, and the Political Function of Emotion," *Hypatia* 31, no. 3 (2016): 582.

7   World Wildlife Fund, *Appetite for Destruction*, 7, 11, https:// www.wwf.org.uk/sites/default/files/2017-11/WWF_ AppetiteForDestruction_Full_Report_Web_0.pdf.

8   See for example, Wayne Martindale, "Trendy Foods Should Come with a Recipe for Sustainability," *The Conversation*, September 28, 2016, https://theconversation.com/trendy-foods-should-come-with-a-recipe-for-sustainability-65766; Alex Park and Julia Lurie, "It Takes How Much Water to Grow an Almond?" *Mother Jones*, February 24, 2014, https://www.motherjones.com/environment/2014/02/ wheres-californias-water-going/; "Palm Oil: What are the Issues?" *BBC* April 10, 2018, https://www.bbc.co.uk/

newsround/39492207.

9   Patricia MacCormack, *Posthuman Ethics* (Farnham: Ashgate 2012), 76, note 1.

10 Sunaura Taylor, *Beasts of Burden: Animal and Disability Liberation* (New York: New Press, 2017), 81.

11 Isabella Tree, "If You Want to Save the World, Veganism isn't the Answer," *Guardian*, August 25, 2018, https://www.theguardian.com/commentisfree/2018/aug/25/veganism-intensively-farmed-meat-dairy-soya-maize?CMP=Share_iOSApp_Other.

12 Petter, "Number of Vegans in the UK."

13 Tree, "If You Want to Save the World."

14 Isabella Tree, *Wilding: The Return of Nature to a British Farm* (London: Picador, 2018). Electronic Book, 295.3. See also Kate Good, "Explain Like I'm 5: Why Tofu Consumption Is Not Responsible for Soy-Related Deforestation," *One Green Planet*, January 22, 2015, http://www.onegreenplanet.org/environment/why-tofu-consumption-is-not-responsible-for-soy-related-deforestation/.

15 Tree, "If You Want to Save the World."

16 Tara Garnett, "Why Eating Grass-fed Beef isn't Going to Help Fight Climate Change," *The Conversation,* October 3, 2017, https://theconversation.com/why-eating-grass-fed-beef-isnt-going-to-help-fight-climate-change-84237.

17 Vasile Stanescu, "'Green' Eggs and Ham? The Myth of Sustainable Meat and the Danger of the Local," *The Journal for Critical Animal Studies* VIII, 1/2 (2010): 9, 12. See also Caroline Saunders, Andrew Barber and Greg Taylor, "Food Miles – Comparative Energy/Emissions Performance of New Zealand's Agriculture Industry," Research Report 285 (Lincoln University, New Zealand, July 2006), 93.

18 Stanescu, "'Green' Eggs and Ham?" 12–13. See also Christopher L. Weber and H. Scott Matthews, "Food-Miles and the Relative Climate Impacts of Food Choices in the

United States," *Environmental Science and Technology* 42, no. 10 (2008): 3508, http://pubs.acs.org.

19 Stanescu, "'Green' Eggs and Ham?," 15.

20 For example, "The Very Highest Animal Welfare Standards," *The Soil Association*, https://www.soilassociation.org/organic-living/whyorganic/better-for-animals/.

21 Vasile Stanescu, "Why 'Loving' Animals is Not Enough: A Response to Kathy Rudy, Locavorism, and the Marketing of 'Humane' Meat," *The Journal of American Culture* 36, no. 2 (2013): 103.

22 Stanescu, "Why 'Loving' Animals is Not Enough", 108.

23 Barbara Noske, *Humans and Other Animals: Beyond the Boundaries of Anthropology* (London: Pluto Press, 1989).

24 Sartya Rodriguez, "Interview with John Sanbonmatsu, Associate Professor at Worcester Polytechnic Institute," *Direct Action Everywhere*, December 1, 2014, https://www.directactioneverywhere.com/theliberationist/2014/12/1/interview-with-john-sanbonmatsu-associate-professor-of-philosophy-at-worcester-polytechnic-institute.

25 Cora Diamond, "Eating Meat and Eating People," *Philosophy* 53, no. 206 (1978): 470; Chloë Taylor, "Foucault and the Ethics of Eating," *Foucault Studies* 9 (2010): 75.

26 Henning Steinfeld *et al, Livestock's Long Shadow: Environmental Issues and Options* (Rome: Food and Agriculture Organization of the United Nations, 2006), xx.

27 Steinfeld *et al, Livestock's Long Shadow*, xx.

28 For example, Elke Stehfest *et al,* "Climate Benefits of Changing Diet," *Climatic Change* 95 (2009): 99; P. Smith, et al, "How Much Land-based Greenhouse Gas Mitigation Can be Achieved without Compromising Food Security and Environmental Goals?" *Global Change Biology Bioenergy* 19, no. 8 (2013): 2285–2302; P. J. Gerber *et al, Tackling Climate Change through Livestock: A Global Assessment of Emissions and Mitigation Opportunities* (Rome: Food

and Agriculture Organization of the United Nations, 2013); Martin C. Heller *et al*, "Greenhouse Gas Emissions and Energy Use Associated with Production of Individual Self-selected U.S. Diets," *Environmental Research Letters* 13 044004 (2018), no page numbers; William J. Ripple *et al*, and 15, 364 Scientist Signatories from 184 Countries, "World Scientists' Warning to Humanity: A Second Notice," *BioScience* 67, no. 12 (2017): 1026–28; Joseph Poore and Thomas Nemecek, "Reducing Food's Environmental Impacts through Producers and Consumers," *Science* 360, 6392 (2018): 987–92.

29 George Monbiot, "There's a Population Crisis All Right. But Probably Not the One You Think," *Guardian*, November 19, 2015, https://www.theguardian.com/commentisfree/2015/nov/19/population-crisis-farm-animals-laying-waste-to-planet. See also Corey J. A. Bradshaw and Barry W. Brook, "Human Population Reduction is not a Quick Fix for Environmental Problems," *PNAS* 111, no. 46 (2014): 16610–15, http://www.pnas.org/content/pnas/111/46/16610.full.pdf.

30 Kip Anderson and Keegan Kuhn, *Cowspiracy: The Sustainability Secret* (United States, 2014); Dan Hancox, "The Unstoppable Rise of Veganism: How a Fringe Movement went Mainstream," *Guardian,* April 1, 2018, https://www.theguardian.com/lifeandstyle/2018/apr/01/vegans-are-coming-millennials-health-climate-change-animal-welfare; Tree, "If You Want to Save the World." On *Cowspiracy's* impact on popular discussions around climate change, see Danny Chivers, "Cowspiracy: Stampeding in the Wrong Direction?" *New Internationalist*, February 10, 2016, https://newint.org/blog/2016/02/10/cowspiracy-stampeding-in-the-wrong-direction.

31 Chivers, "Cowspiracy." The study claiming the 51% statistic used in *Cowspiracy* is Robert Goodland and Jeff Anhang,

"Livestock and Climate Change," *World Watch* (2009): 10–19.

32 Chivers, "Cowspiracy."

33 Chivers, "Cowspiracy."

34 "The Evidence: Should We All be Vegetarians?" BBC World Service, London, April 19, 2017, https://www.bbc.co.uk/sounds/play/p04yzvnx.

35 "The Evidence: Should We All be Vegetarians?"

36 I am indebted as well to Gerardo Tristán for discussions about the problems with the call to "Go Vegan!"

37 Bina Agarwal, *Gender Challenges: Agriculture, Technology, and Food Security* (Oxford: Oxford University Press, 2016), 316–21; Ilse Köhler-Rollefson, *Invisible Guardians: Women Manage Livestock Diversity* (Rome: Food and Agriculture Organisation Animal Production and Health Paper No. 174, 2012), ix. See also *The State of Food and Agriculture 2010-2011: Women in Agriculture* (Rome: Food and Agriculture Organisation, 2011); Steinfeld *et al, Livestock's Long Shadow*, xx, 4, 268.

38 Gerber, *et al, Tackling Climate Change*, 1, 85.

39 Poore and Nemecek, "Reducing Food's Environmental Impacts," 987, 991.

40 For example, Martin Lukas, "Neoliberalism has Conned us into Fighting Climate Change as Individuals," *Guardian*, July 17, 2017, https://www.theguardian.com/environment/true-north/2017/jul/17/neoliberalism-has-conned-us-into-fighting-climate-change-as-individuals.

41 Ramachandra Guha, *How Much Should a Person Consume? Environmentalism in India and the United States* (Los Angeles: University of California Press, 2006), 244.

42 Guha, *How Much Should a Person Consume?* 233–34, 244.

43 Taylor, *Beasts of Burden*, 182.

44 *El Maíz en Tiempos de Guerra,* http://elmaizentiempos deguerra.org.

45 Alberto Cortés interviewed by Carmen Aristegui, CNN en Español, February 14, 2018, http://www.elmaizentiemposdeguerra.org/blog/entrevista-con-aristegui-video/. Mexico both produces and imports corn, primarily from the United States. According to anthropologist Elizabeth Fitting, the discovery of transgenes in Mexican corn in 2001, initiated "highly charged debates about the extent to which GM corn poses a threat to native varieties in the crop's centre of origin, domestication, and biodiversity." Fitting, *The Struggle for Maize: Campesinos, Workers, and Transgenic Corn in the Mexican Countryside* (Durham: Duke University Press, 2011), 1.

46 Vandana Shiva, *Stolen Harvest: The Hijacking of the Global Food Supply* (Cambridge, MA: South End Press, 2000).

47 Val Plumwood, "Integrating Ethical Frameworks for Animals, Humans, and Nature," *Ethics and the Environment* 5, no. 2 (2000): 301.

48 Alfred W. Crosby, Jr., *The Columbian Exchange: Biological and Cultural Consequences of 1492* (London: Praeger, 2003 [1973]), 75–76.

49 Stephen Burgen, "Fears for Environment in Spain as Pigs Outnumber People," *Guardian*, August 19, 2018, https://www.theguardian.com/world/2018/aug/19/fears-environment-spain-pigs-outnumber-humans-pork-industry.

50 A.G. Holdier, "Speciesist Veganism: An Anthropocentric Argument," in *Critical Perspectives on Veganism,* eds. Jodey Castricano and Rasmus R. Simonsen (Basingstoke: Palgrave MacMillan, 2016), 41–66.

51 Val Plumwood, *Environmental Culture: The Ecological Crisis of Reason* (London: Routledge, 2002), 14.

52 Nixon, *Slow Violence*, 2.

53 For example, "Ex-slaughterhouse Worker, Virgil Butler," *Animal Voices*, February 15, 2005; https://animalvoicesradio.wordpress.com/2005/02/15/

ex-slaughterhouse-worker-virgil-butler/.

54   Marion Stamp-Dawkins, *Animal Suffering* (London: Chapman & Hall, 1980); Jacky Turner, *Stop — Look — Listen: Recognising the Sentience of Farm Animals* (Petersfield: Compassion in World Farming Trust, 2003).

55   Taylor, *Beasts of Burden*, 59.

56   Erika Cudworth, *Social Lives with Other Animals: Tales of Sex, Death and Love* (Basingstoke: Palgrave Macmillan, 2011), 76.

57   Gillespie, "Witnessing Animal Others," 576.

58   See Taylor, *Beasts of Burden*, 63.

59   Gillespie, "Witnessing Animal Others," 579; 584–85.

60   Nixon, *Slow Violence*, 2.

61   See also, "The Evidence: Should We All Be Vegetarians?"; Julia Best, Mike Feider and Jacqueline Pitt, "Introducing Chickens – Arrival, Uptake and Use in Prehistoric Britain," *Past: The Newsletter of the Prehistoric Society* 84 (2016): 1–3, http://www.prehistoricsociety.org/files/PAST_84_for_web.pdf.

62   Cudworth, *Social Lives with Other Animals*.

63   Ben Fine, Michael Heasman and Judith Wright, *Consumption in the Age of Affluence: The World of Food* (London: Routlegde, 1996), 204; Compassion in World Farming, *The Life of Broiler Chickens, Farm Animal Welfare Compendium*, May 1, 2013, https://www.ciwf.org.uk/media/5235306/The-life-of-Broiler-chickens.pdf; Ruth Harrison, *Animal Machines* (Wallingford: CABI, 2013 [1964]), 41–55.

Chapter 4
Caring through species

1   Tom Regan, *The Case for Animal Rights* (London: Routledge & Kegan Paul, 1983), xii; Peter Singer, *Animal Liberation* (New York: Discus/Avon Books, 1977 [1975]), ix–x. See also

this book, chapter 2.

2   Josephine Donovan and Carol J. Adams, eds., *Beyond Animal Rights: A Feminist Caring Ethic for the Treatment of Animals* (New York: Continuum, 1996); Josephine Donovan and Carol J. Adams, eds., *The Feminist Care Tradition in Animal Ethics* (New York: Columbia University Press, 2007).

3   Kathy Rudy, *Loving Animals: Toward a New Animal Advocacy* (Minneapolis: University of Minnesota Press, 2011), 101, 35, xii, 21–31, 36.

4   For more on "locavorism," see this book, chapter 3.

5   Rudy, *Loving Animals*, 99.

6   Vasile Stanescu, "Why 'Loving' Animals is Not Enough: A Response to Kathy Rudy, Locavorism, and the Marketing of 'Humane' Meat," *The Journal of American Culture* 36, no. 2 (2013): 103. See also this book, chapter 3.

7   Stanescu, "Why 'Loving' Animals is Not Enough," 106.

8   Thanks to Chloë Taylor for her useful and incisive comments on emotions and reason in animal ethics.

9   Stanescu, "Why 'Loving' Animals is Not Enough," 108.

10 Stanescu, "Why 'Loving' Animals is Not Enough," 100, 109.

11 Rudy, *Loving Animals*, 75–76.

12 Elspeth Probyn, *Carnal Appetites: FoodSexIdentities* (London: Routledge, 2000), 51.

13 Rudy, *Loving Animals*, 75–6.

14 Rudy, *Loving Animals*, 85.

15 A 2017 study estimated vegans at under 1% of the American population. "Vegan Demographics 2017 — U.S., and the World," http://veganbits.com/vegan-demographics-2017/.

16 Rudy, *Loving Animals*, 76.

17 Michelle R. Loyd-Paige, "Thinking and Eating at the Same Time: Reflections of a Sistah Vegan," in *Sistah Vegan: Black Female Vegans Speak on Food, Identity, Health, and Society,* ed. A. Breeze Harper (New York: Lantern Books, 2010), 1–2.

18 Loyd-Paige, "Thinking and Eating," 6, 3.

19 A. Breeze Harper, "Introduction: The Birth of the Sistah Vegan Project," in *Sistah Vegan: Black Female Vegans Speak on Food, Identity, Health, and Society,* ed. A. Breeze Harper (New York: Lantern Books, 2010), xv.

20 Teresa O'Connor, "Traditional Indigenous Mexican Food is among the World's Healthiest — but it's Misunderstood in the U.S. It's Time to Decolonize Your Diet," *Yes Magazine,* July 28, 2017, https://www.alternet.org/food/traditional-indigenous-mexican-food-among-worlds-healthiest-its-misunderstood-us. See also this book, chapter 6.

21 Harper stresses that many advertisements for veganism or alternative foods in the United States feature thin, white bodies. Harper, "Introduction," xv.

22 Amélie Frost Benedikt, "On Doing the Right Thing at the Right Time: Toward an Ethics of *Kairos,*" in *Rhetoric and Kairos: Essays in History, Theory, and Practice,* eds. Phillip Sipiora and James S. Baumlin (Albany: State University of New York Press, 2002), 229.

23 Melissa Santosa, "Identity, Freedom, and Veganism," in *Sistah Vegan: Black Female Vegans Speak on Food, Identity, Health, and Society,* ed. A. Breeze Harper (New York: Lantern Books, 2010), 75.

24 Probyn, *Carnal Appetites.*

25 Vaughan Monamy, *Animal Experimentation: A Guide to the Issues,* 3rd Edition (Cambridge: Cambridge University Press, 2017): 61–67; "Safety & Testing," *AnimalResearch.Info,* http://www.animalresearch.info/en/drug-development/safety-testing/; Marjorie Morgan, "We Need More Vegan Medication," *gal–dem,* June 28, 2018, http://gal-dem.com/need-vegan-medication/.

26 "UK Animal Research Statistics" (2017) https://speakingofresearch.com/facts/uk-statistics/.

27 Monamy, *Animal Experimentation,* 15.

28 Sunaura Taylor, *Beasts of Burden: Animal and Disability Liberation* (New York: New Press, 2017) 194–96.

29 For example, Jean Swingle Greek and C. Ray Greek, *Sacred Cows and Golden Geese: The Human Cost of Experiments on Animals* (London: Continuum, 2000). In the United Kingdom the website Animal Free Research provides an excellent overview of current developments. https://www.animalfreeresearchuk.org.

30 "List of Animal-Free Medications," *The Vegan Society*, https://www.vegansociety.com/resources/nutrition-and-health/medications/list-animal-free-medications; Morgan, "We Need More Vegan Medication."

31 "Being Vegan and Medicine," Fat Gay Vegan, November 30, 2015, http://fatgayvegan.com/2015/11/30/being-vegan-and-medicine/. Indira died in early 2016. "Sad News," *Fat Gay Vegan*, November 11, 2016, http://fatgayvegan.com/2016/11/11/sad-news-2/.

32 "Being Vegan and Medicine."

33 "Being Vegan and Medicine."

34 Taylor, *Beasts of Burden*, 171, 209.

35 "Hello World," *Cancer Guinea Pig*, July 5, 2012, https://cancerguineapig.com/2012/05/07/hello-world/.

36 "Holding it Together: Hope in the Darkness," *Cancer Guinea Pig*, August 9, 2017, https://cancerguineapig.com/2017/08/09/holding-it-together-hope-in-the-darkness/.

37 "Guinea Pig," *AnimalResearch.Info*; http://www.animalresearch.info/en/designing-research/research-animals/guinea-pig/. Guinea pigs were historically used in cancer research, but today have been largely replaced by other rodents (rats and mice). They continue to be used in studies of a range of other medical conditions. James B. Rogers and Herman T. Blumenthal, "Studies of Guinea Pig Tumors: 1. Report of Fourteen Spontaneous Guinea Pig Tumors, with a Review of the Literature," *Cancer Research*

20 (1960): 191–97; Donna J. Clemons and Jennifer L. Seeman, *The Laboratory Guinea Pig,* 2nd Edition (Boca Raton: CRC Press, 2011); James G. Fox, Lynn C. Anderson, Glen Otto, Kathleen R. Pritchett-Corning, Mark T. Whary, eds., *Laboratory Animal Medicine,* 3rd Edition (Amsterdam: Academic Press, 2016).

38 Daniel Engber, "Test Tube Piggies: How did the Guinea Pig Become a Symbol of Science?" *Slate*, June 18, 2012, http://www.slate.com/articles/health_and_science/science/2012/06/human_guinea_pigs_and_the_history_of_the_iconic_lab_animal_.html.

39 "Hello World."

40 Comment, *Cancer Guinea Pig*, June 19, 2012, https://cancerguineapig.com/about/.

41 "The Carrot or the Stick," *Cancer Guinea Pig,* July 31, 2012, https://cancerguineapig.com/2012/07/31/the-carrot-or-a-stick/.

42 "Reiki and Cancer," *Cancer Guinea Pig*, October 21, 2015, https://cancerguineapig.com/2015/10/23/reiki-and-cancer/.

43 Taylor, *Beasts of Burden*, 200, 202.

44 "Swimming in Source," *Cancer Guinea Pig*, January 17 2017, https://cancerguineapig.com/2018/01/17/2018-swimming-in-source/.

45 Taylor, *Beasts of Burden*, 21, 132.

46 "Queer Femme Time, Part 1," *Cancer Guinea Pig*, November 7, 2012, https://cancerguineapig.com/2012/11/07/queer-femme-time-pt-1/.

47 Brian Luke, "Taming Ourselves or Going Feral? Towards a Nonpatriarchal Metaethic of Animal Liberation," in *Animals and Women: Feminist Theoretical Explorations*, eds. Carol J. Adams and Josephine Donovan (Durham: Duke University Press, 1995), 312–13.

48 "Selfo selfis selfit selfimus selfistis selferunt!" *Cancer*

GuineaPig, March 28, 2014, https://cancerguineapig.
com/2014/03/28selfo-selfis-selfit-selfimus-selfistis-
selferunt/.

49   Taylor, *Beasts of Burden*, 204.

Chapter 5
Creatures we wear

1   Julia Emberley, *Venus and Furs: The Cultural Politics of Fur* (London: I.B. Taurus, 1998).
2   Carol Dyhouse, "Skin Deep: The Fall of Fur," *History Today* 61, no. 11 (2011): 26, 29.
3   Jennifer Farley Gordon and Colleen Hill, *Sustainable Fashion: Past, Present and Future* (London: Bloomsbury Academic, 2014). Electronic Book, 384.5.
4   Dyhouse, "Skin Deep," 27.
5   Gordon and Hill, *Sustainable Fashion*, 384.5–385.7.
6   Maneesha Deckha, "Animal Justice, Cultural Justice: A Posthumanist Response to Cultural Rights in Animals," *Journal of Animal Law and Ethics* 2 (2007): 208–19. See also George Wenzel, *Animal Rights, Human Rights: Ecology, Economy and Ideology in the Canadian Arctic* (London: Belhaven, 1991).
7   See the testimony of Inuit leader John Amagualik in John-Henry Harter, *New Social Movements, Class, and the Environment: A Case Study of Greenpeace Canada* (Newcastle upon Tyne: Cambridge Scholars Publishing, 2011), 36–37.
8   Deckha, "Animal Justice, Cultural Justice," 219, 220.
9   See Wenzel, *Animal Rights* and Harter, *New Social Movements*, 27–44.
10 Wenzel, *Animal Rights*, 1; Gordon and Hill, *Sustainable Fashion*, 379.5.
11 Gordon and Hill, *Sustainable Fashion*, 390.7.

12   See also this book, chapter 1.

13   "Gillian Anderson Is Naked in 'Liberating' New Anti-Fur Campaign," PETA UK, February 7, 2018, https://www.peta.org.uk/blog/gillian-anderson-naked-liberating-new-anti-fur-campaign/.

14   Emberley, *Venus and Furs*, 7, 29, 32.

15   See Wenzel, *Animal Rights* and Harter, *New Social Movements*.

16   Erica Fudge, *Animal* (London: Reaktion Books, 2002), 57.

17   Gordon and Hill, *Sustainable Fashion*, 415.5.

18   "Fake Fur Becomes a Novelty Fabric," *New York Times*, September 13, 1950, 12; cited in Gordon and Hill, *Sustainable Fashion*, 418.0.

19   Susan Sontag, "Notes On Camp," in *Against Interpretation and Other Essays* (London: Andre Deutsch, 1987), 275, 277, 278.

20   Sontag, "Notes On Camp," 287–88.

21   Steve Baker, *Picturing the Beast: Animals, Identity and Representation* (Chicago: University of Illinois Press, 2001 [1993]), 190-91.

22   Baker, *Picturing the Beast*, 232.

23   Gordon and Hill, *Sustainable Fashion*, 389.4

24   On contemporary totems, see Baker, *Picturing the Beast*, 180.

25   "The Skinny on Tattoos," *The Vegan Society*, https://www.vegansociety.com/resources/lifestyle/fashion/vegan-tattoos.

26   Sabrina Barr, "Woman with 'Vegan' Face Tattoo Astounds the Internet," *Independent*, January 28, 2018, https://www.independent.co.uk/life-style/vegan-face-tattoo-veganism-kate-alice-jordan-mccrea-a8181976.html.

27   Jack Clayton, "42 Good, Bad and Questionable Tattoos for Vegans and Vegetarians," *Mpora*. https://mpora.com/style/42-good-bad-questionable-tattoos-vegans-vegetarians/.

28   "Importance of Moths," Butterfly Conservation, http://www.

mothscount.org/text/16/importance_of_moths.html.

29 Claude Lévi-Strauss, "The Totemic Illusion," in *The Animals Reader: The Essential Classic and Contemporary Writings*, ed. Linda Kalof and Amy Fitzgerald (London: Bloomsbury, 2007), 268.

30 Gloria Anzaldúa, "Metaphors in the Tradition of the Shaman," in *The Gloria Anzaldúa Reader* (London: Duke University Press, 2009). See also this book, chapter 1.

31 Niels van Doorn, "The Fabric of Our Memories: Leather, Kinship, and Queer Material History," *Memory Studies* 9, no. 1 (2015): 85.

32 All About Leather, http://www.all-about-leather.co.uk/index.html; "Don't Hide from the Truth," *Guardian*, August 27, 2008, https://www.theguardian.com/lifeandstyle/2008/aug/27/ethicalfashion.leather; Gordon and Hill, *Sustainable Fashion*, 396.9–398.1.

33 Gordon and Hill, *Sustainable Fashion*, 396.9.

34 Drude-Katrine Plannthin, "Animal Ethics and Welfare in the Fashion and Lifestyle Industries," in *Green Fashion: Environmental Footprints and Eco-design of Products and Processes*, eds. Subramanian Senthilkanna Muthu and Miguel A. Gardetti (Singapore: Springer Science and Business Media, 2016), 73.

35 Marla Rose, "The Myth of Harmlessness: The Leather, Wool and Down Industries are the Meat Industry," *Medium*, August 30, 2018, https://medium.com/@marla_rose/the-myth-of-harmlessness-the-leather-wool-and-down-industries-are-the-meat-industry-b0a997f0756e.

36 "All About Leather"; "Don't Hide from the Truth"; Plannthin, "Animal Ethics and Welfare," 73–76; Rose, "The Myth of Harmlessness."

37 For a critique of the "forgotten violence" of leather, with reference to Karl Marx's writing on production and commodity fetishism, see Dinesh Joseph Wadiwel, *The War*

Against Animals (Leiden: Brill Rodopi, 2015), 160, 168–71.

38 van Doorn, "Fabric of Our Memories," 87.

39 Gayle Rubin, "The Catacombs: A Temple of the Butthole," in *Deviations: A Gayle Rubin Reader* (Durham: Duke University Press, 2011 [1991]), 225.

40 Rubin, "The Catacombs," 228, 226, 238, 239.

41 Rubin, "The Catacombs," 228–29.

42 van Doorn, "Fabric of Our Memories," 90, 91; emphasis in original.

43 van Doorn, "Fabric of Our Memories," 89, 95, 89–90.

44 Carol J. Adams, *The Sexual Politics of Meat: A Feminist-Vegetarian Critical Theory* (New York: Continuum, 2000 [1990]).

45 Gary Steiner, *Animals and the Limits of Postmodernism* (New York: Columbia University Press, 2013), 206.

46 Gordon and Hill, *Sustainable Fashion*, 400.6–405.6.

47 Chloë Taylor, "Respect for the (Animal) Dead," in *Animal Death*, eds. Jay Johnston and Fiona Probyn-Rapsey (Sydney: Sydney University Press, 2013), 88, 94, 96–97. See also this book, chapter 2.

48 Taylor, "Respect for the (Animal) Dead," 99.

49 Bob Torres and Jenna Torres, *Vegan Freak: Being Vegan in a Non-Vegan World,* 2nd Edition (Oakland: PM Press, 2010), 198.

Interlude 2
Carnage

1 Simon Amstell, *Carnage: Swallowing the Past* (United Kingdom, 2017).

2 Joshua Schuster, "The Vegan and the Sovereign," in *Critical Perspectives on Veganism*, eds. Jodey Castricano and Rasmus R. Simonsen (Basingstoke: Palgrave MacMillan, 2016), 219.

Chapter 6
Dangers and pleasures

1   On the vegan "green pound" see Zoey Henderson, "Welcome to the Mainstream: The Vegan Revolution is Coming to a High Street Near You," *Bright Zine/Ethical Lifestyle*, October 26, 2017, https://www.brightzine.co/news/2017/10/26/mainstream-vegan-revolution; Marjorie Morgan, "We Need More Vegan Medication," *gal-dem*, June 28, 2018, http://gal-dem.com/need-vegan-medication/.

2   Tara Lomax, "Vegan Consumerism and Going 'Mainstream,'" ProgressivePodcastAustralia.com; July 11, 2015, https://archive.org/details/VeganConsumerism. I focus on posts from English-speaking countries in the global north — including Australia, Canada, the UK and the US — where the vegan consumer brand has taken off and spread most rapidly.

3   Jodey Castricano and Rasmus Rahbek Simonsen, "Food for Thought," in *Critical Perspectives on Veganism*, eds. Jodey Castricano and Rasmus R. Simonsen (Basingstoke: Palgrave MacMillan, 2016), 2.

4   Lomax, "Vegan Consumerism."

5   Wayne Hsiung, "Buying Our Movement," *Direct Action Everywhere,* January 10, 2014, https://www.directactioneverywhere.com/theliberationist/2014/1/10/buying-our-movement?rq=consumerism.

6   Kelly Atlas, "How the 'Go Vegan' Message Perpetuates the Objectification of Nonhumans," *Direct Action Everywhere*, February 27, 2014, https://www.directactioneverywhere.com/theliberationist/2014/2/27/how-vegans-perpetuate-the-objectification-of-animals?rq=consumerism.

7   Adamas, "A Critique of Consumption-Centered Veganism," *H.E.A.L.T.H: Humans, Earth, and Animals Living Together Harmoniously,* June 3, 2011, http://eco-health.blogspot.com/2011/06/crtique-of-consumption-centered.html;

Lomax, "Vegan Consumerism."

8   Ali Sleiter, "Veganism and Consumerism," *Chickpeas and Change,* December 22, 2014, https://chickpeasandchange. wordpress.com/2014/12/22/veganism-consumerism/.

9   For example, Robert C. Jones, "Veganisms," in *Critical Perspectives on Veganism,* eds. Jodey Castricano and Rasmus R. Simonsen (Basingstoke: Palgrave MacMillan, 2016), 15–39.

10 For an explanation of some of the difficulties with such claims, as well as the weaknesses of objections to them, see Jones, "Veganisms."

11 Atlas, "How the 'Go Vegan' Message Perpetuates the Objectification of Nonhumans."

12 Sartya Rodriguez, "Interview with John Sanbonmatsu, Associate Professor at Worcester Polytechnic Institute," *Direct Action Everywhere,* December 1, 2014, https://www. directactioneverywhere.com/theliberationist/2014/12/1/ interview-with-john-sanbonmatsu-associate-professor-of- philosophy-at-worcester-polytechnic-institute.

13 Brigid Brophy, "The Rights of Animals," in *Animal Rights: A Historical Anthology,* eds. Andrew Linzey and Paul Barry Clarke (New York: Columbia University Press, 2004 [1990]), 157–58, 159.

14 Juawana Grant and Brittni MacKenzie-Dale, "Lisa Simpson and Darlene Conner: Television's Favorite Killjoys," in *Critical Perspectives on Veganism,* eds. Jodey Castricano and Rasmus Rahbek Simonsen (Basingstoke: Palgrave MacMillan, 2016), 307-30; Rasmus Rahbek Simonsen, "A Queer Vegan Manifesto," *Journal for Critical Animal Studies* 10, no. 3 (2012): 51–81; James Stanescu, "Vegan Feminist Killjoys (Another Willful Subject)," *Critical Animal,* September 23, 2013, http://criticalanimal.blogspot.co.uk/2013/09/ vegan-feminist-killjoys-another-willful.html; Richard Twine "Vegan Killjoys at the Table — Contesting Happiness and

Negotiating Relationships with Food Practices," *Societies* 4, no. 4 (2014): 623–39.

15 Sara Ahmed, *The Promise of Happiness* (Durham: Duke University Press, 2010), 65.

16 Twine, "Vegan Killjoys at the Table," 626.

17 Stanescu, "Vegan Feminist Killjoys."

18 Carol J. Adams, *The Sexual Politics of Meat: A Feminist-Vegetarian Critical Theory* (New York: Continuum, 2000 [1990]).

19 Patricia MacCormack, *Posthuman Ethics* (Farnham: Ashgate, 2012), 73, n. 8.

20 Cathryn Bailey, "We Are What We Eat: Feminist Vegetarianism and the Reproduction of Racial Identity," *Hypatia* 22, no. 2 (2007): 45–47.

21 Bailey, "We Are What We Eat," 53.

22 Maneesha Deckha, "Toward a Postcolonial, Posthumanist Feminist Theory: Centralizing Race and Culture in Feminist Work on Non-human Animals," *Hypatia* 27, no. 3 (2012): 529, 535.

23 Rita Laws, "Returning to the Corn," *Vegetarian News,* September 1994. Available online as "Native Americans and Vegetarianism," https://ivu.org/history/native_americans.html. See also Rita Laws, "Mother Corn, Father Pumpkin, Sister Bean..." *Vegan Publishers,* 17 September, 2017, https://veganpublishers.com/mother-corn-father-pumpkin-sister-bean-circles-of-compassion/. Excerpted from Will Tuttle, ed. *Circles of Compassion: Essays Connecting Issues of Justice* (Danvers, MA: Vegan Publishers, 2014).

24 Tanya Talaga, *Seven Fallen Feathers: Racism, Death and Hard Truths in a Northern City* (Toronto: House of Anansi Press, 2017), 19. See also Zoe Tennant, "Breaking Bread: Bannock's Contentious Place in Aboriginal Cuisine," *The Walrus,* August 23, 2017, https://thewalrus.ca/breaking-bread/.

25 Margaret Robinson, "Veganism and Mi'kmaq Legends," *The Canadian Journal of Native Studies* 33, no. 1 (2013): 190–91.

26 Robinson, "Veganism and Mi'kmaq Legends," 190, 191.

27 For a critical account, including the key posts referred to here, see Heather Barrett, "White Veganism Doesn't Care about Black Lives," *gal–dem,* July 31, 2017, http://gal-dem.com/white-veganism-black-lives/.

28 Heather Barrett, "White Veganism."

29 "Women of Colour Speak Out," Facebook page, January 11, 2017, https://www.facebook.com/wocspeakout/posts/white-veganism-is-a-reference-to-mainstream-veganismwhich-is-undeniably-very-whi/1905832942978521/.

30 Miranda Larbi, "Please Don't Forget that Veganism Hasn't Always Been a White, Middle-Class Thing," *Metro,* January 14, 2018, https://metro.co.uk/2018/01/14/please-dont-forget-veganism-hasnt-always-white-middle-class-thing-7228027/. See also Nancy Huang, "Veganism and Animal Whites," *Palatinate,* January 27, 2017, https://www.palatinate.org.uk/veganism-and-animal-whites/

31 Barrett, "White Veganism."

32 Bailey, "We Are What We Eat," 53.

33 Bailey "We Are What We Eat," 39–40.

34 Bailey "We Are What We Eat," 47–48.

35 Bailey "We Are What We Eat," 53, 56.

36 Simonsen, "Queer Vegan Manifesto," 54–55.

37 Bailey "We Are What We Eat," 57.

38 Sunaura Taylor, *Beasts of Burden: Animal and Disability Liberation* (New York: New Press, 2017), 173.

39 Jamie Robertson, "Greggs: How its Vegan Sausage Roll Stormed Social Media," BBC News, January 11, 2019, https://www.bbc.co.uk/news/business-46809868.

40 For example, "Stella McCartney Takes on the Leather Trade," PETA, https://www.peta.org/videos/stella-mccartney-takes-on-the-leather-trade/.

41 All of the references to writing on white veganism cited in the section above mention the frequency with which comparisons between factory farming, slavery and the Holocaust circulate on the internet.

42 Alexis de Coning, "Why So Many White Supremacists Are into Veganism," *Vice,* October 20, 2017, https://www.vice.com/en_uk/article/evb4zw/why-so-many-white-supremacists-are-into-veganism; "White Nationalism, Anti-Semitism and the Vegan Movement," *The Vegan Vanguard,* podcast; January 3, 2018, http://veganvanguardpodcast.com/2018/01/03/white-nationalism-anti-semitism-and-the-vegan-movement/.

43 For a historical study of animals and National Socialism, see Boria Sax, *Animals in the Third Reich: Pets, Scapegoats, and the Holocaust* (London: Continuum, 2000). Sax argues that Hitler was a vegetarian, probably following the example of the composer Richard Wagner, but acknowledges that the Fürher's vegetarianism was inconsistent and remains a matter of historical debate (35).

44 "White Nationalism, Anti-Semitism and the Vegan Movement."

45 de Coning, "Why So Many White Supremacists Are into Veganism."

46 Iselin Gambert and Tobias Linné, "From Rice Eaters to Soy Boys: Race, Gender, and Tropes of 'Plant Food Masculinity,'" *Animal Studies Journal* 7, no. 2 (2018): 129–79; Vasile Stanescu, "'White Power Milk': Milk, Dietary Racism, and the 'Alt-Right,'" *Animal Studies Journal* 7, no. 2 (2018): 103–28.

47 Carol J. Adams, *The Sexual Politics of Meat: A Feminist-Vegetarian Critical Theory* (New York: Continuum, 2000 [1990]).

48 For example, Amy Harmon, "Why White Supremacists Are Chugging Milk (and Why Geneticists Are Alarmed)," *New York Times,* October 17, 2018, https://www.nytimes.

com/2018/10/17/us/white-supremacists-science-dna.html; Ashitha Nagesh, "Secret Nazi Code Kept Hidden by 'Milk' and 'Vegan Agenda,'" *Metro,* February 21, 2017, https://metro.co.uk/2017/02/21/secret-nazi-code-kept-hidden-by-milk-and-vegan-agenda-6463079/.

49   "Call You and Yours: Are you Sticking to a Vegan Diet?," BBC Radio 4, February 5, 2019, https://www.bbc.co.uk/programmes/m0002bn2.

50   Jasbir Puar, *Terrorist Assemblages: Homonationalism in Queer Times* (Durham: Duke University Press, 2007).

51   Jacques Derrida and Elisabeth Roudinesco, *For What Tomorrow... A Dialogue,* trans. Jeff Fort (Stanford: Stanford University Press, 2004 [2001]), 68.

52   Jeffrey Pilcher, *Planet Taco: A Global History of Mexican Food* (Oxford: Oxford University Press, 2010), 130–31.

53   *Happy Cow,* https://www.happycow.net.

54   China Despain, "Anthony Bourdain: Vegetarians Make 'Bad Travellers and Bad Guests,'" *Ecorazzi,* October 17, 2011, http://www.ecorazzi.com/2011/10/17/anthony-bourdain-vegetarians-make-bad-travelers-and-bad-guests/.

55   Gary Steiner, *Animals and the Limits of Postmodernism* (New York: Columbia University Press, 2013), 211.

56   See Katie MacDonald and Kelly Struthers Montford, "Eating Animals to Build Rapport: Conducting Research as Vegans or Vegetarians," *Societies* 4 (2014): 737–52.

57   Sean O'Callaghan, *Fat Gay Vegan: Eat, Drink and Live Like You Give a Shit* (New York: Nourish, 2018), Electronic Book, 105.0–113.0, 127.0.

58   MacDonald and Montford, "Eating Animals to Build Rapport."

59   Gino Jafet Quintero Vanegas and Alvaro López López, "The (Unethical) Consumption of a Newborn Animal: *Cabrito* as a Tourist and Recreational Dish in Monterrey, Mexico," in *Animals, Food and Tourism,* ed. Carol Kline (Oxford: Routledge, 2018), 40, 36, 42, 45.

60 Ophélie Véron, "From Seitan Bourguignon to Tofu Blaquette: Popularizing Veganism in France with Food Blogs," in *Critical Perspectives on Veganism,* eds. Jodey Castricano and Rasmus R. Simonsen (Basingstoke: Palgrave MacMillan, 2016), 287–305.

61 David M. Peña-Guzmán, "Anti-Colonial Food Politics: A Case Study In Action From Mexico," *faunalytics,* October 24, 2018, https://faunalytics.org/anti-colonial-food-politics-a-case-study-in-action-from-mexico/.

62 FaunAcción, http://faunaccion.org/en/.

63 Peña-Guzmán, "Anti-Colonial Food Politics." For a similar project founded by a Mexican American in the United States, see *Vegan Mexican Food,* https://www.veganmexicanfood.com, part of the Food Empowerment Project, http://www.foodispower.org.

64 Laws, "Returning to the Corn" and Robinson, "Veganism and Mi'kmaq Legends."

65 Personal communication from Wotko/Gerardo Tristán, October 2018. Translation from Spanish to English by author.

Conclusion
Doing veganism

1   "Call You and Yours: Are you Sticking to a Vegan Diet?," BBC Radio 4, February 5, 2019, https://www.bbc.co.uk/programmes/m0002bn2.

BIBLIOGRAPHY

Adamas. "A Critique of Consumption-Centred Veganism." *H.E.A.L.T.H: Humans, Earth, and Animals Living Together Harmoniously*. June 3, 2011. http://eco-health.blogspot.com/2011/06/crtique-of-consumption-centered.html.

Adams, Carol J. *The Pornography of Meat*. New York: Continuum, 2003.

Adams, Carol J. *The Sexual Politics of Meat: A Feminist-Vegetarian Critical Theory*. New York: Continuum, 2000 (1990).

Agarwal, Bina. *Gender Challenges: Agriculture, Technology, and Food Security*. Oxford: Oxford University Press, 2016.

Ahmed, Sara. *The Promise of Happiness*. Durham: Duke University Press, 2010.

All About Leather. http://www.all-about-leather.co.uk/index.html.

Amstell, Simon. *Carnage: Swallowing the Past*. United Kingdom, 2017.

Anderson, Kip and Keegan Kuhn. *Cowspiracy: The Sustainability Secret*. United States, 2014.

Anzaldúa, Gloria. "Metaphors in the Tradition of the Shaman." In *The Gloria Anzaldúa Reader*, 121–23. Durham: Duke University Press, 2009.

Atlas, Kelly. "How the 'Go Vegan' Message Perpetuates the Objectification of Nonhumans." *Direct Action Everywhere*.

February 27, 2014. https://www.directactioneverywhere. com/theliberationist/2014/2/27/how-vegans-perpetuate-the-objectification-of-animals?rq=consumerism.

Bailey, Cathryn. "We Are What We Eat: Feminist Vegetarianism and the Reproduction of Racial Identity." *Hypatia* 22, no. 2 (2007): 39–59.

Baker, Steve. *Picturing the Beast: Animals, Identity, and Representation.* Chicago: University of Illinois Press, 2001 (1993).

Barrett, Heather. "White Veganism Doesn't Care about Black Lives." *gal-dem* July 31, 2017. http://gal-dem.com/ white-veganism-black-lives/.

"Being Vegan and Medicine." *Fat Gay Vegan.* November 30, 2015. http://fatgayvegan.com/2015/11/30/being-vegan-and-medicine/.

Benedikt, Amélie Frost. "On Doing the Right Thing at the Right Time: Toward an Ethics of Kairos." In *Rhetoric and Kairos: Essays in History, Theory, and Practice,* edited by Phillip Sipiora and James S. Baumlin. 226–35. Albany: State University of New York Press, 2002.

Bourke, Joanna. *What it Means to be Human: Reflections from 1791 to the Present.* London: Virago, 2011.

Brophy, Brigid, "In Pursuit of a Fantasy." In *Animals, Men and Morals: An Enquiry into the Maltreatment of Non-Humans,* edited by Stanley and Rosalind Godlovitch and John Harris, 125–45. London: Victor Gollancz Ltd, 1971.

Brophy, Brigid. "The Rights of Animals." In *Animal Rights: A Historical Anthology,* edited by Andrew Linzey and Paul Barry

Clarke, 156–62. New York: Columbia University Press, 2004 [1990]). Originally published in *Sunday Times*. October 10, 1965.

Burgen, Stephen. "Fears for Environment in Spain as Pigs Outnumber People." *Guardian,* August 19, 2018. https://www.theguardian.com/world/2018/aug/19/fears-environment-spain-pigs-outnumber-humans-pork-industry.

Calarco, Matthew. "Being Toward Meat: Anthropocentrism, Indistinction, and Veganism." *Dialectical Anthropology* 38, no. 4 (2014): 415–29.

"Call You and Yours: Are You Sticking to a Vegan Diet?" BBC Radio 4. February 5, 2019. https://www.bbc.co.uk/programmes/m0002bn2.

Cancer Guinea Pig. https://cancerguineapig.com.

Castricano, Jodey and Rasmus R. Simonsen, eds. *Critical Perspectives on Veganism*. Basingstoke: Palgrave MacMillan, 2016.

Castricano, Jodey and Rasmus Rahbek Simonsen. "Introduction: Food for Thought." In *Critical Perspectives on Veganism*, edited by Jodey Castricano and Rasmus R. Simonsen, 1–11. Basingstoke: Palgrave MacMillan, 2016.

Chivers, Danny. "Cowspiracy: Stampeding in the Wrong Direction?" *New Internationalist*. February 10, 2016. https://newint.org/blog/2016/02/10/cowspiracy-stampeding-in-the-wrong-direction.

Clark, Nigel and Kathryn Yusoff. "Queer Fire: Ecology, Combustion and Pyrosexual Desire." *Feminist Review* 118 (2018): 7–24.

Cole, Matthew. "Asceticism and Hedonism in Research Discourses of Veg*anism." *British Food Journal* 110, no. 7 (2008): 706–16.

Corman, Lauren. "Capitalism, Veganism, and the Animal Industrial Complex." *Species and Class*. April 21, 2014. http://rabble.ca/blogs/bloggers/vegan-challenge/2014/04/capitalism-veganism-and-animal-industrial-complex.

Cortés, Alberto. *El Maíz en Tiempos de Guerra*. Mexico, 2016.

Cudworth, Erika. *Social Lives with Other Animals: Tales of Sex, Death and Love*. Basingstoke: Palgrave MacMillan, 2011.

Curtin, Deane. "Toward an Ecological Ethic of Care." *Hypatia* 6, no. 1 (1991): 60–74.

de Coning, Alexis. "Why So Many White Supremacists Are into Veganism." *Vice*. October 20, 2017. https://www.vice.com/en_uk/article/evb4zw/why-so-many-white-supremacists-are-into-veganism.

Deckha, Maneesha. "Animal Justice, Cultural Justice: A Posthumanist Response to Cultural Rights in Animals." *Journal of Animal Law and Ethics* 2 (2007): 189–229.

Deckha, Maneesha. "Toward a Postcolonial, Posthumanist Feminist Theory: Centralizing Race and Culture in Feminist Work on Non-human Animals." *Hypatia* 27, no. 3 (201): 527–45.

Derrida, Jacques and Elisabeth Roudinesco. *For What Tomorrow… A Dialogue*. Translated by Jeff Fort. Stanford: Stanford University Press, 2004 (2001).

Despain, China. "Anthony Bourdain: Vegetarians Make 'Bad Travellers and Bad Guests.'" *Ecorazzi*. October 17, 2011. http://www.ecorazzi.com/2011/10/17/

anthony-bourdain-vegetarians-make-bad-travelers-and-bad-
guests/.

Diamond, Cora. "Eating Meat and Eating People." *Philosophy* 53,
no. 206 (1978): 465–79.

Donovan, Josephine and Carol J. Adams, eds. *Beyond Animal
Rights: A Feminist Caring Ethic for the Treatment of Animals.*
New York: Continuum, 1996.

Donovan, Josephine and Carol J. Adams, eds. *The Feminist Care
Tradition in Animal Ethics.* New York: Columbia University Press,
2007.

"Don't Hide from the Truth." *Guardian,* August 27, 2008. https://
www.theguardian.com/lifeandstyle/2008/aug/27/ethicalfashion.
leather.

Ducournau, Julia. *Raw.* France-Belgium, 2016.

Dyhouse, Carol. "Skin Deep: The Fall of Fur." *History Today* 61,
no. 11 (2011): 26–29.

Emberley, Julia. *Venus and Furs: The Cultural Politics of Fur.*
London: I.B. Tauris, 1998.

"The Evidence: Should We All be Vegetarians?" BBC Wolrd Service
London. April 19, 2017. https://www.bbc.co.uk/sounds/play/
p04yzvnx.

Francione, Gary L. "Veganism as a Moral Imperative." *Animal
Rights: The Abolitionist Approach.* May 12, 2016. https://www.
abolitionistapproach.com/veganism-moral-imperative/.

Fudge, Erica. *Animal.* London: Reaktion Books, 2002.

Gambert, Iselin and Tobias Linné. "From Rice Eaters to Soy Boys: Race, Gender, and Tropes of 'Plant Food Masculinity.'" *Animal Studies Journal* 7, no. 2 (2018): 129–79.

Garnett, Tara. "Why Eating Grass-fed Beef isn't Going to Help Fight Climate Change." *The Conversation.* October 3, 2017. https://theconversation.com/why-eating-grass-fed-beef-isnt-going-to-help-fight-climate-change-84237.

Gerber, P. J., H. Steinfeld, B. Henderson, A. Mottet, C. Opio, J. Dijkman, A. Falcucci and G. Tempio. *Tackling Climate Change through Livestock: A Global Assessment of Emissions and Mitigation Opportunities.* Rome: Food and Agriculture Organization of the United Nations, 2013.

Gillespie, Kathryn. "Witnessing Animal Others: Bearing Witness, Grief, and the Political Function of Emotion." *Hypatia* 31, no. 3 (2016): 573–88.

Gordon, Jennifer Farley and Colleen Hill. *Sustainable Fashion: Past, Present and Future.* London: Bloomsbury Academic, 2014. Electronic Book.

grace, d. "Vegetarianism and the PETA Incident." *[meory] me. theory. together.* April 16, 2006. http://barelyesoteric.blogspot.com/2006/04/vegetarianism-peta-incident.html.

Griffin, Nathan Stephens. *Understanding Veganism: Biography and Identity.* Basingstoke: Palgrave MacMillan, 2016.

Gruen, Lori. "Facing Death and Practicing Grief." In *Ecofeminism: Feminist Intersections with Other Animals and the Earth,* edited by Carol J. Adams and Lori Gruen, 127–41. New York: Bloomsbury, 2014.

Guha, Ramachandra. *How Much Should a Person Consume? Environmentalism in India and the United States*. Los Angeles: University of California Press, 2006.

Hall, Stuart. "Gramsci's Relevance for the Study of Race and Ethnicity." *Journal of Communication Enquiry* 10, no. 5 (1986): 5-27.

Hamilton, Carrie. "Sex, Work, Meat: The Feminist Politics of Veganism." *Feminist Review* 114 (2016): 112–29.

Hancox, Dan. "The Unstoppable Rise of Veganism: How a Fringe Movement went Mainstream." *Guardian*. April 1, 2018. https://www.theguardian.com/lifeandstyle/2018/apr/01/vegans-are-coming-millennials-health-climate-change-animal-welfare.

Harper, A. Breeze. "Introduction: The Birth of the Sistah Vegan Project." In *Sistah Vegan: Black Female Vegans Speak on Food, Identity, Health, and Society,* edited by A. Breeze Harper. xii–xix. New York: Lantern Books, 2010.

Harper, A. Breeze, ed. *Sistah Vegan: Black Female Vegans Speak on Food, Identity, Health, and Society*. New York: Lantern Books, 2010.

Harrison, Ruth. *Animal Machines*. Wallingford: CABI, 2013 (1964).

Harter, John-Henry. *New Social Movements, Class, and the Environment: A Case Study of Greenpeace Canada*. Newcastle upon Tyne: Cambridge Scholars Publishing, 2011.

Henderson, Zoey. "Welcome to the Mainstream: The Vegan Revolution is Coming to a High Street Near You." *Bright Zine/ Ethical Lifestyle*. October 26, 2017. https://www.brightzine.co/news/2017/10/26/mainstream-vegan-revolution.

Holdier, A.G. "Speciesist Veganism: An Anthropocentric Argument." In *Critical Perspectives on Veganism*, edited by Jodey Castricano and Rasmus R. Simonsen, 41–66. Basingstoke: Palgrave MacMillan, 2016.

Hsiung, Wayne. "Buying Our Movement." *Direct Action Everywhere*, January 10, 2014. https://www.directactioneverywhere.com/theliberationist/2014/1/10/buying-our-movement?rq=consumerism.

Kean, Hilda. *Animal Rights: Politics and Social Change in Britain since 1800*. London: Reaktion Books, 1998.

Kim, Claire Jean. "Moral Extensionism or Racist Exploitation? The Use of Holocaust and Slavery Analogies in the Animal Liberation Movement." *New Political Science* 33, no. 3, (2011): 311–33.

Köhler-Rollefson, Ilse. *Invisible Guardians: Women Manage Livestock Diversity*. Rome: Food and Agriculture Organisation Animal Production and Health Paper no. 174, 2012.

Jones, Robert C. "Veganisms." In *Critical Perspectives on Veganism,* edited by Jodey Castricano and Rasmus R. Simonsen, 15–39. Basingstoke: Palgrave MacMillan, 2016.

Joy, Melanie and Jens Tuider. "Foreword." In *Critical Perspectives on Veganism*, edited by Jodey Castricano and Rasmus R. Simonsen, x–xv. Basingstoke: Palgrave MacMillan, 2016.

Larbi, Miranda. "Please Don't Forget that Veganism Hasn't Always Been a White, Middle-Class Thing." *Metro,* January 14, 2018. https://metro.co.uk/2018/01/14/please-dont-forget-veganism-hasnt-always-white-middle-class-thing-7228027/.

Laws, Rita. "Returning to the Corn." *Vegetarian News.* September 1994. Available online as "Native Americans and Vegetarianism." https://ivu.org/history/native_americans.html.

Leneman, Leah. "No Animal Food: The Road to Veganism in Britain, 1909–1944." *Society & Animals* 7, no. 3 (1999): 219–28.

Lévi–Strauss, Claude. "The Totemic Illusion." In *The Animals Reader: The Essential Classic and Contemporary Writings,* edited by Linda Kalof and Amy Fitzgerald, 262-69. London: Bloomsbury, 2007.

Lomax, Tara. "Vegan Consumerism and Going 'Mainstream.'" *ProgressivePodcastAustralia.com.* July 11, 2015. https://archive.org/details/VeganConsumerism.

Loyd-Paige, Michelle R. "Thinking and Eating at the Same Time: Reflections of a Sistah Vegan." In *Sistah Vegan: Black Female Vegans Speak on Food, Identity, Health, and Society,* edited by A. Breeze Harper, 1–7. New York: Lantern Books, 2010.

Luke, Brian. "Taming Ourselves or Going Feral? Towards a Nonpatriarchal Metaethic of Animal Liberation." In *Animals and Women: Feminist Theoretical Explorations,* edited by Carol J. Adams and Josephine Donovan, 290–319. Durham: Duke University Press, 1995.

MacCormack, Patricia. *Posthuman Ethics.* Farnham: Ashgate, 2012.

MacDonald, Katie and Kelly Struthers Montford. "Eating Animals to Build Rapport: Conducting Research as Vegans or Vegetarians." *Societies* 4 (2014): 737–52.

McJetters, Christopher-Sebastian. "Slavery. It's Still a Thing." *Vegan Publishers.* June 11, 2014. http://veganpublishers.com/slavery-its-still-a-thing-christopher-sebastian-mcjetters/.

Monamy, Vaughan. *Animal Experimentation: A Guide to the Issues.* 3rd edition. Cambridge: Cambridge University Press, 2017.

Monbiot, George. "There's a Population Crisis All Right. But Probably Not the One You Think." *Guardian.* November 19, 2015. https://www.theguardian.com/commentisfree/2015/nov/19/population-crisis-farm-animals-laying-waste-to-planet.

Montford, Kelly Struthers. "The 'Present Referent': Nonhuman Animal Sacrifice and the Constitution of Dominant Albertan Identity." *PhaenEx* 8, no. 2 (2013): 105–34.

Morgan, Marjorie. "We Need More Vegan Medication." *gal-dem.* June 28, 2018. http://gal-dem.com/need-vegan-medication/.

Nixon, Rob. *Slow Violence and the Environmentalism of the Poor.* Cambridge, MA: Harvard University Press, 2011.

O'Callaghan, Sean. *Fat Gay Vegan: Eat, Drink and Live Like You Give a Shit.* New York: Nourish, 2018. Electronic Book.

Quintero Venegas, Gino Jafet and Álvaro López López. "The (Unethical) Consumption of a Newborn Animal: *Cabrito* as a Tourist and Recreational Dish in Monterrey, Mexico." In *Animals, Food and Tourism,* edited by Carol Kline, 36–51. Abingdon: Routledge, 2018.

Parry, Jovan. "Gender and Slaughter in Popular Gastronomy." *Feminism & Psychology* 20, no. 3 (2010): 381–96.

Parry, Jovan and Annie Potts. "Vegan Sexuality: Challenging Heteronormative Masculinity through Meat-free Sex." *Feminism & Psychology* 20, no. 1 (2010): 53–72.

Patterson, Charles. *Eternal Treblinka: Our Treatment of Animals and the Holocaust.* New York: Lantern Books, 2002.

Peña-Guzmán, David M. "Anti-Colonial Food Politics: A Case Study in Action From Mexico." *faunalytics.* October 24, 2018. https://faunalytics.org/anti-colonial-food-politics-a-case-study-in-action-from-mexico/.

Petter, Olivia. "Number of Vegans in UK Soars to 3.5 million, Survey Finds." *Independent.* April 3, 2018. https://www.independent.co.uk/life-style/food-and-drink/vegans-uk-rise-popularity-plant-based-diets-veganism-figures-survey-compare-the-market-a8286471.html.

Phillips, Layli. "Veganism and Ecofeminism." In *Sistah Vegan: Black Female Vegans Speak on Food, Identity, Health, and Society,* edited by A. Breeze Harper, 8–19. New York: Lantern Books, 2010.

Pick, Anat. "Turning to Animals between Love and Law." *New Formations* 76 (2012): 68–85.

Plannthin, Drude-Katrine. "Animal Ethics and Welfare in the Fashion and Lifestyle Industries." In *Green Fashion: Environmental Footprints and Eco-design of Products and Processes,* edited by Subramanian Senthilkanna Muthu and Miguel A. Gardetti, 49–122. Singapore: Springer Science and Business Media, 2016.

Plumwood, Val. "Animals and Ecology: Towards a Better Integration." *Australian National University Digital Collection: Working/Technical Paper*, 2003. https://core.ac.uk/download/pdf/156617082.pdf. No page numbers.

Plumwood, Val. "Being Prey." (2011 [1999]). https://kurungabaa.wordpress.com/2011/01/18/being-prey-by-val-plumwood/. No page numbers.

Plumwood, Val. "Ecofeminism." In *Encyclopedia of Feminist Theories,* edited by Lorraine Code, 151–52. London: Routldege, 2000.

Plumwood, Val. *Environmental Culture: The Ecological Crisis of Reason.* London: Routledge, 2002.

Plumwood, Val. *Feminism and the Mastery of Nature.* London: Routledge, 1993.

Plumwood, Val. "Integrating Ethical Frameworks for Animals, Humans, and Nature." *Ethics and the Environment* 5, no. 2 (2000): 285–322.

Poore, Joseph and Thomas Nemecek. "Reducing Food's Environmental Impacts through Producers and Consumers." *Science* 360, 6392 (2018): 987–92.

Probyn, Elspeth. *Carnal Appetites: FoodSexIdentities.* London: Routledge, 2000.

Probyn, Elspeth. *Eating the Ocean.* Durham: Duke University Press, 2016.

Probyn, Elspeth. "Swimming with Tuna: Human-Ocean

Entanglements." *Australian Humanities Review* 51 (2011): 97–114.

Regan, Tom. *The Case for Animal Rights*. London: Routledge & Kegan Paul, 1983.

Robinson, Margaret. "Veganism and Mi'kmaq Legends." *Canadian Journal of Native Studies* 33, no. 1 (2013): 189–96.

Rodriguez, Sartya. "Interview with John Sanbonmatsu, Associate Professor at Worcester Polytechnic Institute." *Direct Action Everywhere*. December 1, 2014. https://www.directactioneverywhere.com/theliberationist/2014/12/1/interview-with-john-sanbonmatsu-associate-professor-of-philosophy-at-worcester-polytechnic-institute.

Rose, Marla. "The Myth of Harmlessness: The Leather, Wool and Down Industries are the Meat Industry." *Medium*. August 30, 2018. https://medium.com/@marla_rose/the-myth-of-harmlessness-the-leather-wool-and-down-industries-are-the-meat-industry-b0a997f0756e.

Ross, Mirha-Soleil. "Shaking Things Up: Queer Rights/Animal Rights." Interview with Claudette Vaughn. *Vegan Voice* (September-November 2003). http://www.satyamag.com/oct03/ross.html.

Ross, Mirha-Soleil. "Yapping Out Loud for Animals and Prostitutes!" Interview with Nadja Lubiw. ANIMAL VOICES Radio, CIUT 89.5 FM, Toronto, April 26, 2002. Transcript available at https://kersplebedeb.com/posts/yap_int-2/.

Rubin, Gayle. "The Catacombs: A Temple of the Butthole." In *Deviations: A Gayle Rubin Reader*, 224–40. Durham: Duke University Press, 2011 (1991).

Rudy, Kathy. *Loving Animals: Toward a New Animal Advocacy*. Minneapolis: University of Minnesota Press, 2011.

Santosa, Melissa. "Identity, Freedom, and Veganism." In *Sistah Vegan: Black Female Vegans Speak on Food, Identity, Health, and Society,* edited by A. Breeze Harper, 73–77. New York: Lantern Books, 2010.

Schuster, Joshua. "The Vegan and the Sovereign." In *Critical Perspectives on Veganism*, edited by Jodey Castricano and Rasmus R. Simonsen, 203–23. Basingstoke: Palgrave MacMillan, 2016.

Sebo, Jeff. "Multi-Issue Food Activism." In *The Oxford Handbook of Food Ethics*, edited by Anne Barnhill, Mark Budolfson and Tyler Doggett, 399–424. Oxford: Oxford University Press, 2018.

Simonsen, Rasmus R. "A Queer Vegan Manifesto." *Journal for Critical Animal Studies* 10, no. 3 (2012): 51-81.

Singer, Peter. *Animal Liberation*. New York: Discus/Avon Books, 1977 (1975).

Singer, Peter. *Animal Liberation*. Revised Edition. London: The Bodley Head, 2015 (1990).

Sleiter, Ali. "Veganism and Consumerism." *Chickpeas and Change*. December 22, 2014. https://chickpeasandchange.wordpress.com/2014/12/22/veganism-consumerism/.

Sontag, Susan. "Notes On Camp." In *Against Interpretation and Other Essays,* 275–92. London: Andre Deutsch, 1987.

Spiegel, Marjorie. *The Dreaded Comparison: Human and Animal*

Slavery. New York: Mirror Books, 1997.

Stanescu, James. "Vegan Feminist Killjoys (Another Willful Subject)." *Critical Animal.* September 23, 2013. http://criticalanimal.blogspot.co.uk/2013/09/vegan-feminist-killjoys-another-willful.html.

Stanescu, Vasile. "'Green' Eggs and Ham? The Myth of Sustainable Meat and the Danger of the Local." *The Journal for Critical Animal Studies* 8, no. 1/2 (2010), 8–32.

Stanescu, Vasile. "'White Power Milk': Milk, Dietary Racism, and the 'Alt-Right'." *Animal Studies Journal* 7, no. 2 (2018): 103–28.

Stanescu, Vasile. "Why 'Loving' Animals is Not Enough: A Response to Kathy Rudy, Locavorism, and the Marketing of 'Humane' Meat." *The Journal of American Culture* 36, no. 2 (2013): 100–10.

Stehfest, Elke, Lex Bouwman, Detlef P. van Vuuren, Michel G. J. den Elzen, Bas Eickhout and Pavel Kabat. "Climate Benefits of Changing Diet." *Climatic Change* 95 (2009): 83–102.

Steiner, Gary. "Animal, Vegetable, Miserable." *New York Times.* November 22, 2009.

Steiner, Gary. *Animals and the Limits of Postmodernism.* New York: Columbia University Press, 2013.

Steinfeld, Henning, Pierre Gerber, Tom Wassenaar, Vincent Castel, Mauricio Rosales and Cees de Haan. *Livestock's Long Shadow: Environmental Issues and Options.* Rome: Food and Agriculture Organization of the United Nations, 2006.

Talaga, Tanya. *Seven Fallen Feathers: Racism, Death and Hard*

Truths in a Northern City. Toronto: House of Anansi Press, 2017.

Taylor, Chloë. "Foucault and the Ethics of Eating." *Foucault Studies* 9 (2010): 71–88.

Taylor, Chloë. "Respect for the (Animal) Dead." In *Animal Death,* edited by Jay Johnston and Fiona Probyn-Rapsey, 85–102. Sydney: Sydney University Press, 2013.

Taylor, Sunaura. *Beasts of Burden: Animal and Disability Liberation.* New York: New Press, 2017.

Tennant, Zoe. "Breaking Bread: Bannock's Contentious Place in Aboriginal Cuisine." *The Walrus.* August 23, 2017. https://thewalrus.ca/breaking-bread/.

Torres, Bob and Jenna Torres. *Vegan Freak: Being Vegan in a Non-Vegan World.* 2nd edition. Oakland: PM Press, 2010.

Tree, Isabella. "If You Want to Save the World, Veganism isn't the Answer." *Guardian,* August 25, 2018. https://www.theguardian.com/commentisfree/2018/aug/25/veganism-intensively-farmed-meat-dairy-soya-maize?CMP=Share_iOSApp_Other.

Twine, Richard. "Vegan Killjoys at the Table: Contesting Happiness and Negotiating Relationships with Food Practices." *Societies* 4, no. 4 (2014): 623–39.

van Doorn, Niels. "The Fabric of Our Memories: Leather, Kinship, and Queer Material History." *Memory Studies* 9, no. 1 (2015): 85–98.

Vance, Carol S., ed. *Pleasure and Danger: Exploring Female*

Sexuality. London: Pandora Press, 1992.

Wadiwel, Dinesh Joseph. "Do Fish Resist?" *Cultural Studies Review* 22, no. 1 (2016): 196–242.

Wadiwel, Dinesh Joseph. *The War Against Animals.* Leiden: Brill Rodopi, 2015.

Wallace, David Foster. "Consider the Lobster." *Gourmet.* August 2004, 50–64.

Wenzel, George. *Animal Rights, Human Rights: Ecology, Economy and Ideology in the Canadian Arctic.* London: Belhaven, 1991.

"White Nationalism, Anti-Semitism and the Vegan Movement." *The Vegan Vanguard.* Podcast. January 3, 2018. http://veganvanguardpodcast.com/2018/01/03/white-nationalism-anti-semitism-and-the-vegan-movement/.

World Wildlife Fund. *Appetite for Destruction.* https://www.wwf.org.uk/sites/default/files/2017-11/WWF_AppetiteForDestruction_Full_Report_Web_0.pdf.

Wright, Laura. *The Vegan Studies Project.* Athens: University of Georgia Press, 2015.

INDEX

64, 68, 123, 140, 165

anthropophagy, 72–76, 166, 217
note 1

anti-capitalism, 6, 24, 64, 114,
161, 190
    and veganism, 14–15, 54,
    177, 195–96

anti-colonialism, 6, 9, 54, 173
    and veganism, 14, 20, 54

anti-racism, 6, 9, 17, 174
    and veganism, 20, 166,
    179–81, 197

anti-Semitism, *see* Jewish
people

Anzaldúa, Gloria, 43–44, 142

Australia, 46–56, 66
    see also Indigenous people

B

Bailey, Cathryn, 170, 175–76

Baker, Steve, 39–41, 43, 140

Barrett, Heather, 174–75

birds, 191
    in scientific experiments, 118

Black people, 12, 31–33
    compared to animals, 33,
    174
    women, 112, 138
    see also African Americans;

people of colour; race;
racism

bodies,
    animal, 100, 153
        and care, 104
        dead, 60–61, 111,
        144–45, 149–51, 158–9
        shared experiences with
        human bodies, 124
    and care, 7, 104, 116, 130
    human 7, 82, 116, 123–24,
    141–43
        and animal symbols,
        153–54
        body image, 20
        and clothing, 132
        dead, 36, 40, 72, 151
        and disability, 129–30
        eating, 56, 60–61, 132
        exploitation, 24
        healing, 125
        and leather, 145
        metaphors, 43, 142
        non-normative, 146
        older, 110, 146
        queer, 143, 146–48
        vegan, 16, 110
        women's, 110, 168

Brophy, Brigid, 72, 75, 165

butterflies, 141

C

Calarco, Matthew, 51

Canada, 14, 26, 42, 134–36,
172–74, 183, 188, 190

130, 197
see also bodies; time

dogs, 189
  companions, 101–103,
  106–107
  images of suffering, 39–40
  in scientific experiments, 30,
  118

donkeys, 189

drugs, *see* medication

E

eating, 197
  animals,
    meanings of, 170–71
  ethics, 55–58, 62–64, 73,
  166
  and human connections,
  60–61, 166
    vegan food, 123
  and sex, 56, 66–67, 72–74,
  116
  see also bodies; pleasure

ecofeminism, *see* feminism

eggs, 10, 22, 84, 127, 145, 166,
185, 187, 197
  Britishness, 181
  and environment, 86–87,
  111
  "feminized protein," 27
  and human health, 82, 111
  organic, 86, 110
  production, 53, 81, 155

elephants, 79

emotions,
  animal,
    and other animals, 106
    and people, 105
  see also sentience
  human, 99
    and human-animal
    relations, 11, 63, 65,
    70, 102–103, 105–107,
    153–54
    and veganism,
      anger, 22–23, 167
      joy, 193–95
      pain, 152, 167
      shame,152

environment, 61, 77–103
passim, 165
  and animals, 78, 142
  and fashion, 140
  and veganism, 96, 107, 109,
  114
  and vegetarianism, 172
  see also care; climate
  change; dairy; eggs;
  emotions; environmental
  destruction;
  environmentalism; health
  care; leather; meat;
  meat-eating; stories and
  storytelling

environmental destruction, 82,
98
  and animals, 77–80
  and food production, 80, 112
  and inequality among
  people, 78, 93–94
  and veganism, 197
  see also omnivores and
  omnivorism

concentration compared to
factory farms, 31, 35–37, 40
vegetarianism, 179, 182
neo-Nazis, see far right
see also Holocaust; Jewish
people

neoliberalism, *see* capitalism

Nixon, Rob, 78, 98, 101

non-binary people, 196
see also queer

nutrition, *see* health

O

O'Callaghan, Sean (Fat Gay
Vegan), 120, 184

omnivores and omnivorism, 9,
15, 22, 25, 51, 60, 66–67, 74,
109, 115, 155, 166
and care, 104
discrediting veganism, 173,
181, 185
and environmental
destruction, 93–94
eroticised, 56
ethical aspects, 47, 181
and rituals using animal
products, 145, 168–69

oysters
as food, 64–67
sentience, 65–67

P

Patterson, Charles, 33–34, 37
Peña-Guzman, David, 187

people of colour, 8, 33
compared to animals, 43
see also Black people;
Indigenous people; race;
racism

PETA (People for the Ethical
Treatment of Animals), 31, 38,
157, 162
"Animal Liberation Project"
exhibition, 32–33, 36–37
anti-fur campaigns, 135–36

pets, see animals, companion

pigs, 80, 87, 189
as food, 26, 97–100, 156
as metaphors for police, 41

pigeons, 1

plant-based diets, 2–3, 20, 57
and climate change, 86, 92
ethics of, 58, 73
and femininity, 180
Mexican and Mexican
American, 97, 112, 187–88
outside the West, 10, 12–13,
171, 174
in precolonial North
America, 171–72, 188
represented in tattoos, 141
see also veganism

plants, 50, 52–53, 78, 142
ethical aspects, 96–97
see also sentience

pleasure, 6, 197
  and animal products, 16, 26, 153
  and eating, 67–68 168–69
  politics of, 25
  and politics, 108, 166
  of veganism, 8–9, 18–19, 21, 152, 158, 177–78, 186, 188, 193, 195
  see also sex

Plumwood, Val, 46–56, 58, 64–65, 70–71, 74–75, 94, 96–98, 151
  see also feminism, ecofeminism

pornography, 28–29
  see also feminism; sex workers

power relations
  see relations

predators, 46–51
  people as, 53, 73–75
  see also prey

prey, 46–51, 54
  people as 48–49, 52, 56, 73–75, 151
  see also predators

primates, in scientific experiments, 118

Probyn, Elspeth, 56–62, 64–66, 68–70, 108–109, 116

Q

queer,
  activism, 66
    and veganism, 12, 14, 15, 24
  camp, 138–40
  communities, 143, 148–50
  culture, 41–44, 139
    and food, 58
  fems, 128–29, 139–43
  history, 146–49, 150, 152
  "homonationalism," 181
  lesbians, 148
  people, 8
    violence against, 143
  politics and veganism, 20, 24–25
  subcultures, 20, 133, 143–52
  theory, 8, 161
    and veganism, 9, 195
  veganism as, 9, 60
  see also anarchism; bodies; consumerism; disability; feminism; identity; memory; men; mourning; racism; relations; sex; time

Quintero Venegas, Gino Jafet, 185

R

race,
  and food, 68
  and health care, 119
  and veganism, 5, 17, 19, 171, 174–78
  vegetarianism, 170–71
  see also Black people; feminism; fur; Indigenous

88–89, 92–98
and food, 169–70, 189
and tourism, 186
and veganism, 9, 19, 23, 24,
95
on the internet, 120, 124

T

Talaga, Tanya, 172–73

tattoos,
animal, 133, 141–43
vegan, 141
see also plant-based diets;
totems

Taylor, Chloë, 18, 57, 86,
150–51

Taylor, Sunaura, 16, 65, 81, 94,
99, 121–22, 128–30

tigers, fur, 134

time,
and disability, 129
medical, 129
queer femme, 128–29
and veganism, 128–30, 186

totems, animal,154
leather, 149
tattoos, 142

Tristán, Gerardo/Wotko,
188–91, 193

tourism and travel,
and animals, 184–85
and food ethics, 169, 183–86
and meat-eating, 184–85

and veganism, 7, 182–87
see also social media; stories
and storytelling

transgender people, 7, 26, 196
in queer spaces, 146
see also queer
trauma,
and historical violence, 33,
35, 37
transpecies, 157

Tree, Isabella, 83–84

U

United Kingdom, 2–3, 10–11,
30, 36, 39, 58, 75, 79, 83, 86,
101–102, 114, 117–18, 134,
135–37, 161, 174, 178, 180–81

United States, 2–3, 8, 11, 25,
28, 30–34, 42, 86, 88–89,
92–93, 95, 106, 109–10, 112,
118–19, 134–35, 143–49, 162,
171–72, 174, 179-80,183, 190

utilitarian philosophy, 11, 12,
65, 71
critiques of, 51, 54, 105
see also Singer, Peter

V

van Doorn, Niels, 143–50

vegan, word, 10, 14
as logo, 162
problems with, 164
symbol of gentrification, 175
see also vegans; veganism